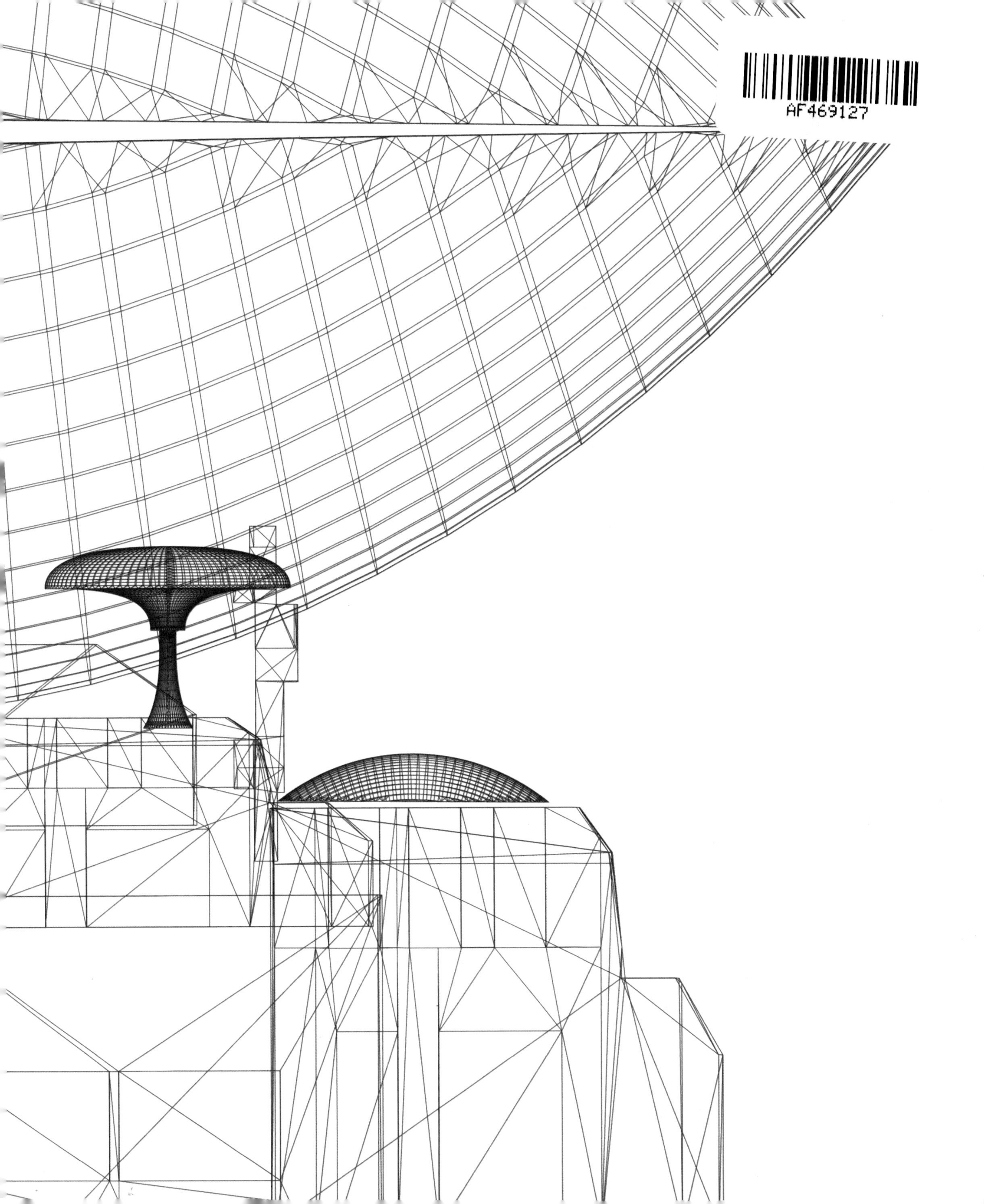
AF469127

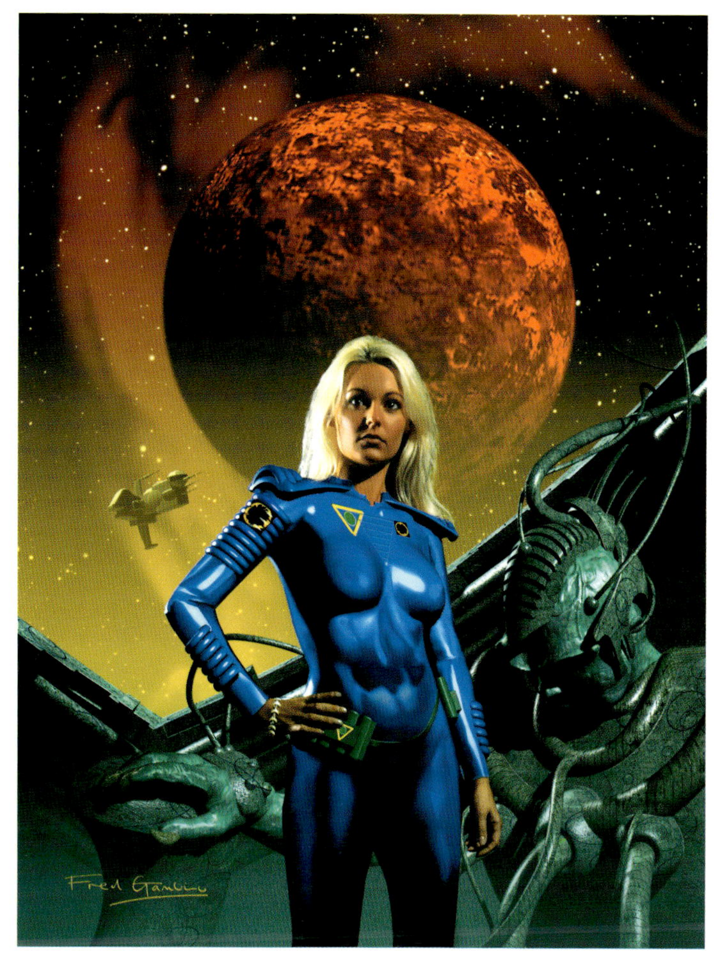

GROUND ZERO

Fred Gambino

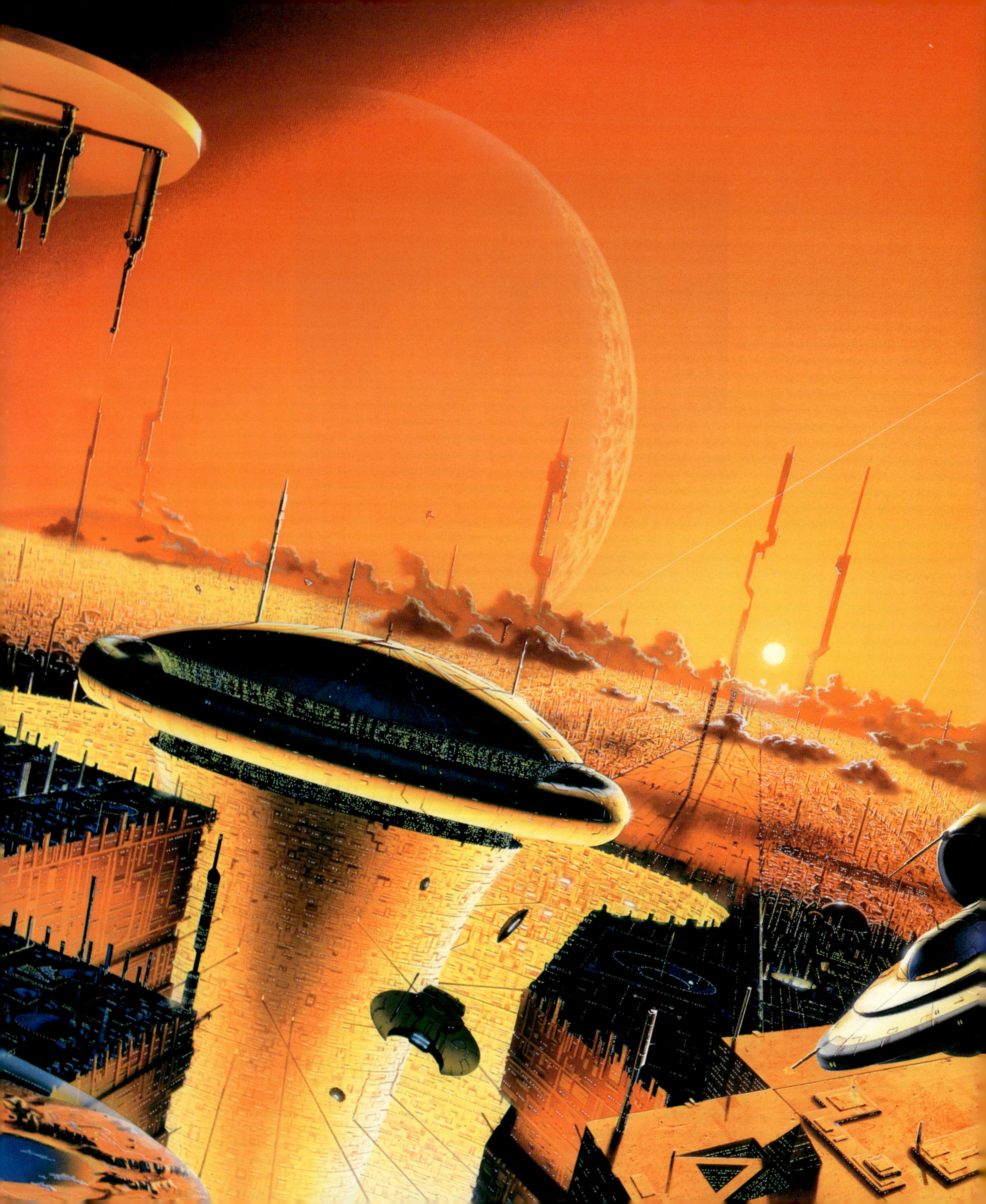

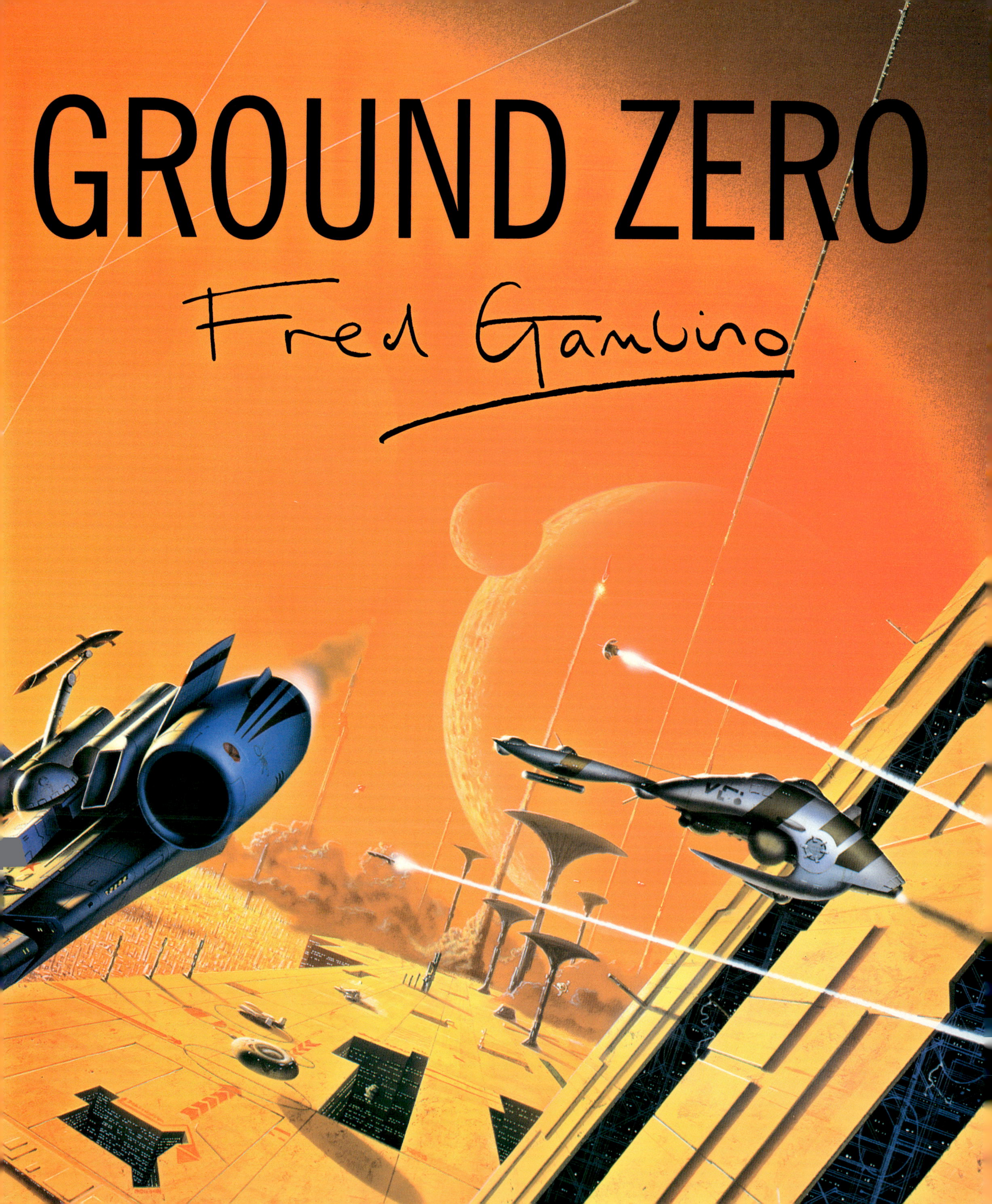
GROUND ZERO
Fred Gambino

Acknowledgements
In the course of twenty plus years pursuing my career as an illustrator, there have been many people to whom I owe a huge debt of thanks, so, to all those who have encouraged, supported, inspired, endured, tolerated, suffered, posed – usually above and beyond the call of duty – financed, maintained and generally bolstered me during the last two decades, thank you all very much indeed!

A special mention must go to Nigel Gibson, photographer extraordinaire and (tor) mentor Laura, my ex-wife, who oversaw the start of it all; Chris Moore, a serendipitous meeting that changed everything; Brian Fennely and Carol Butfoy of the Sarah Brown Agency, without whom the raw material for this book would not have existed; Alison Eldred, without whose persistence this book may not have existed at all, and especially to Jenny, who now enjoys all the above duties and then some.

First published in Great Britain in 2001
by Paper Tiger
an imprint of Collins & Brown Limited
London House
Great Eastern Wharf
Parkgate Road
London SW11 4NQ
www.papertiger.co.uk

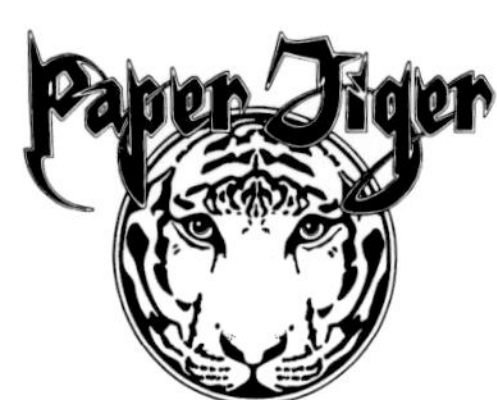

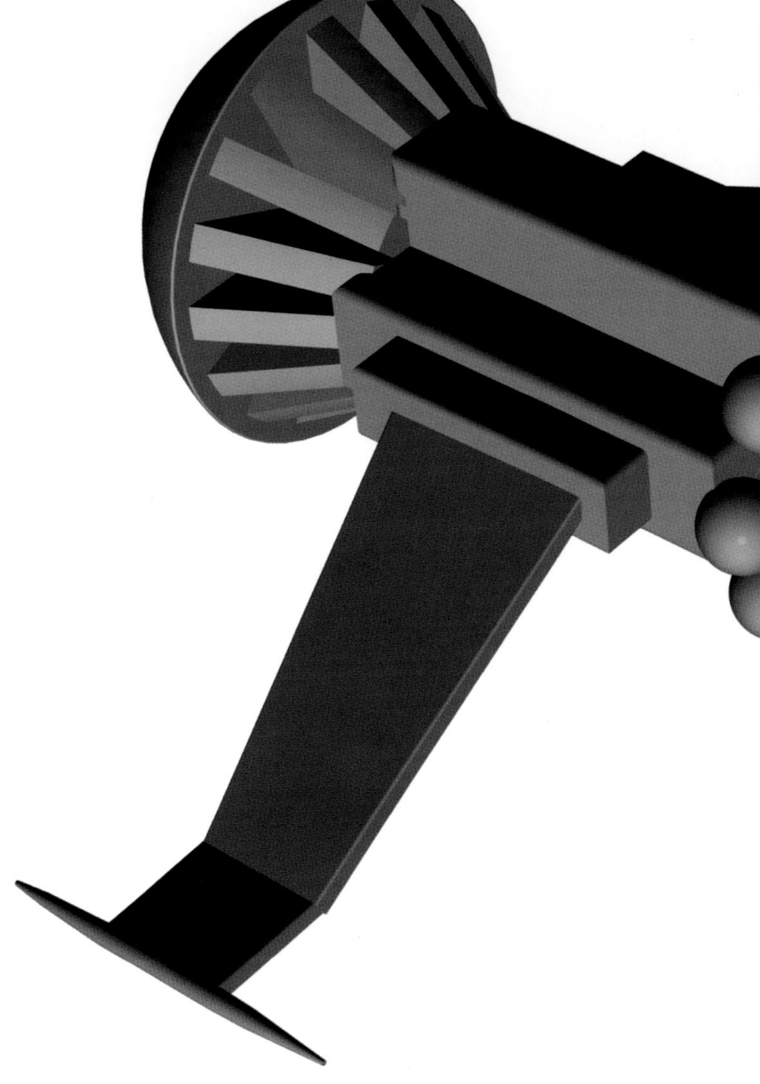

Distributed in the United States and Canada by Sterling Publishing Co, 387 Park Avenue South, New York, NY 10016, USA

2 4 6 8 9 7 5 3 1

British Library Cataloguing-in-Publication Data: A catalogue record for this book is available from the British Library.

ISBN 1 85585 891 6 (hb)
ISBN 1 85585 907 6 (pb)

Commissioning Editor: Katie Hardwicke
Designer: David Eldred

Reproduction by Classic Scan Pte Ltd, Singapore
Printed and bound in China by L-Rex Printing Company

Contents

Foreword

By Dick Jude

Sitting in my office as the then manager of Forbidden Planet, I was filtering the morning's mail a couple of years ago. Among the envelopes addressed to me was one that contained a particular surprise in the form of an invitation to write a book on current fantasy art.

I felt the only way to hold such an anthology together was to tell a story, and I started to sift through a seemingly endless list of people talented, well known and individual enough to fit the bill. Pigment and paper were the only logical starting points that would lead to the use of computer rendered images as the conclusion. I started contacting a variety of the artists I knew personally, mostly painters since a combination of the comparatively recent advent of computers as artist's tools and the deeply conservative nature of art editors had limited the number of published digital images. All paths led to Fred Gambino, his work was everywhere and his name constantly cropped up when discussing digital art within the context of science fiction. Many of the artists had spoken to him for advice as they too added the computer to their range of art tools.

A friendly and enthusiastic telephone conversation resulted in a very pleasurable weekend in his company in the surreal atmosphere of the British Science Fiction convention, in Liverpool. His vivid, intense images were jammed into a tiny maze of a room with several other key artists in the current British SF art scene. The lack of space did none of them justice, but it was a pleasure to view their work uncluttered by the typography of title, author and publisher's blurb that so often hides the true composition of the original, and also to see them on a much larger scale than their typical reproduction as book cover illustrations.

Fred was as charming and friendly as was promised by our introductory conversation and responded very quickly and thoroughly to my requests for information and images. Huge files of far more pictures than could ever be included flooded from my mail box – although casting my eye over the sheer range of images in this book makes me now wish I had asked to view far more. There was no hesitation on Fred's part in sending not only final image files but numerous supporting thumbnails, wire frames and renders – the digital equivalent of sketches. His answers to my questions were equally generous. The Fred Gambino section came together very smoothly and immediately became the commissioning editor's favourite because of the detail and breadth of the images. The book also worked as a fine shop window for Fred's talents (see opposite).

It was only towards the end of our collaboration that I discovered a central strength of the Fred Gambino technique – model-making. The imagination of young Fred was so stimulated by the puppet shows of Gerry and Sylvia Anderson, *Thunderbirds* in particular, that he spent many hours making hundreds of detailed drawings of vehicles and equipment, his imagination

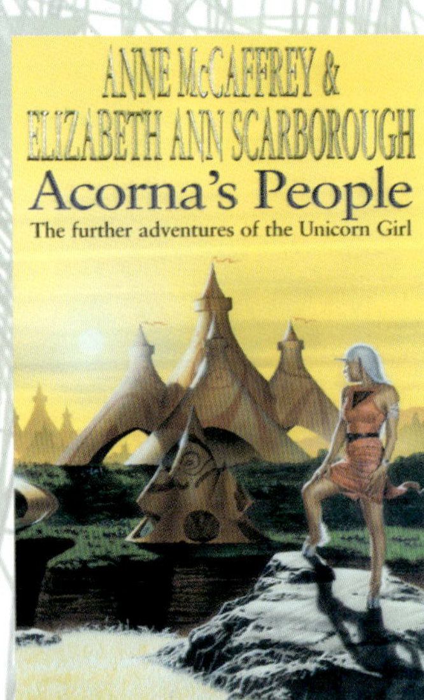

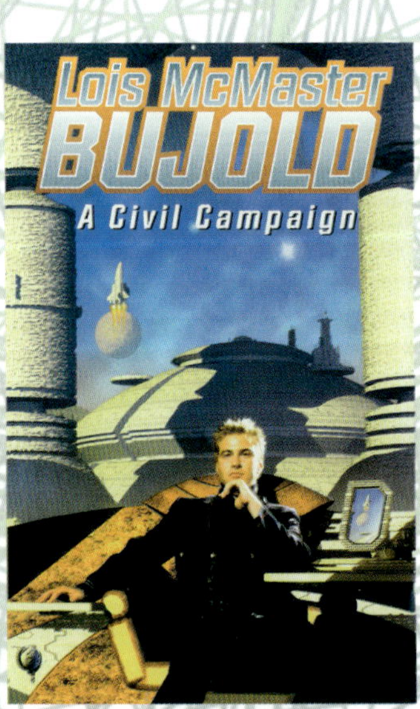

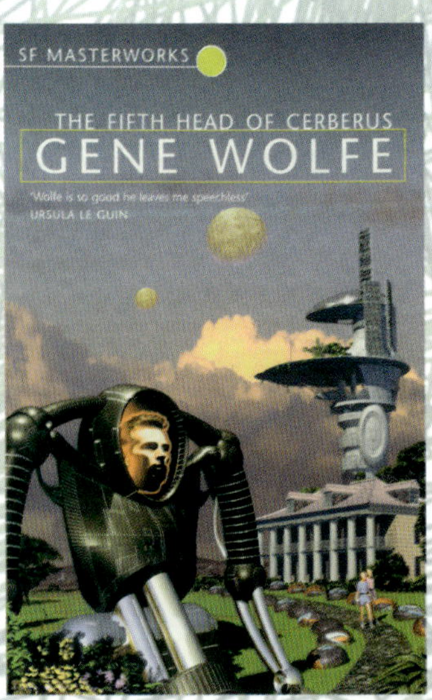

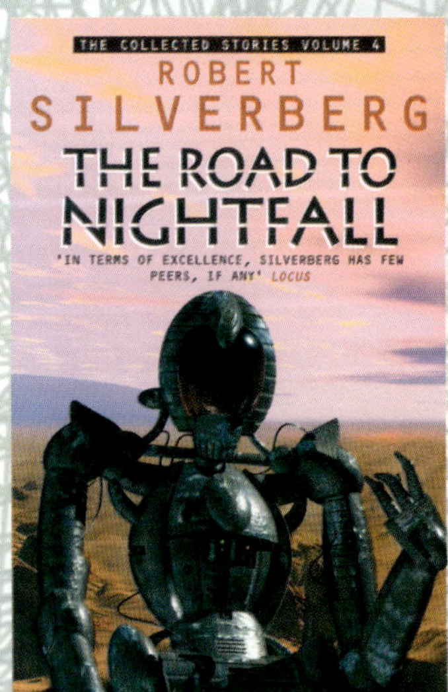

constantly refining the hardware. Echoes of these interests surfaced again in his later illustrative approach, as he would sometimes choose to build model spaceships from a wide variety of odd-shaped, every-day packages. He searched the supermarket aisles for containers exciting enough to become exotic vehicles in his meticulous acrylic paintings, performed mad surgery in the privacy of his studio – cutting and gluing other bits and pieces on until he'd created an object that, when lit correctly, could be photographed and used as reference for the painting he had planned.

This was a time-consuming preparation but a necessary one, since so much of the impact in Fred's paintings is caused by the complex light play dancing off the surfaces within the image. A quick study of the illustrations for the Foundation Series (see pages 99–105), will reveal why such accurate reference was needed. Ultimately though, it was time constraints that made Fred realize that the use of computers in his art was the only way to avoid a seven-day working week. Being among the first of the working illustrators to consider the computer as an art tool, he knew no one who could tutor him, but discovered that his working practice to date transferred naturally into digital form, in particular his talent for model-making. The pages throughout this book have many screen dumps of wire frame models awaiting the cladding of a skin of texture samples or paint as evidence that Fred's model-making approach to picture-making continues.

The Foundation Series and David Brin pictures (see pages 34–9) within this collection provide a good contrast and comparison of Fred's painted art with his digital art. His work disproves both the idiocies that firstly, a computer is only used to produce art by those who cannot really paint or draw, and secondly, that digital art cannot have the sensitivity of an oil or acrylic. He is no slave of the application, dependent on the machine to produce images that his technique cannot realize, but a painter and modeller who decided earlier than most of his peers to use late 20th-century tools to achieve his ends. And what a technique he's developed with them.

The surround sound, high-volume media age in which we live has grown a buying public so thoroughly conditioned by increasingly sophisticated, obscenely expensive Hollywood special effect spectaculars that many of them expect science fiction to be highly detailed intricate hardware with intimidating, impersonal, endless cities and breathtaking big sky backgrounds all delivered in impossibly sharp focus. SF illustration has to keep pace with this visual extravagance and, regardless of the tools he chooses to use, Fred Gambino has the discipline, imagination, patience and technique to satisfy and delight this very demanding audience.

It's great to see this book in print.

Dick Jude, November 2000

"At the beginning of 2000, I was going through one of my occasional quiet periods. I had just had one of my most successful years ever, but it doesn't seem to matter how good things have been, when things go quiet, I panic. Instead of using the time productively, I mope about wondering if my career is over and if I have done my last job.

One Saturday, as I contemplated a life as a brickie's mate or bartender, I was checking my email. I had one headed 'Neutron calling'. 'What's this now', I thought, 'someone trying to sell me something again?'

Instead, it was from John A. Davis, head of DNA animation studios in Dallas, who had just had one of his animations picked up by Paramount. He had seen my work in Dick Jude's anthology of fantasy art and was looking for artists to come up with some conceptual designs for the new film. He said he thought I might have some fun with this and was I interested?

Well, I considered it about as long as it took me to get to the phone, which is situated about 12 inches from my keyboard. There followed several months of thoroughly enjoyable design in an area of work that I think most illustrators would give their right arm for. At the time of writing, the film is still a work in progress and nothing can be shown until after its release, scheduled for late 2001. Look out for it."

Fred Gambino

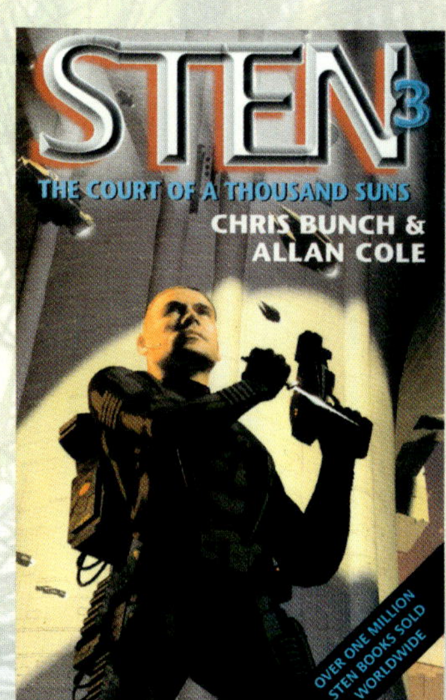

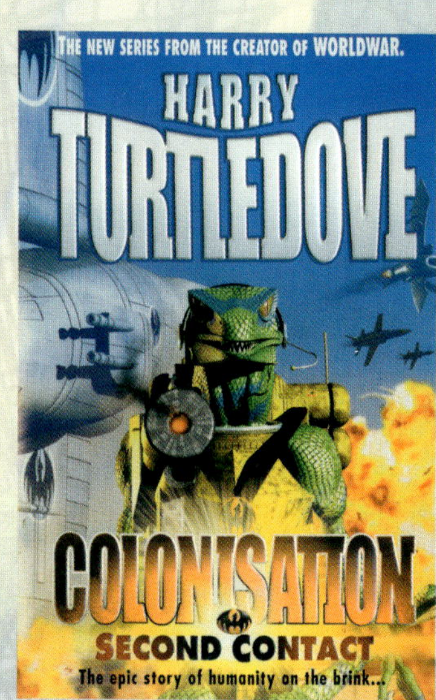

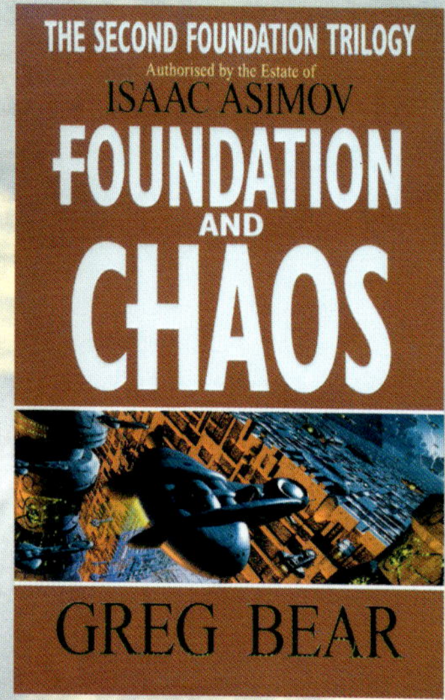

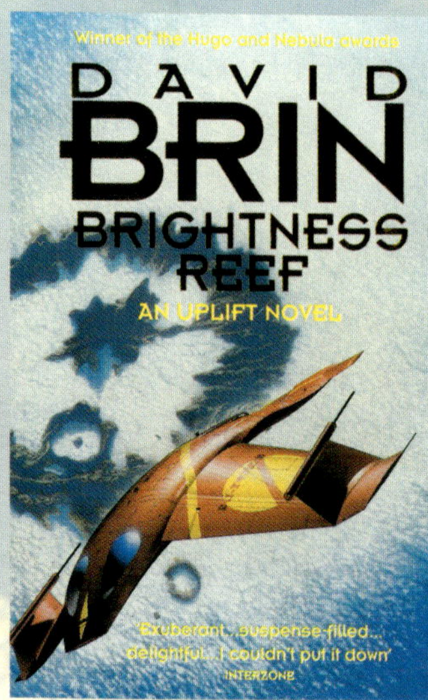

Heroes and Heroines

By Elizabeth Moon

What does a hero look like?

Real heroes and heroines come in all shapes and sizes and colours, speak in all languages and accents. Yet a strong tradition of physical perfection lingers in our minds: we know, or think we know, what heroes and heroines look like.

Years ago, when I first read science fiction, many genre book covers and magazine illustrations emphasized the conventional marks of greatness, posing a ruggedly handsome male (often with torn shirt or spacesuit that revealed his bulging muscles) in front of large complicated machines. A scantily clad and lushly endowed damsel might cower behind him. The same ruggedly handsome male physique showed up on the covers of romance novels, historical adventures and spy novels, garbed in appropriate period attire, and accompanied by the same lushly endowed damsel-in-distress. However smudged with dirt or blood, the hero never looked frightened or tired: his expression ranged somewhere between grim determination and steady confidence.

When women other than damsels-in-distress made it to the covers of science-fiction books, they first appeared as the same scantily clad and lushly endowed damsel – but this time holding a sword or blaster. Just as the male hero had to be jut-jawed and broad-shouldered, the heroine had to be curvaceous. Now she might look triumphant or confident but, like the hero, she never looked tired, confused, or worried.

Writers of adventure and military science fiction mutter into their teacups about this; we all have horror stories about the way some artist dressed (or undressed) our characters. We make the effort to create intelligent, capable, emotionally complex characters of various ages and both sexes, and then they appear on the cover looking like the same luscious babe with flowing locks and ample cleavage and the same jut-jawed grim hero.

But not always. Sometimes an exceptional artist sees beyond the stereotype and creates for us the outward and visible form of our imagination. There she is – tired, hair matted from the helmet, her steady gaze expressing everything she's been through. Someone who thinks and worries. Someone who suffers. Someone who survives.

When I saw the first cover Fred Gambino had done for one of my books, I could hardly believe how perfectly he had expressed my vision of her. Not the luscious babe heroine with the cleavage, but a complex grown woman, capable of real heroism.

When I saw what he had done for other writers' books, which needed a different treatment, I knew that he was not a one-trick pony: here is an artist whose style can adapt to the material, who can and does take the time to give each book his best. There's still a place for the jut-jawed hero and the curvaceous heroine – no one style suits every book – but his ability to go beyond that stereotype and show real people makes this artist extraordinary.

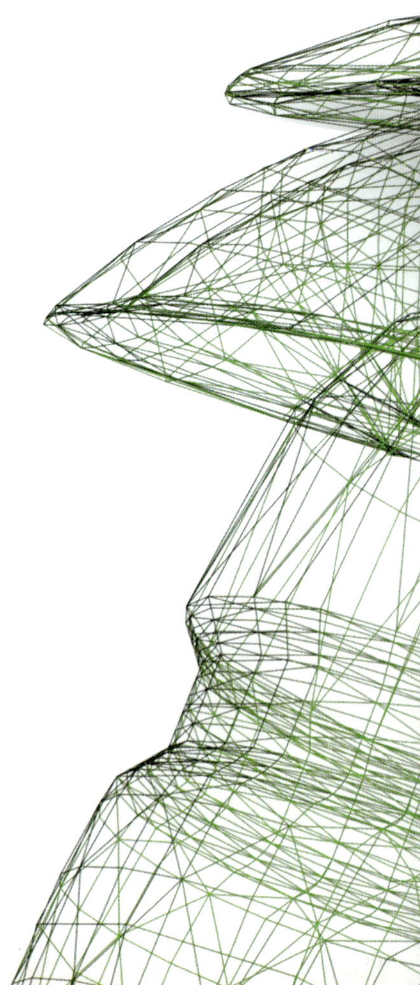

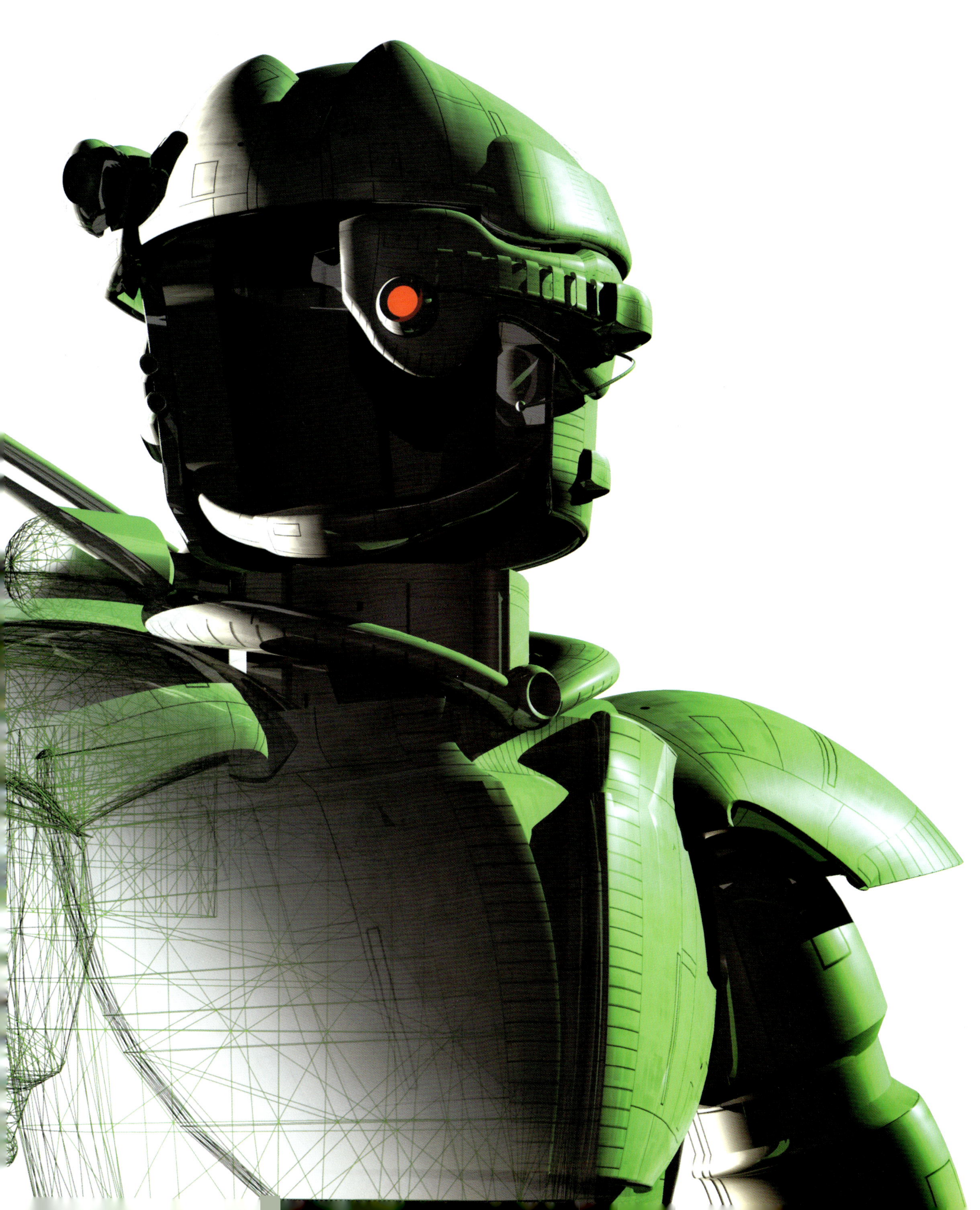

SERRANO LEGACY SERIES

Elizabeth Moon
Little, Brown UK
Digital

In 1999, Peter Cotton of Little, Brown commissioned me to do the first three covers of Elizabeth Moon's space epic concerning the adventures of Heris Serrano and The Fleet. The brief was fairly straightforward; the leading character should feature centre stage, surrounded by hardware and spaceships from the story.

By now I had become pretty adept with the computer and the various softwares I was using. The novelty had worn off, and the computer had pretty much become just another tool. I had felt that, in some of my earlier digital images, there was far too much of the machine and not enough of me. This was due largely to my spending too much time thinking about the software, and not enough time thinking about the image.

With these new commissions I adopted a revolutionary new strategy – I went back to the drawing board. I started by drawing several thumbnail sketches to establish the composition. Then, when something struck a chord, I scanned that thumbnail into the computer, blew it up to the finished size and coloured it in using Photoshop, thus retaining all those spontaneous lines and squiggles that seem to come straight from the subconscious. The result was a more lively, painterly looking image. With the Elizabeth Moon covers, I began with the main figure, and then drew lines and shapes that enhanced the composition. Only when satisfied with this unified broad look did I begin to add the antennae, panelling and lights necessary to start making my abstract shapes become SF hardware.

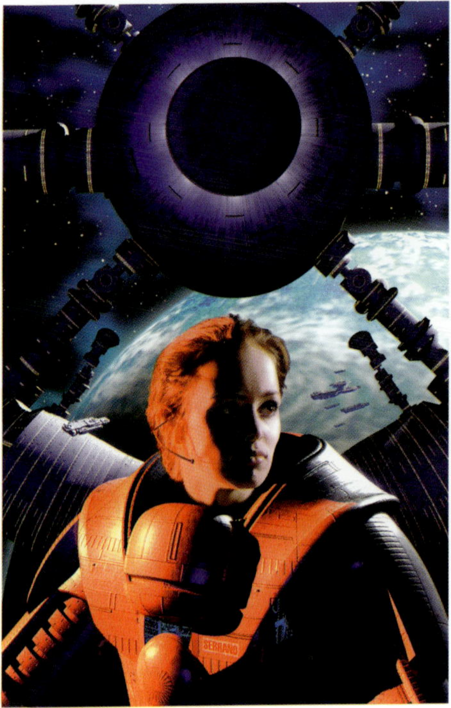

ABOVE

SPORTING CHANCE

Modelled in Alias Sketch and Amapi, and composited in Photoshop, I thought it would work well with all these covers if the hardware extended up behind the type, to give a sense of scale and add interest to the sky. The Earth-like planet is a 3D sphere, texture mapped with a swirling planet texture painted in Photoshop. Matching the photographed head with the perspective of the 3D models needed particular attention with all these images.

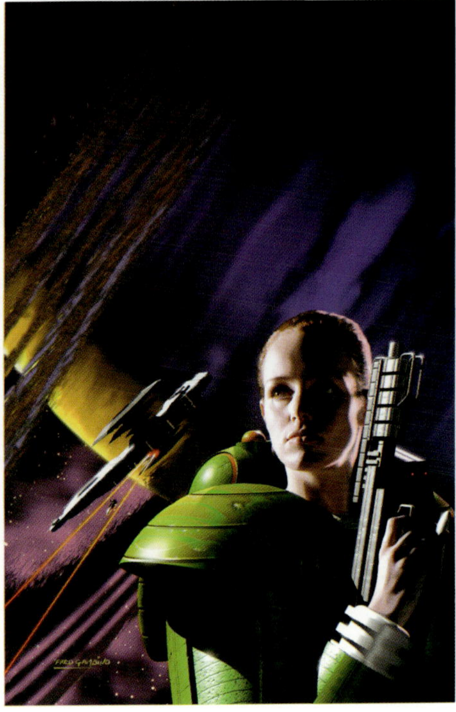

ABOVE

HUNTING PARTY

This was the second I did in the series and a chance to feature a ringed gas giant in the background. I wanted the hardware in the series to have a particular look, as if all the ships in the 'Fleet' universe belonged to the same technology. I felt it would help to give the whole series a more cohesive look.

This was also the first pose to feature a gun. I originally intended this for the second book in the series, *Sporting Chance*. Fans of the series will note the relevance to that book, but the publishers decided that the first cover to appear should have the gun.

RIGHT

RULES OF ENGAGEMENT

Space stations feature heavily in the stories, so a number of the covers show them. I went for a more monochromatic look here – the black suit is almost a silhouette, with only one strong highlight to give it form, helping to concentrate the viewer's eye on Suiza's face.

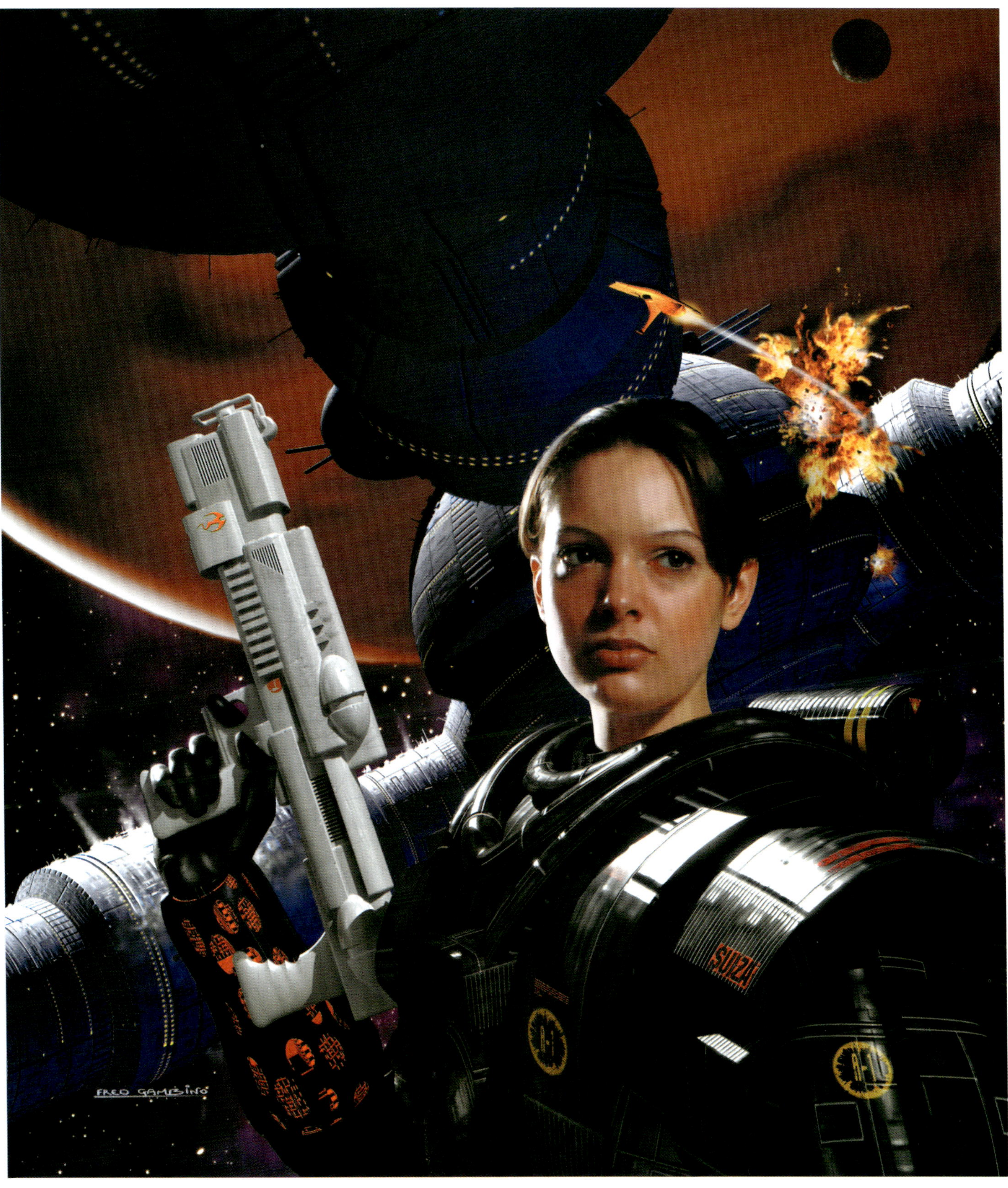
FRED GAMBINO

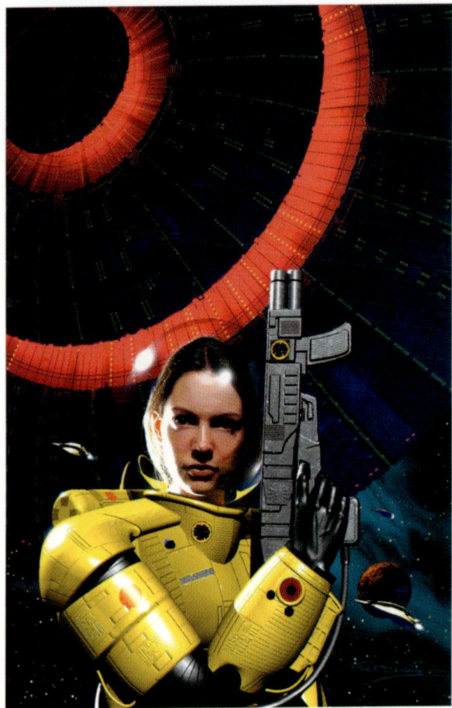

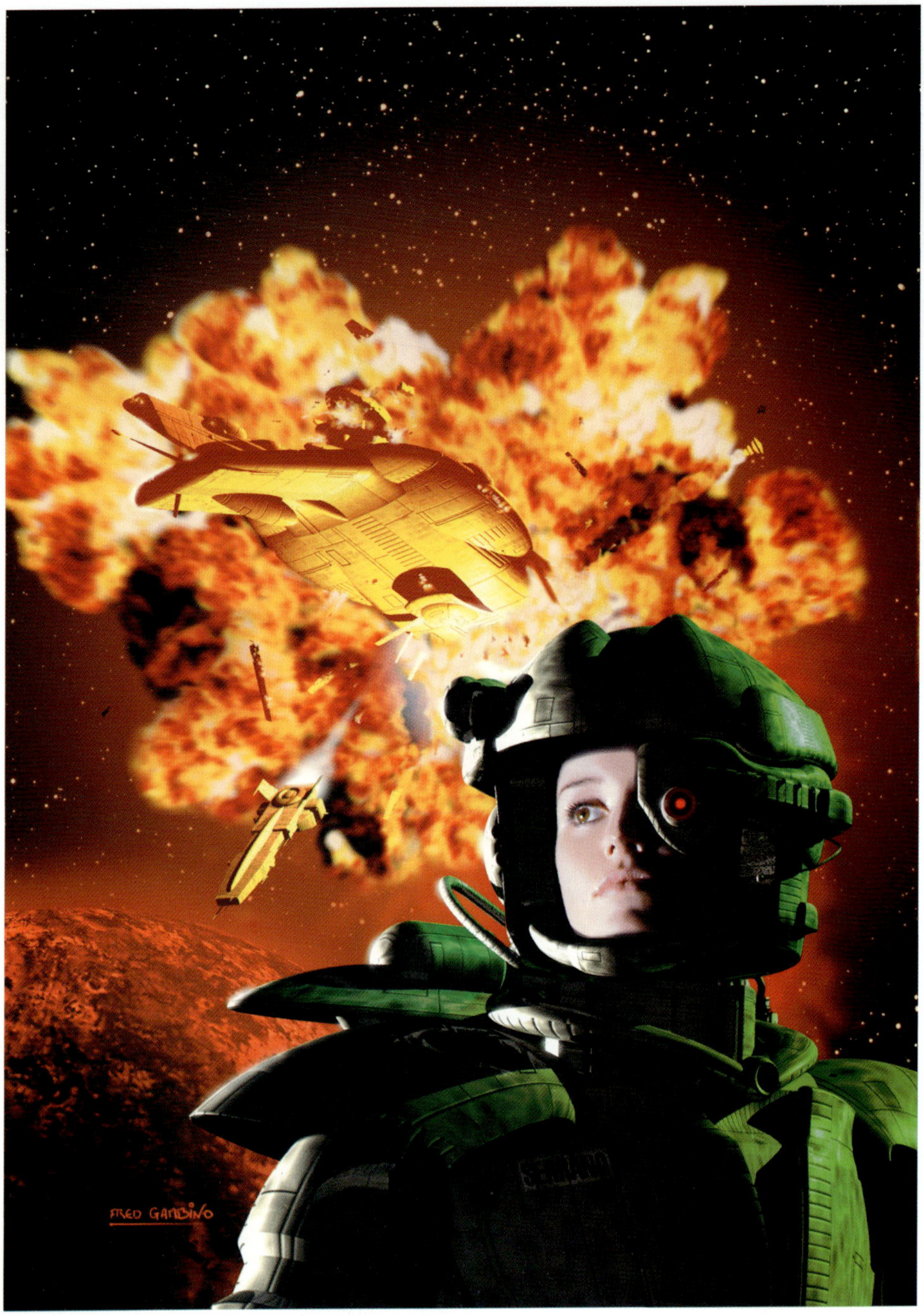

ABOVE

CHANGE OF COMMAND

This was the last Suiza cover, inspired by a TV image of a young boy in the Middle East. I only caught the pose briefly as I walked into the room, but I remember making a mental note and thinking that it would come in useful one day.

RIGHT

WINNING COLOURS

I introduced an exploding space ship this time, just to ring the changes. I particularly enjoyed dismantling the carefully modelled ship in order to simulate the various fragments hurtling away from each other.

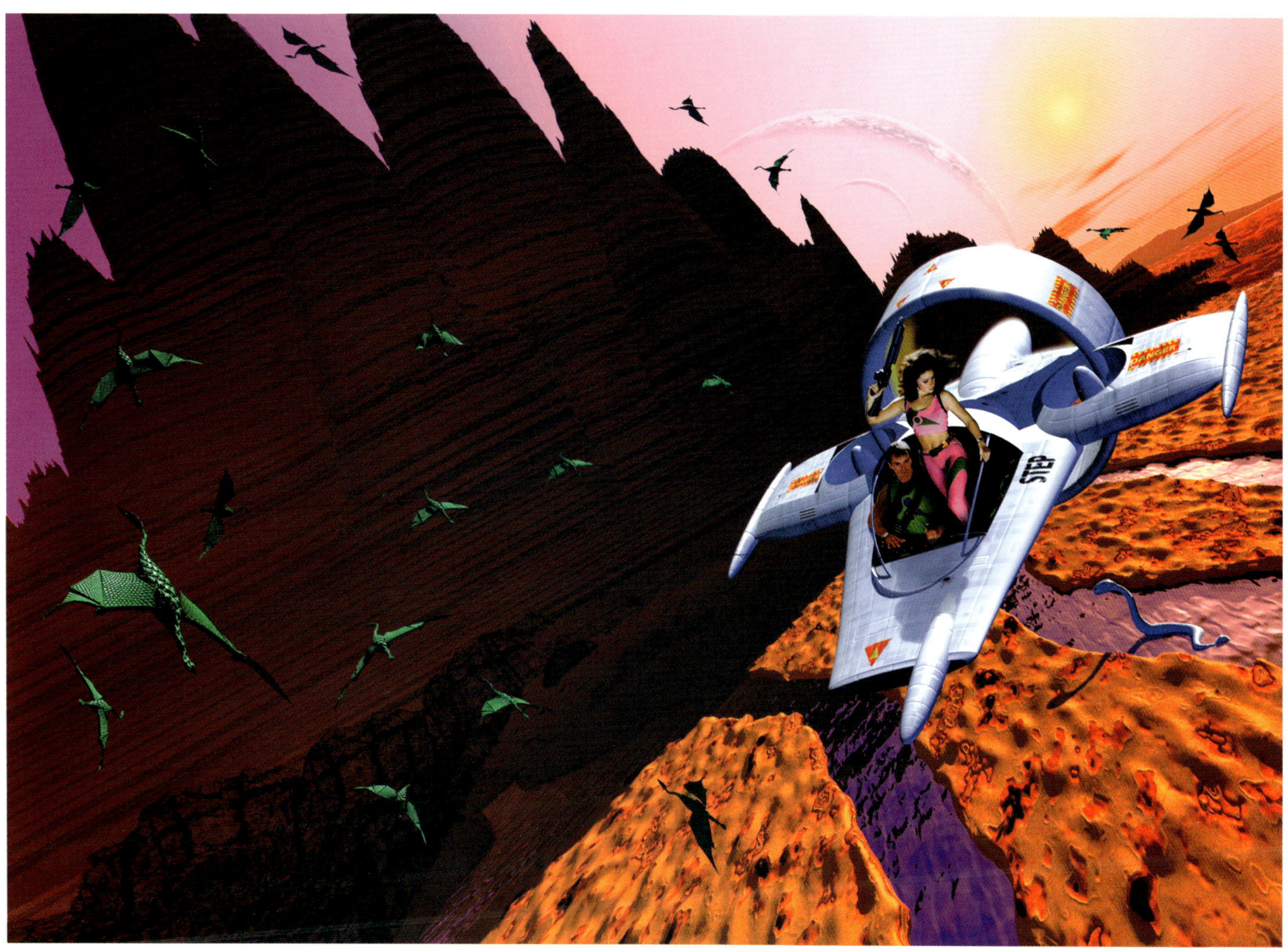

ABOVE

THE DRAGONS OF HEOROT

Larry Niven, Jerry Pournelle
and Steven Barnes
Little, Brown UK
Digital

This was my second printed digital cover and the first that I felt really happy with. At the time, Bryce, a program that specializes in generating landscapes, had only just been released. Its ease of use, relative cheapness, and amazing results made it a huge success, and it quickly became ubiquitous on nearly every aspiring illustrator's hard drive. This, however, was also its downfall; as it was so easy to use, the world was rapidly flooded with millions of Bryce images of varying quality. It became almost impossible for anyone using it to be taken seriously. At the time I did this cover, however, virtually no one else was using it, certainly not in British publishing. I can claim to be one of the first.

 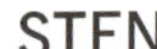

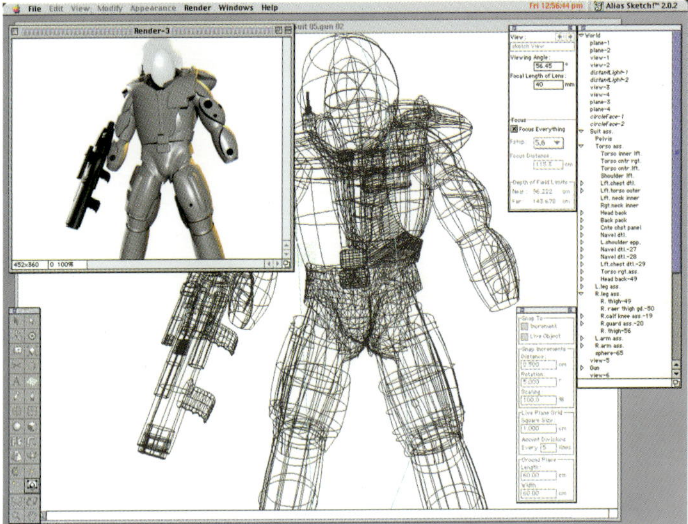

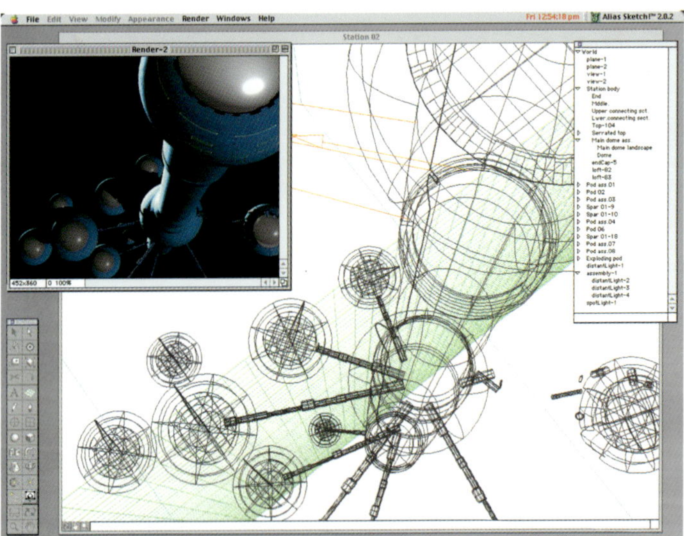

STEN

Allan Cole and Chris Bunch
Little, Brown UK
Digital

After the success of the Serrano Legacy covers (see page 10), Little, Brown gave me a new series. These covers would also feature an eponymous hero, but to make them different from the Elizabeth Moon series, they would wraparound and show more of the figure. I tried to give them a 'James Bond-in-space' feel and 'Sten' set the trend, featuring massive hardware in the background with a large helping of actual or implied violence. I had been to a party a couple of weeks before and had noticed Jamie (below left), who I thought would fit the bill as Sten, perfectly.

The first version featured Sten wearing a bubble helmet, the better to show off Jamie's rugged features – I felt that the hero's face would be crucial to the success of the image. I was somewhat surprised therefore, to get a phone call from the publishers saying that they were worried and that they were even contemplating changing the model. I returned to the illustration, trying to be objective. I first removed the gelled hair, giving him a more military-style crew cut, and then redesigned the helmet, giving it a more aggressive, 'I mean business' look. It improved the image tremendously – funny how one is sometimes blind to the obvious.

LEFT AND BELOW: Early 3D renderings for space suit and space station.

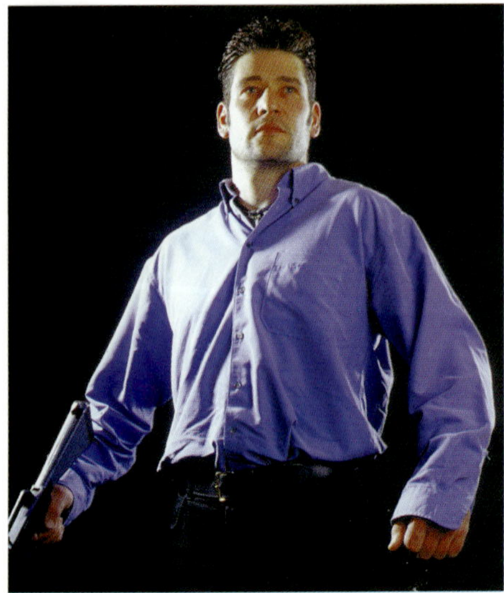

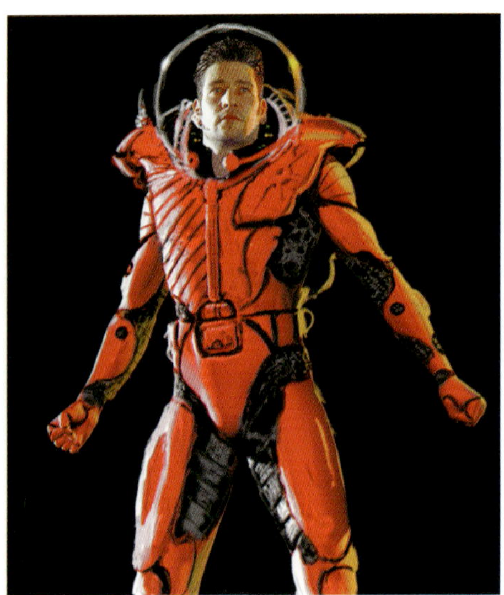

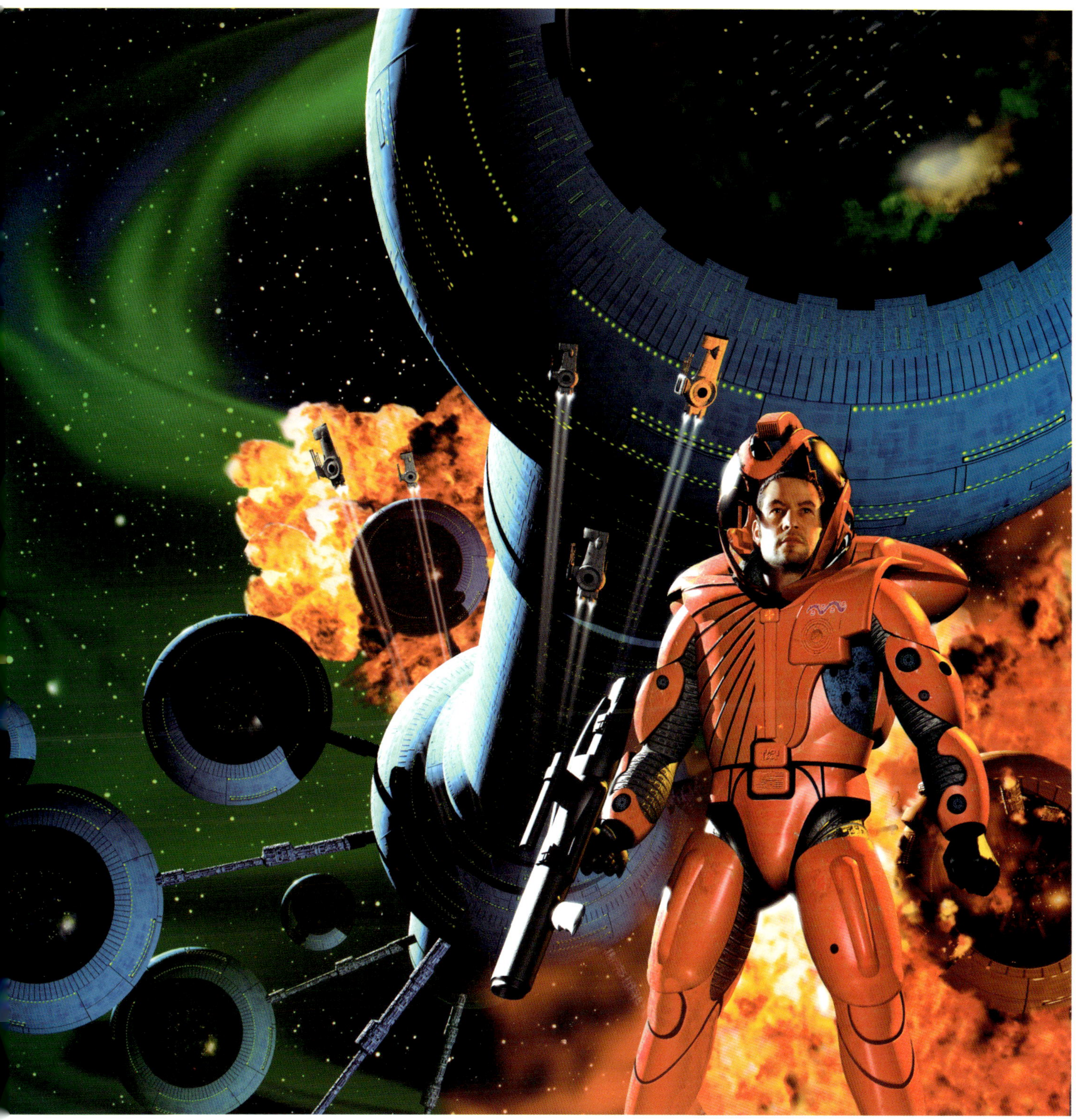

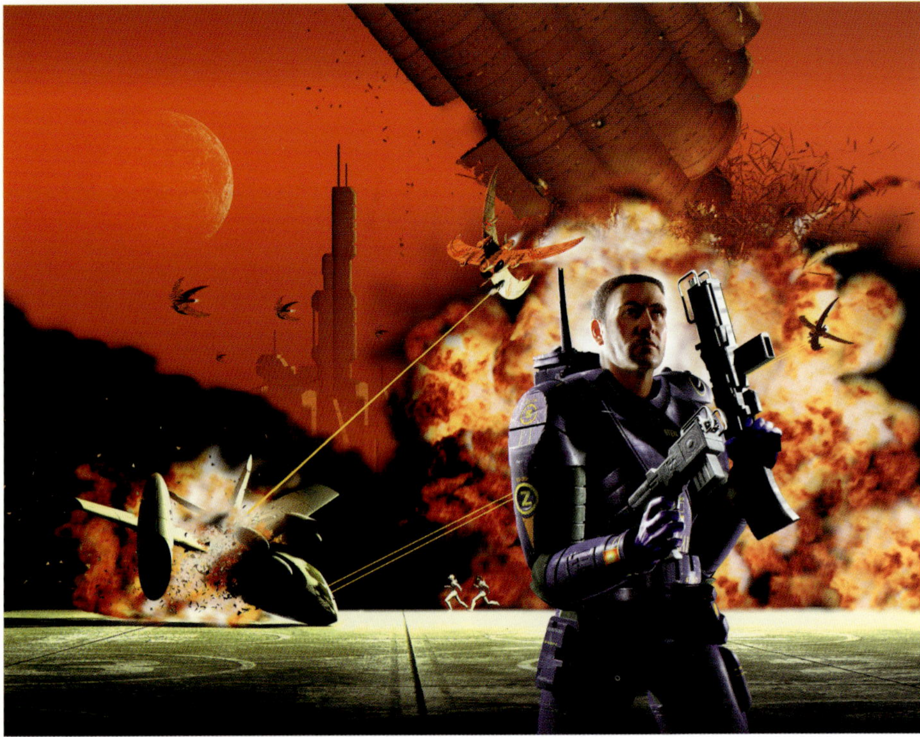

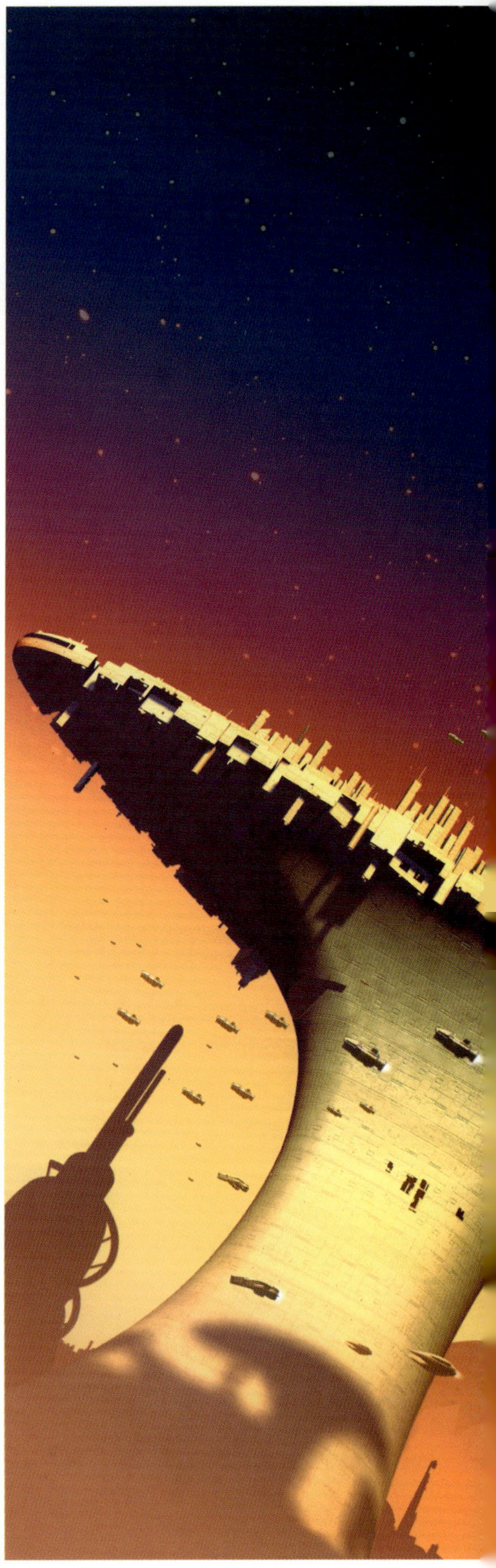

ABOVE

THE WOLF WORLDS

Allan Cole and Chris Bunch
Little, Brown UK
Digital

This was my first attempt to complete a whole cover in Electric Image, the program that has largely superseded Alias Sketch as my main 3D modelling and rendering software.

If you compare this to *Sten* (see page 14), the first cover and the last job I completed in Sketch, I feel that *Wolf Worlds* has a more natural, realistic look. This is partly due to the soft shadows, but also to the way EI shades the geometry.

RIGHT

THE COURT OF A THOUSAND SUNS

Allan Cole and Chris Bunch
Little, Brown UK
Digital

This probably marked the first cover where I felt that I had finally come to grips with Electric Image. It had only taken me six months! Happily, I could now get back to concentrating on the only thing that really matters, the content of the image. Sten's body and military kit were modelled in EI; the only part of Jamie's photograph that survived was his head.

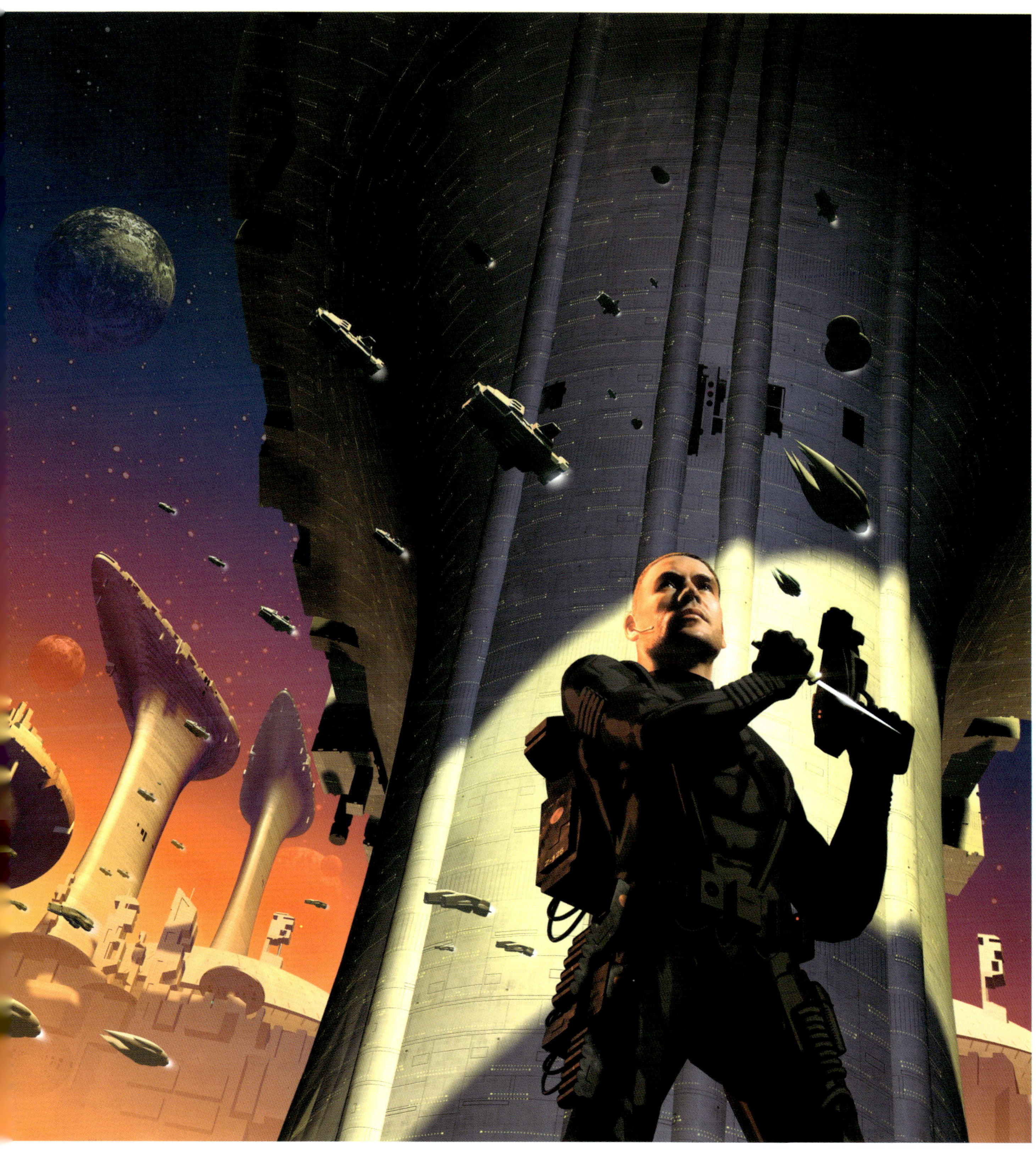

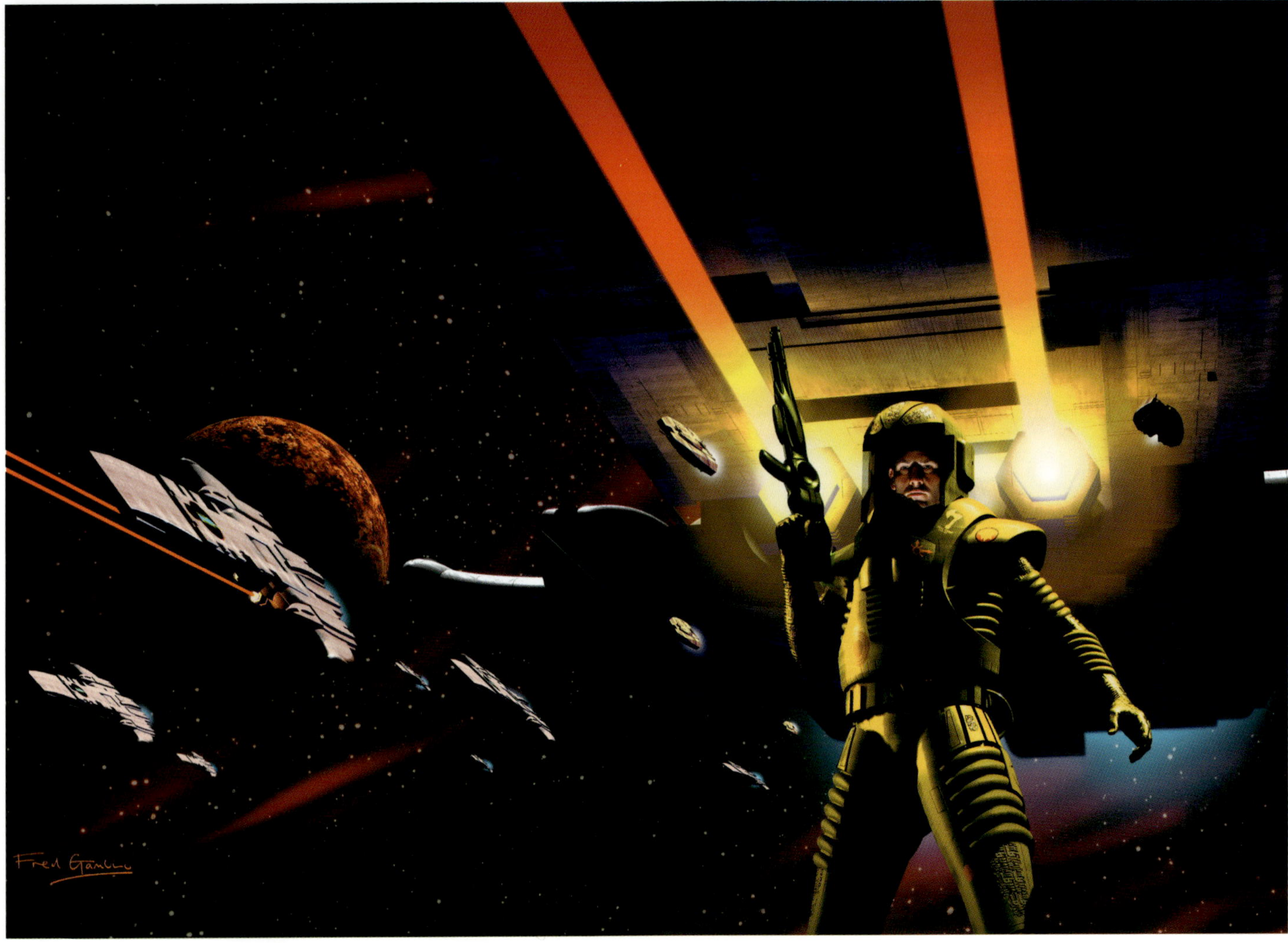

ABOVE

FLEET OF THE DAMNED

Allan Cole and Chris Bunch
Little, Brown UK
Digital

This was another chance to indulge in pure space opera. With guns blazing, the fleet of the damned thunders overhead, while Sten, apparently unperturbed by the proximity of the guns, defiantly stands his ground.

OPPOSITE

A CASE OF CONSCIENCE

James Blish
Orion
Digital

One of the Orion Masterworks series and another space suit design. This time the character called for was of South American appearance. I was up against a very tight deadline and was about to go on holiday, so even if I could think of someone who would fit the bill, I would be struggling to set the shot up and get the film processed in time.

Jenny, my partner, suggested that I look through the considerable amount of reference shots I had amassed over the years; as she pointed out, 'What is the use of saving all this stuff if you never use it?' A good question – I nearly always do a specific shoot for every new job, yet I never throw anything away. So I spent a pleasant hour or two going down memory lane – it's amazing how evocative old photos are. Not least the photo I finally used. The perfect Latin looks, even down to the wet hair that I envisioned the character would have – none other than myself from about ten years ago, a time when all that hair was more than just a memory.

One of the advantages of a compilation of one's work in a book like this is that I can redress changes that the art directors asked for that I might not necessarily have agreed with at the time. The art director had a problem with the lizard in this image and asked for him to be removed. Quite often changes like this do improve the image, but in this case I prefer the lizard, so for the first time in print, here is the director's cut of *A Case of Conscience*.

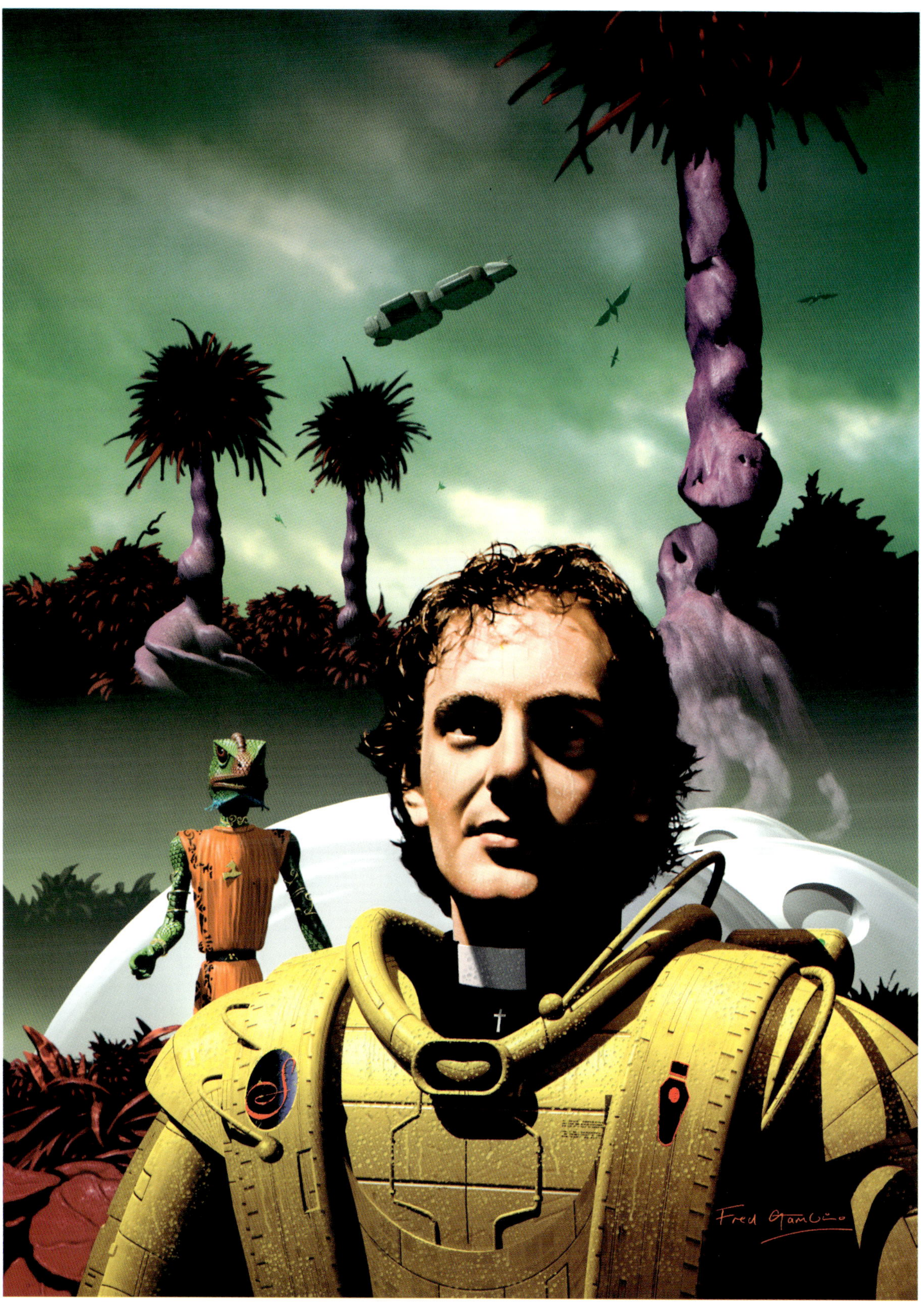
Fred Gambino

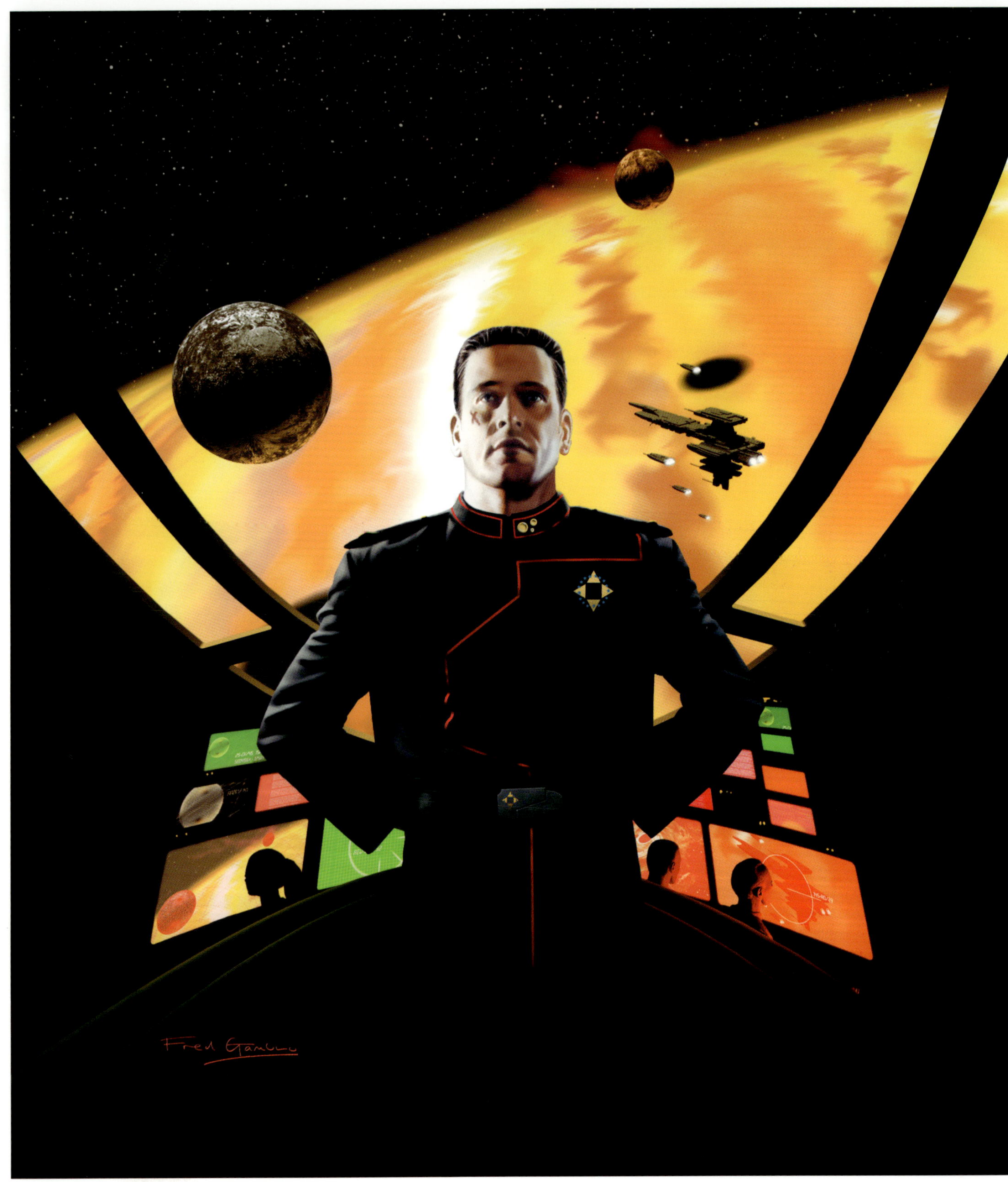
Fred Gambino

OPPOSITE

BROTHERS IN ARMS

Lois McMaster Bujold
HarperCollins USA
Acrylic/digital

Hot on the heels of the Elizabeth Moon and Sten jobs (see pages 10 and 14), I received this cover commission for Avon Books. The brief was fairly tight. Our hero, fresh from the academy, is standing on the bridge of a star ship and behind him is visible a Jupiter-type, gas giant planet.

The art director, who admits he is something of a traditionalist as far as illustration is concerned, was happy for me to do this digitally, as long as the figure definitely *did not* look like a scanned photograph. For most of my career, I have been trying to make my paintings look like photographs, now I'm trying to make my photographs look like paintings! The solution, in this instance, was to paint the figure in acrylics, scan it, and then drop it onto the digital background, which was rendered and modelled in Electric Image.

RIGHT

MERCENARY

Piers Anthony
HarperCollins UK
Acrylic

The second in Anthony's *Bio Of A Space Tyrant* series, featuring Hope Hubris as the tyrant. The five books that make up the sequence cover Hubris's life from a teenager to old age, so I got the chance to progressively age the central figure on each book. In this one he is about twenty-five.

This was painted at a time when I laboriously masked each and every separate element and cut paper masks for virtually every shadow. Hubris's name was accomplished rather more efficiently, by using rubdown lettering. The name had to be placed somewhere on the suit that was almost straight on to the viewer, so there would not be any problems with the perspective.

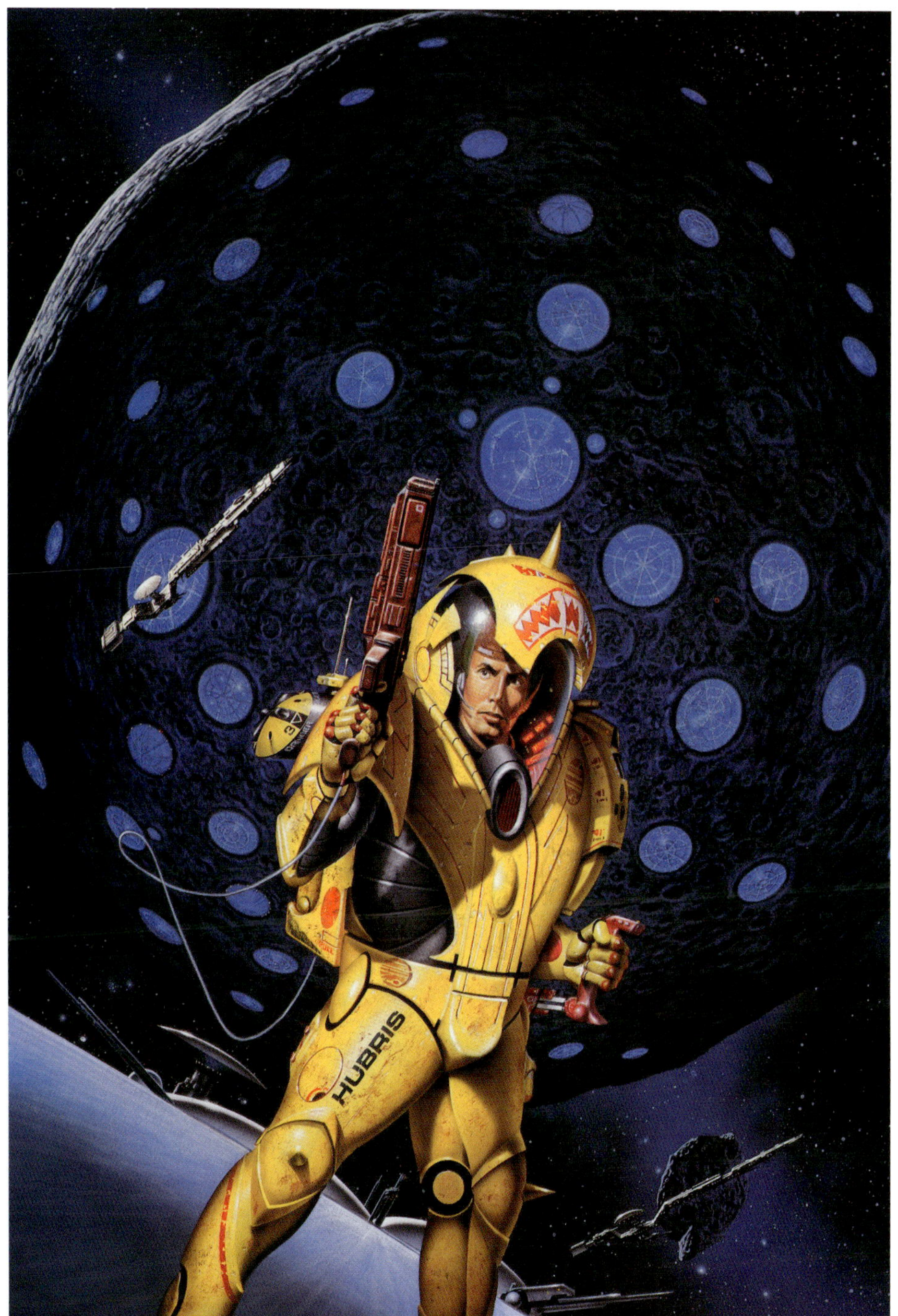

NIGHTWINGS

Robert Silverberg
HarperCollins UK
Digital

This was another of my early digital covers and has been something of a seminal piece, as it seems to be very popular. I always had a problem with it, however, because it was done at a time when I still had not decided on the best way of incorporating my photo reference into the digital image, and I always felt that I should have done more with the figure. This book has now given me the chance. I worked over the body with the airbrush tool to remove the photographic grain, and reworked her hair so that now it looks like it is whirling in the wind. I am much happier with this version. I also took the opportunity to add a ruined building from which the character is launching herself, helping, I think, to give it a more dramatic, vertiginous perspective.

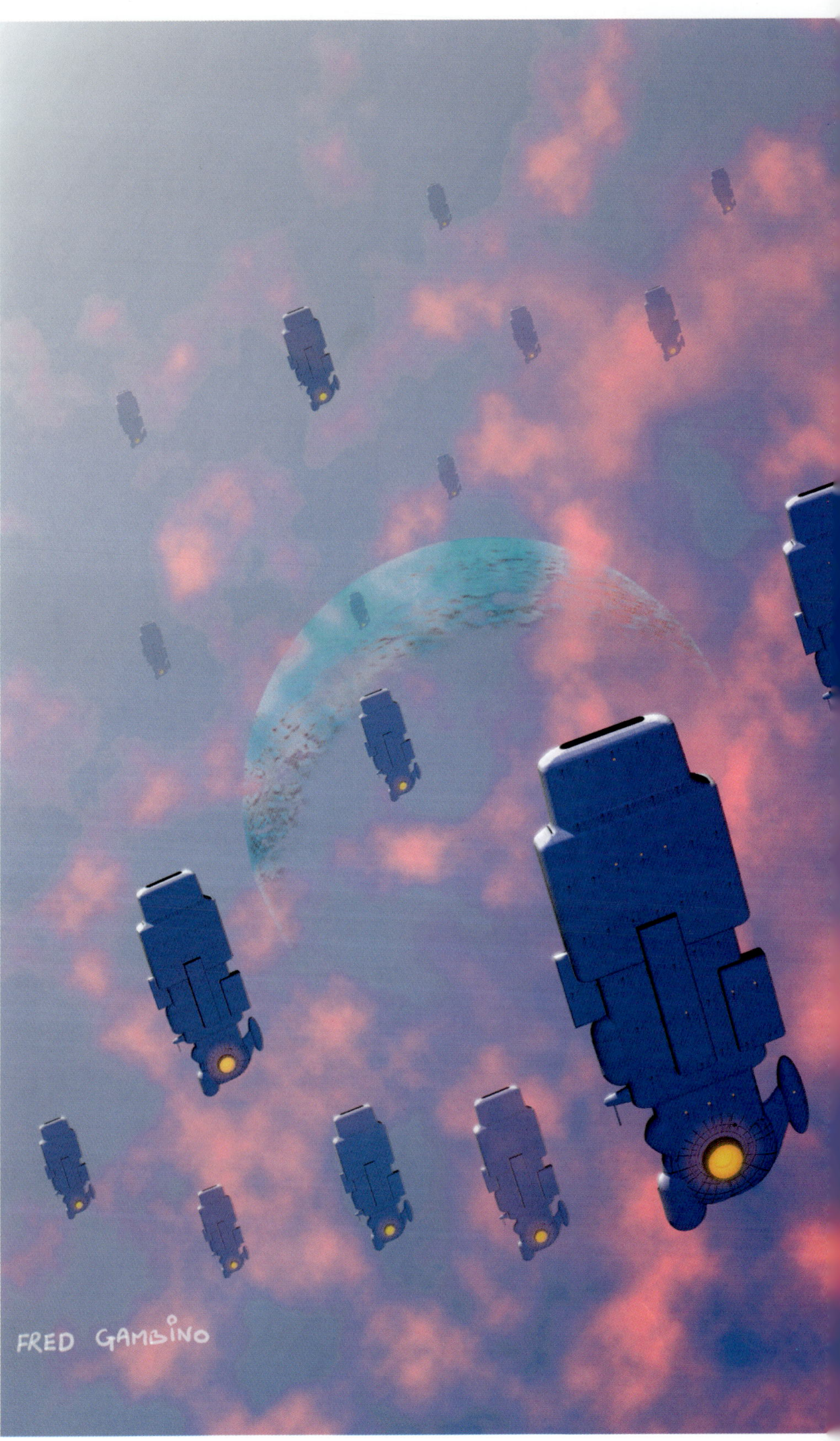

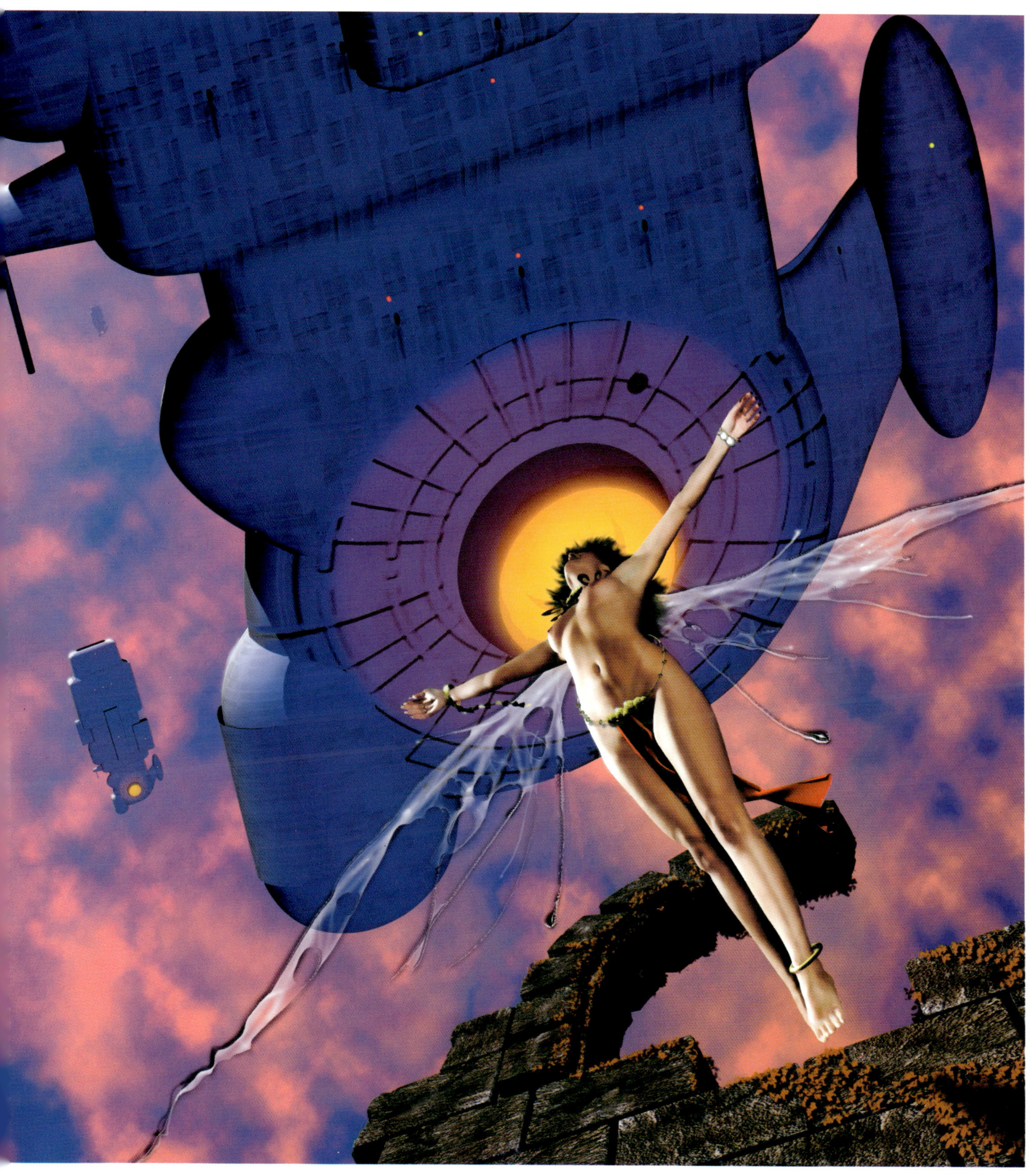

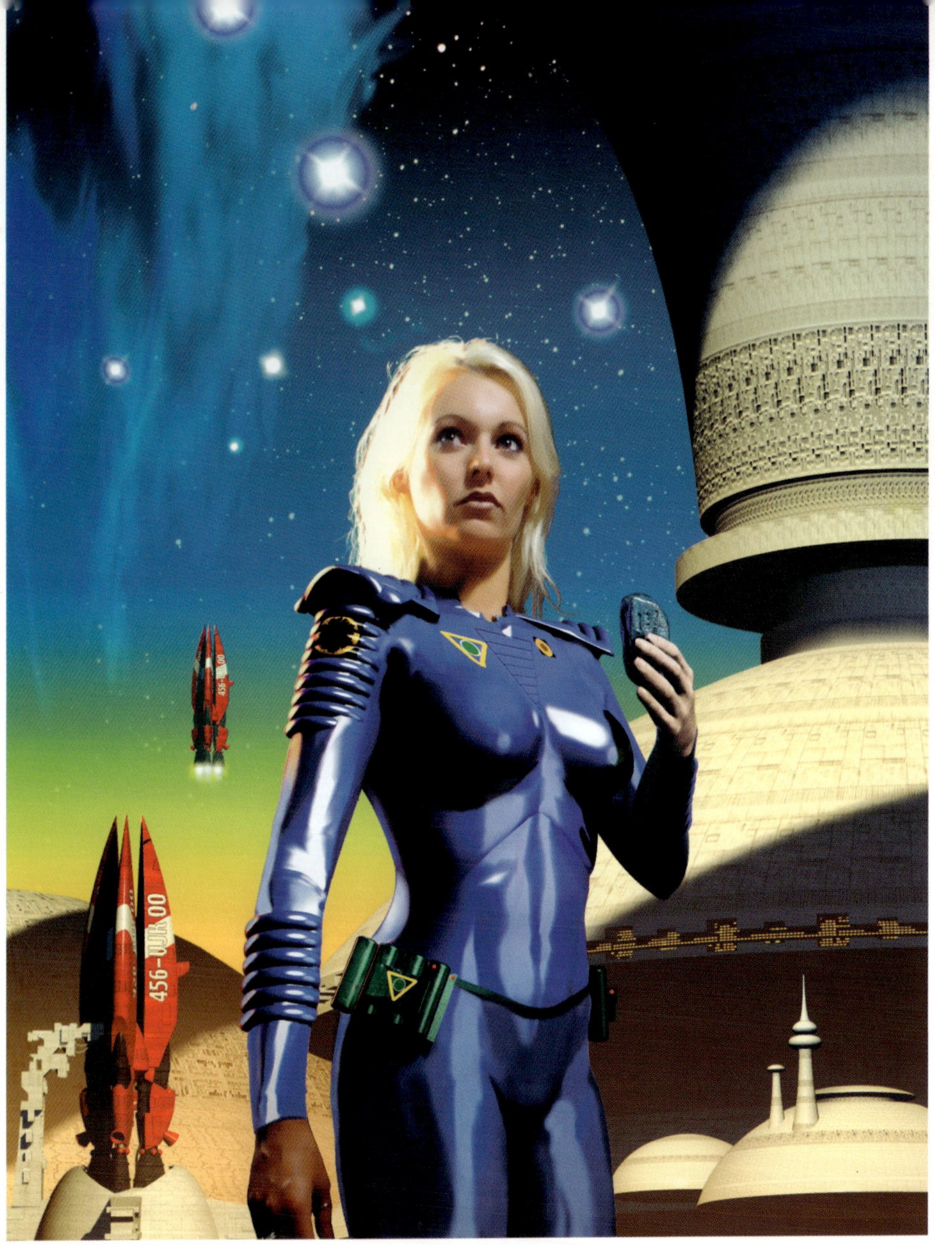

HEART OF STONE

Denny DeMartino
Berkley Books
Digital

For some reason, I've noticed over the years that similar jobs come together. Shortly after I completed *The Court of a Thousand Suns* (page 16), I received this job from Berkley Books in the US. Again, there is a figure in a mega city. The brief stated that the character should look similar to Michele Pfeiffer and it so happened that Salena Jo Marshall, the model who posed for *Nightwings* (see page 22), fitted the bill.

Since I was so pleased with *Court*, and not being one to fail to use a good idea at least twice, I adopted a similar approach, using light and shadow cast on the buildings by objects off camera, so to speak, to direct the viewer's eye to the character's face. I was particularly pleased with the design of the sporty 'boy racer' spaceship in the background and would like to use it again, suitably revised of course, in a more prominent position in something else.

BELOW: Wireframe compilation, model photography and test render of spaceship.

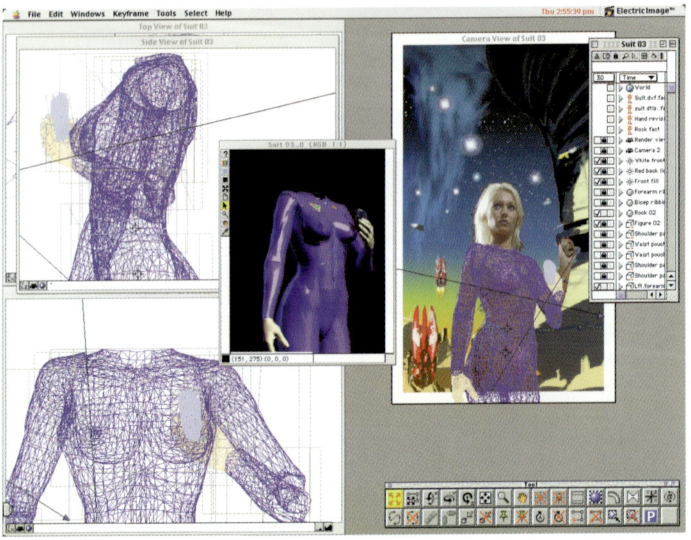

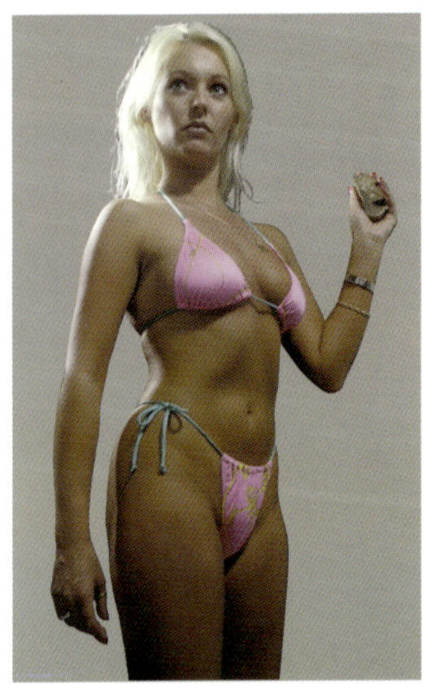

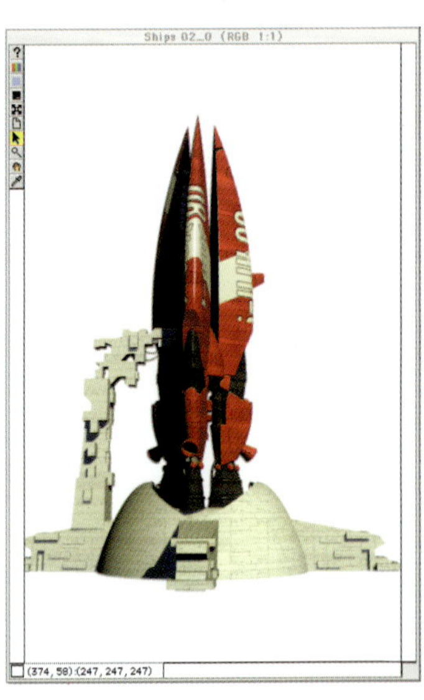

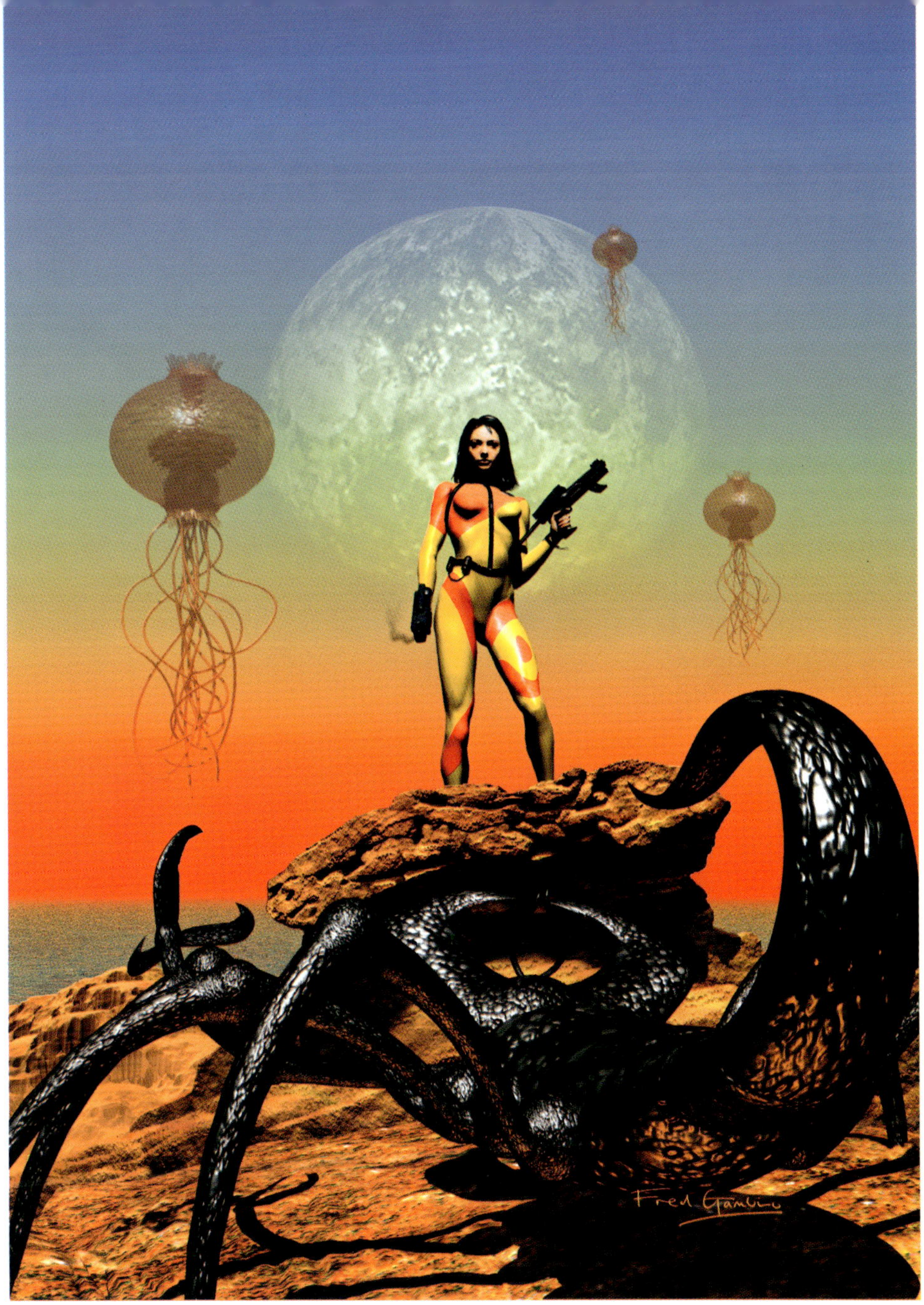

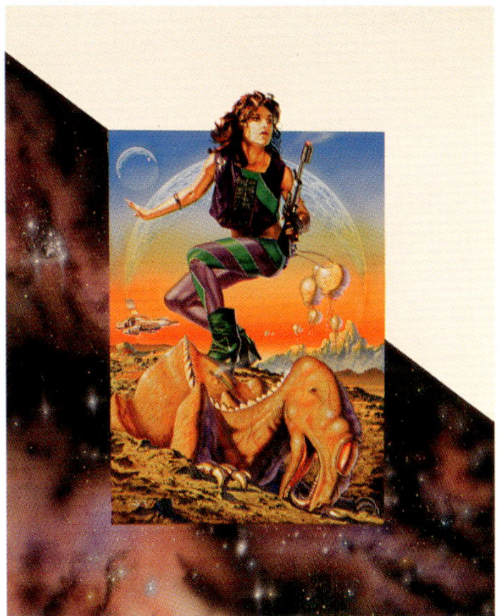

THE JESUS INCIDENT

Frank Herbert
Orion
Digital

At the beginning of the 1980s, I was still trying to establish myself as an illustrator. I had done moderately well soon after leaving college, but the recession had put paid to my budding career, leaving me in the doldrums for a couple of years. A series of covers for Futura marked the beginning of an upward spiral that has continued, more or less, ever since. They commissioned me to illustrate the covers for several Frank Herbert books, amongst them *The Jesus Incident* (above right). Consequently, I remember these covers with affection.

Two decades later, it came as a pleasant surprise to receive *The Jesus Incident* commission again from Orion, as part of their Masterworks series. This image recollects the look of my work of that earlier period, in fact the brief included the passage that described the very same scene that I had illustrated previously, but this time I elected to produce the work digitally. I completed the rough using Poser to generate the figure, intending to produce photographic reference for the final job, as is my usual practice. However, once I had approval, I realized that I would need a lot of space to reproduce this pose, as it would be necessary to get well back from the model. This is not normally a problem, as I have a reciprocal arrangement with a photographic studio where I used to rent office space. But they were too busy and, as I was about to disappear on a three-week trek to Chile, I didn't have the time to wait. My other option is to clear out my dining room and set up lights – fine for close ups, but inadequate in this case. In the event, the solution was simple.

Often when I use Poser, the results are a bit stiff, but occasionally I get a result that I know will be hard to reproduce in the studio. I felt like this about this particular pose. There was a relaxed, but tense, expectant feel to the figure. So, in the end, I elected to keep the Poser body, just using the model's head and hands. I could even use the somewhat plastic feel of the digital image to advantage, as she was supposed to be wearing a skin-tight, synthetic suit. My new-found model, Carly, posed for this – all I needed was her head, and I could manage to photograph that in my dining room without a problem.

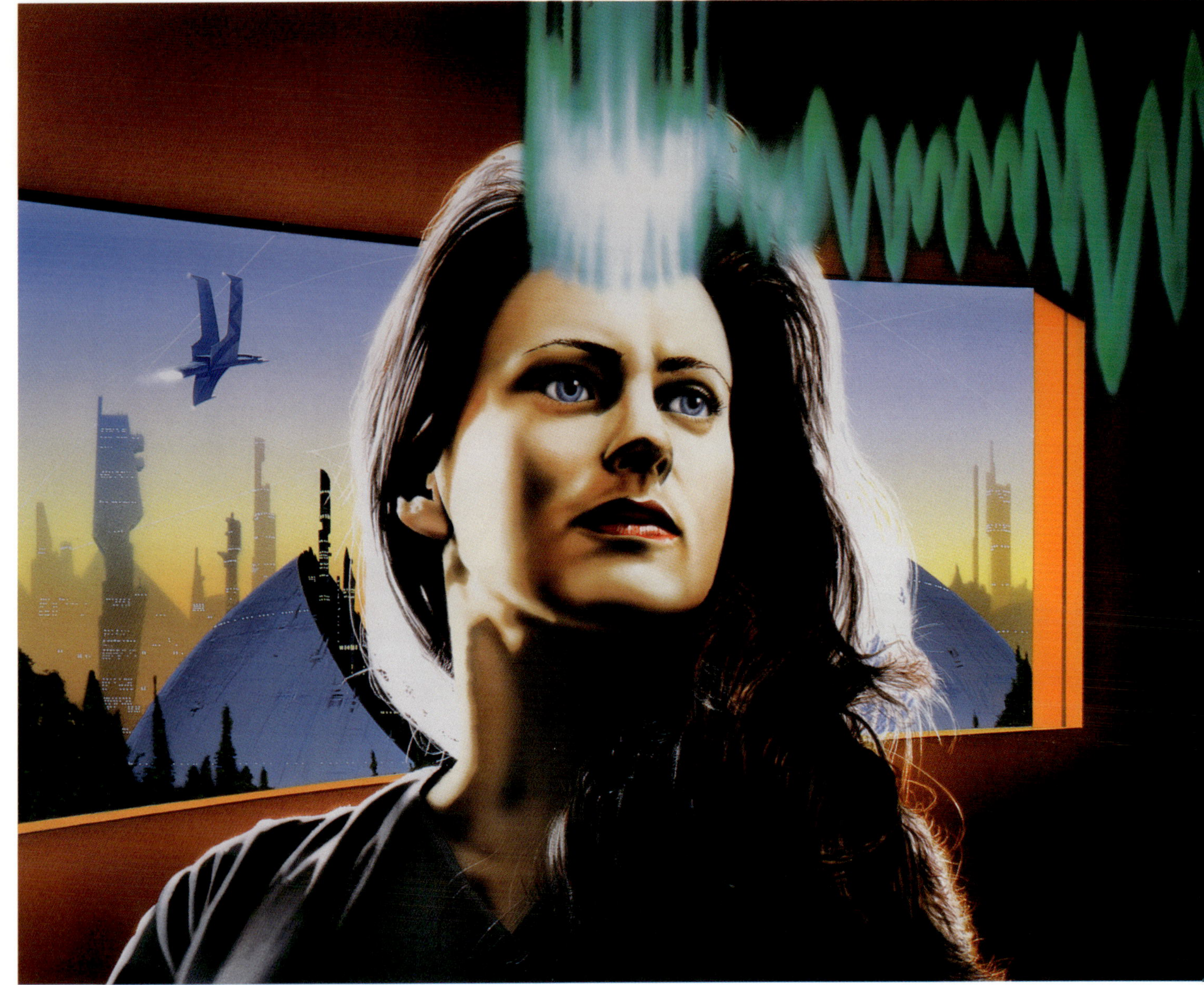

STARBORNE

Robert Silverberg
HarperCollins UK
Acrylic

The premise of this story is that of twin sisters who have the power of telepathic communication, which it turns out is the only way of communicating over stellar distances. The brief was to somehow show the two girls, one on Earth and the other in space, in communication with each other.

My first rough had one face on the front cover, split by a dark shadow, one side lit by cool light, the other by warm light. A view of Earth melted out of the shadow on the warm side, interstellar space on the other. This kept all the action on the front cover.

However, the publishers wanted the two girls separated, with the somewhat contrived device of the 'radio wave' connecting them. Any illustrator will tell you that the roughs they don't choose are the best ones, and I still think that in this case, but an illustrator's job is to give the client what they ask for and they seemed pretty happy with this in the end, which is what counts.

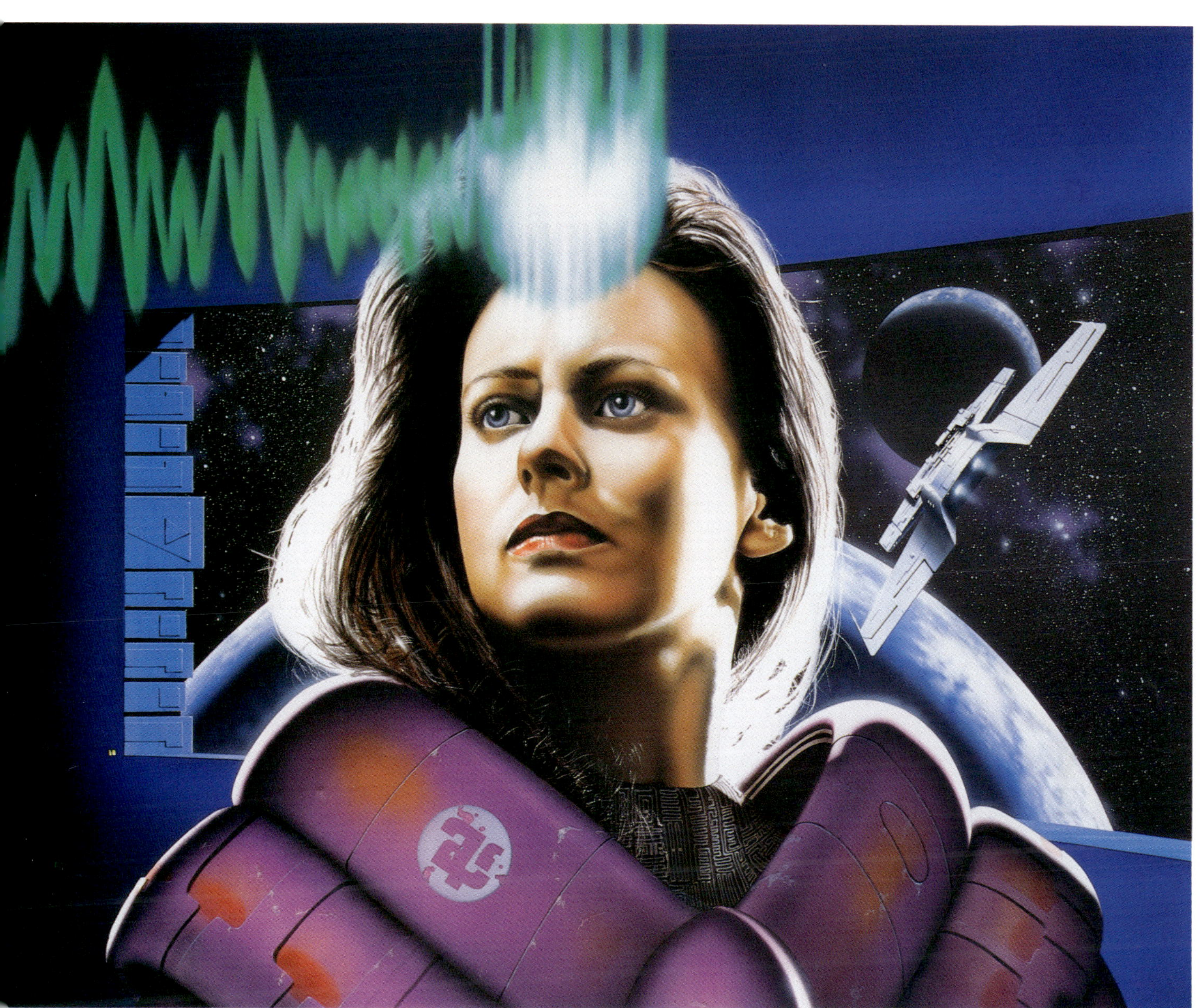

BELOW

NON-STOP

Brian Aldiss
Orion
Digital

For this cover I toyed with the idea of modelling the vines, but in the end decided that the effort involved just wasn't worth the return. Instead, I painted them freehand in Photoshop. I used Poser for the rough of the figure and then originated my own reference for the artwork, using a friend, Chris Green, as the model. This time I felt that the lighting on the retouched Poser head looked much better than my photo, although the body and costume looked fine. So, I did the opposite of *The Jesus Incident* (see page 25), chopping off Chris's head, but keeping his body.

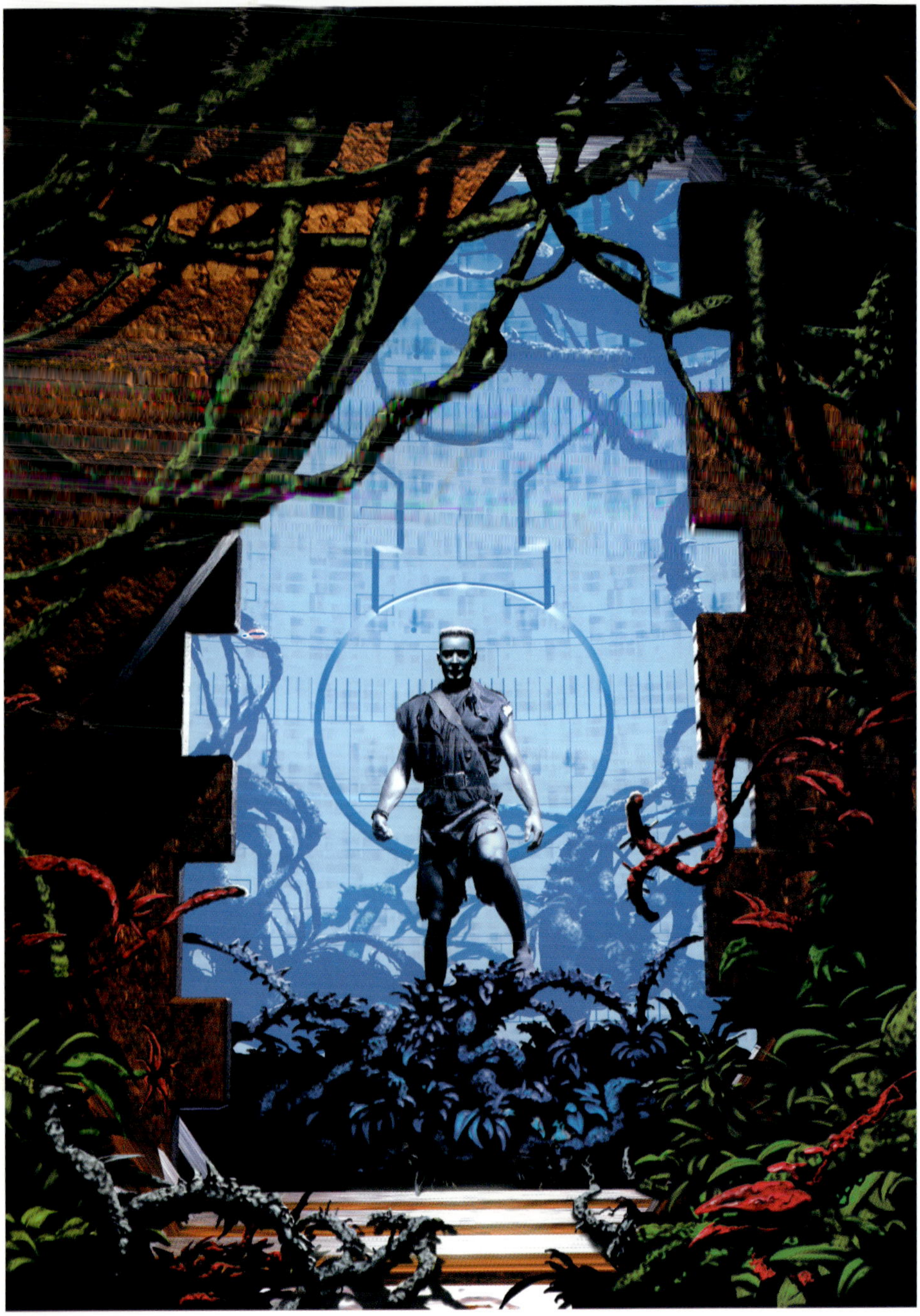

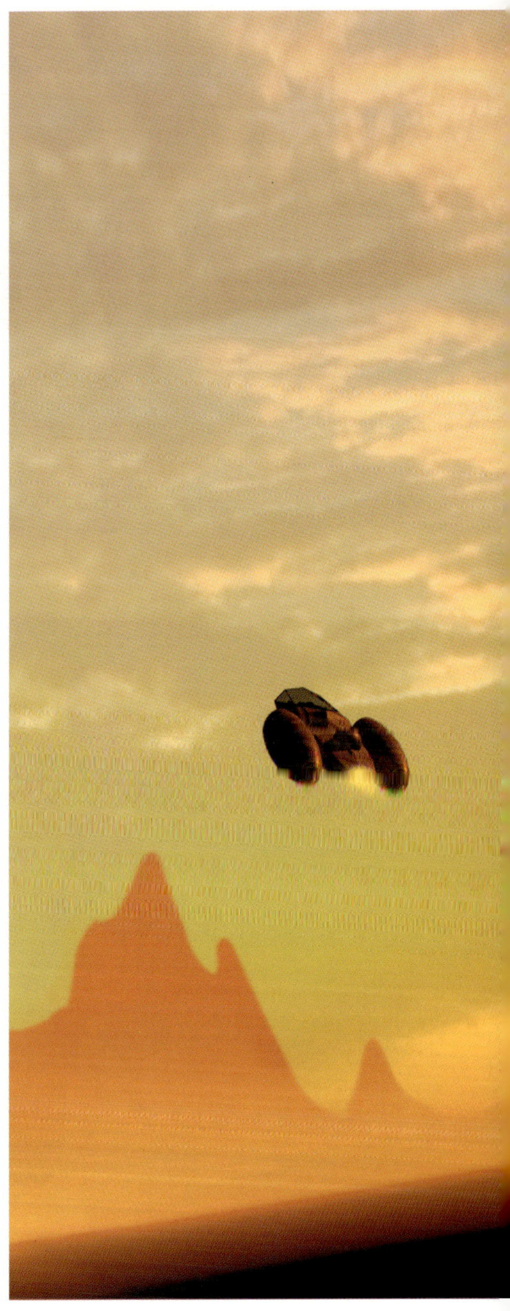

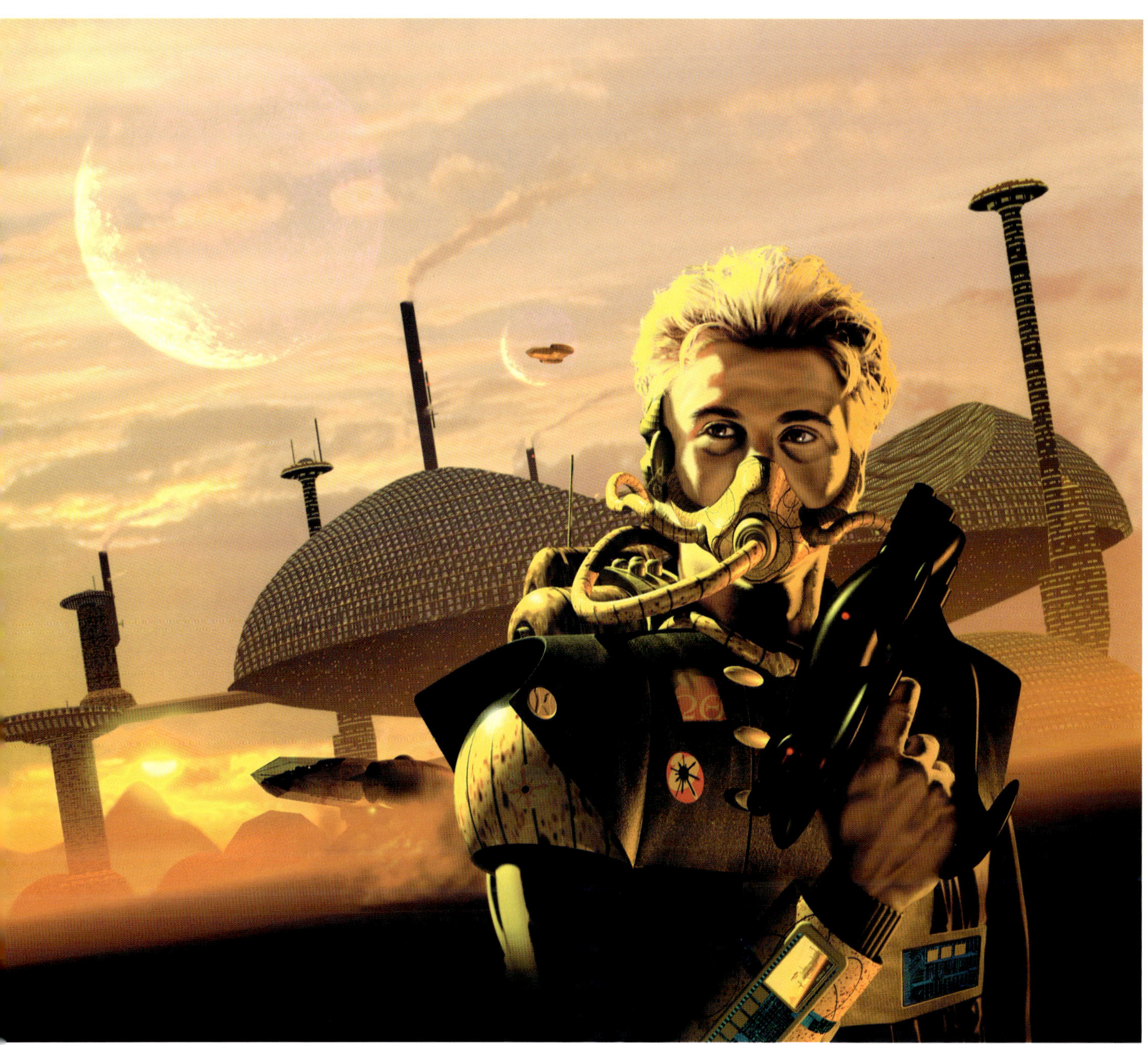

ABOVE

KOMARR

Lois McMaster Bujold
Simon & Schuster UK
Digital

At the time I did this I was battling with my conscience as to how to incorporate my photographic reference into digital images. Although the majority of the photographic reference I use is my own, it still smacks of cheating to simply drop the scanned photo onto the picture. It also tends to stand out like a sore thumb, resulting in an image that looks like a collage. My solution in this instance was to use the various tools in Photoshop to paint over the top of the photograph, in a virtual imitation of what I would have done in the real world. There is nothing left of it in the final illustration. Both the breathing apparatus and gun were modelled and rendered in Alias Sketch.

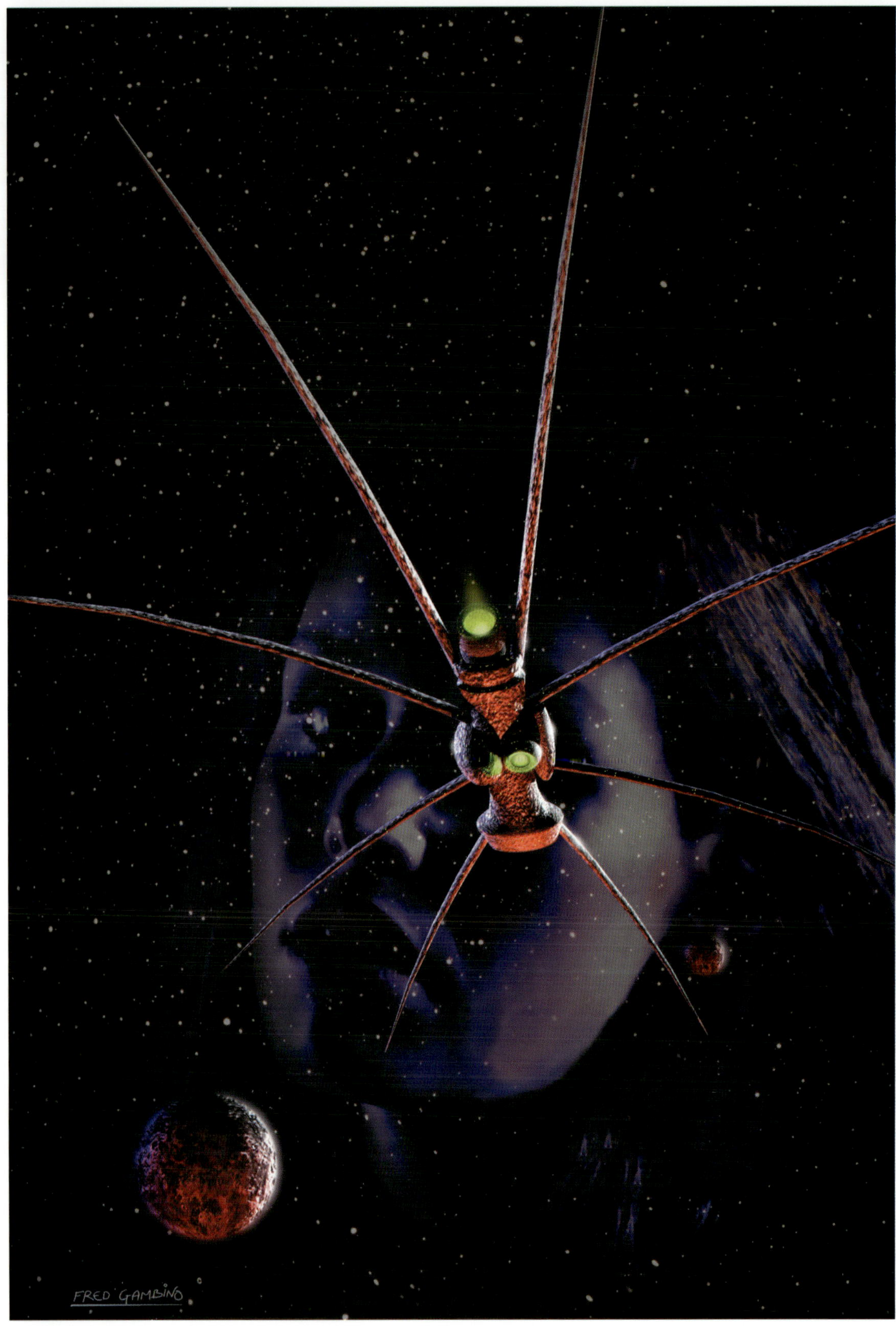
FRED GAMBINO

OPPOSITE

MNEMOSYNE'S KISS

Peter J. Evans
Virgin Books
Digital

Nadine Woodward was the model for this illustration. A professional model, she was due to pose for the Heris Serrano character on the Moon covers (see page 10), when this job came in. It was an ideal opportunity to kill two birds with one stone.

RIGHT

RETURN TO THE FRACTURED PLANET

Dave Stone
Virgin Books
Digital

One of a series of books (see pages 106 and 108) that started life as part of the Doctor Who series. The main character, Bernice Summerfield, or Benny, was the Doctor's sidekick but became so popular that they decided to spin her off in her own series. The first book covers all featured Benny, but sales were not what they had hoped for, so it was deemed that they would try a new tack, using more generic hardware covers.

I don't think I ever had one of the books to read. Usually the brief gave a clear description of what was wanted, with a relevant passage or two from the text. In this case the scene described a pale figure, covered in tattoos, fixed to a circular device redolent of Leonardo da Vinci's famous image showing the proportions of man. Although the device was supposed to be leaning against a wall, I thought it would look much more dramatic floating, as if utilizing some sort of anti-gravity device.

My friend, Chris Green, a veteran of many covers, posed for this one. I bought the trousers from the local Oxfam shop, finding it difficult to meet the saleswoman's eye as she folded them neatly into a bag, saying 'They're very good quality aren't they?', knowing full well that within a few hours they would be shredded and bleached.

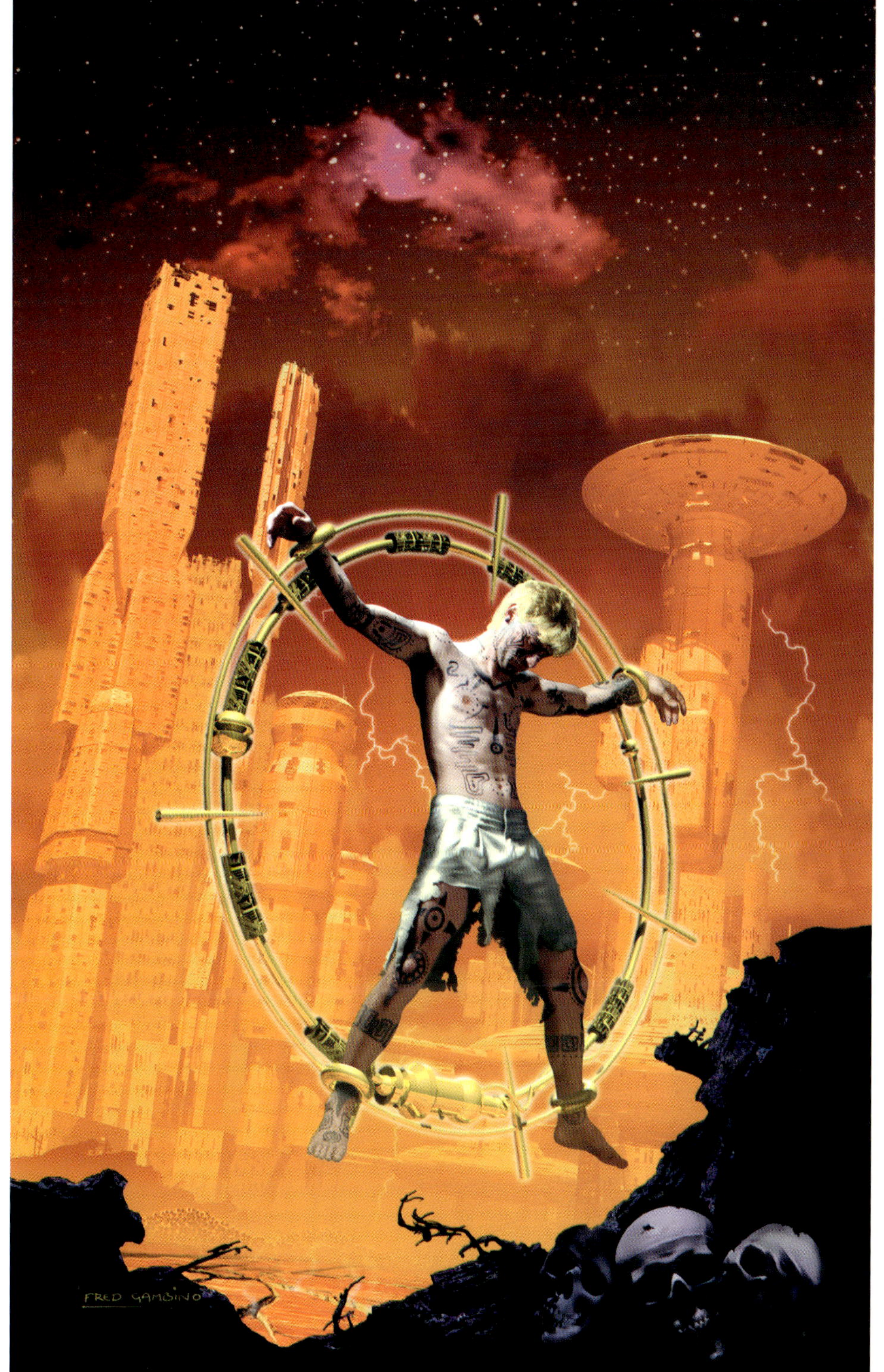

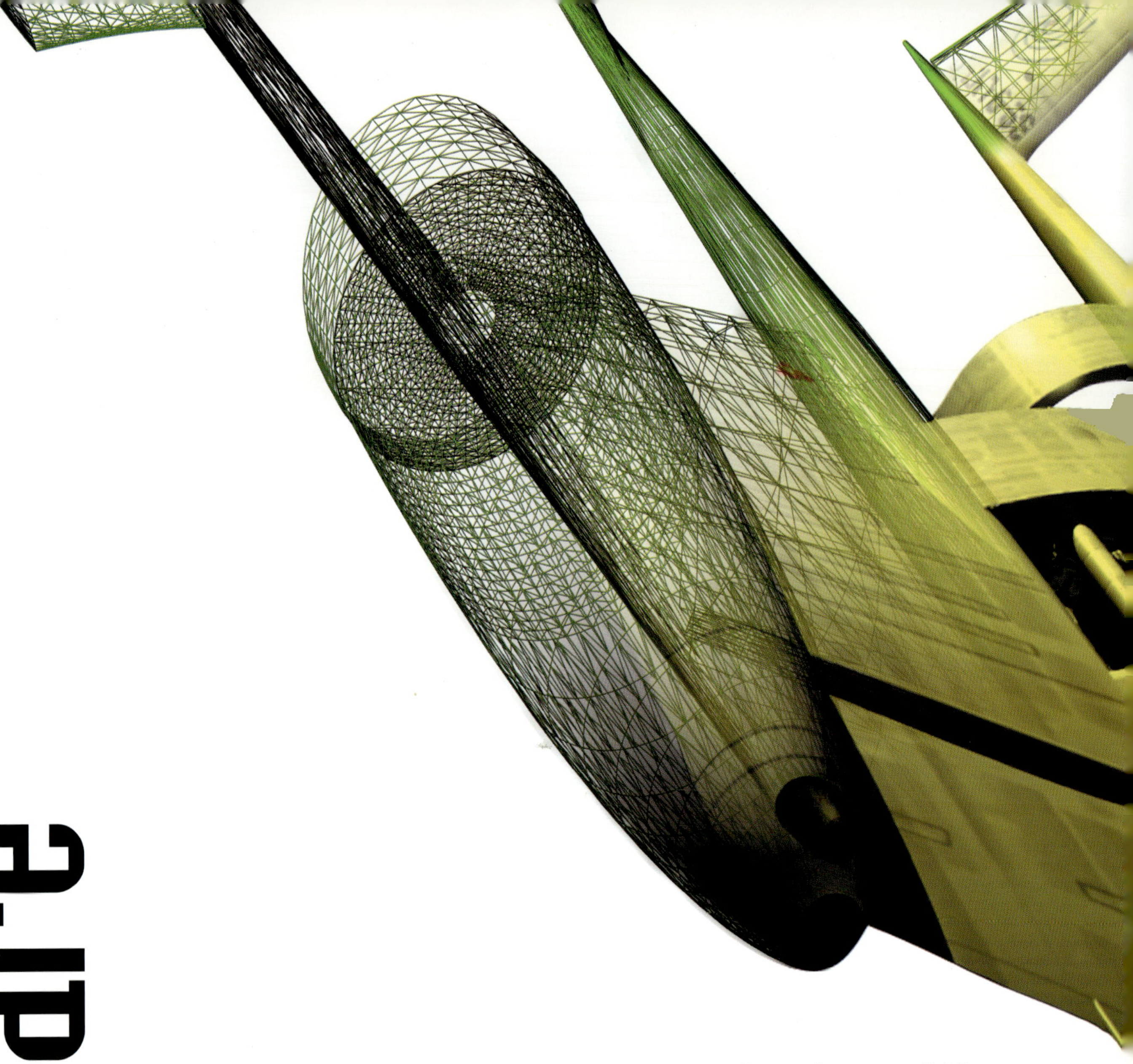

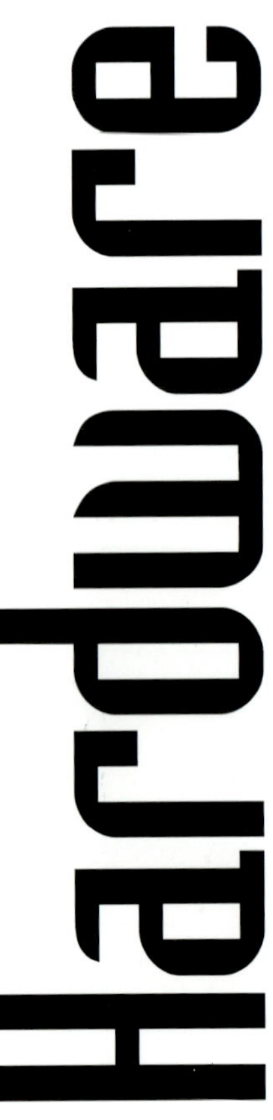

Does art have a role in saving the world?

Let's call effective visual art some work or representation that subtly changes human beings just by the sight of it, transforming hearts and minds without verbal or logical persuasion.

By that reckoning, the 20th century featured two hugely effective works of visual art. First, the terrifying image of the atom bomb changed forever our little-boy romantic attachment to war. The second image was a gift that arrived at the very end of 1968 – a year that brought many of us to the brink of exhaustion and despair – when the Apollo 8 astronauts brought home the first perfect image of the Earth, floating as a blue marble in space, like that gleam of hope shining at the bottom of Pandora's Box.

That picture moved even the most cynical hearts and changed forever our outlook towards this fragile oasis-world.

So yes, art can change people. It can affect you without words and even without representing the human form. Oh, without a doubt the most subtle and interesting objects for depiction are people. People and the wonders of nature. But also leave some room in your heart for things! Planets and storms. Craters and fires. Oceans and nebulae. Serene moonscapes and staggering explosions!

And hardware. Lovely hardware. Bridges, tools, skyscrapers, hotrods, tools and ships ... Especially ships.

Sailing ships and steamers. Spaceships, starships, airships and timeships. Ships of both peace and war. Ships of exploration and rescue and sheer exuberant pleasure. Ships that take you places that no sapient eye has ever seen ... except perhaps the artist's, whose brain somehow peers beyond the narrow valley of our tribe, sieving through images of faraway vistas that our descendants may yet marvel over. If we ever gather up the nerve to go.

Such images persuade us, beckon us. They stoke up the nerve.

Oh, we'll go, all right. Would humans imagine such things, if there weren't already a fiery inner drive to follow where our minds have wandered?

To go in ships, bearing gifts.

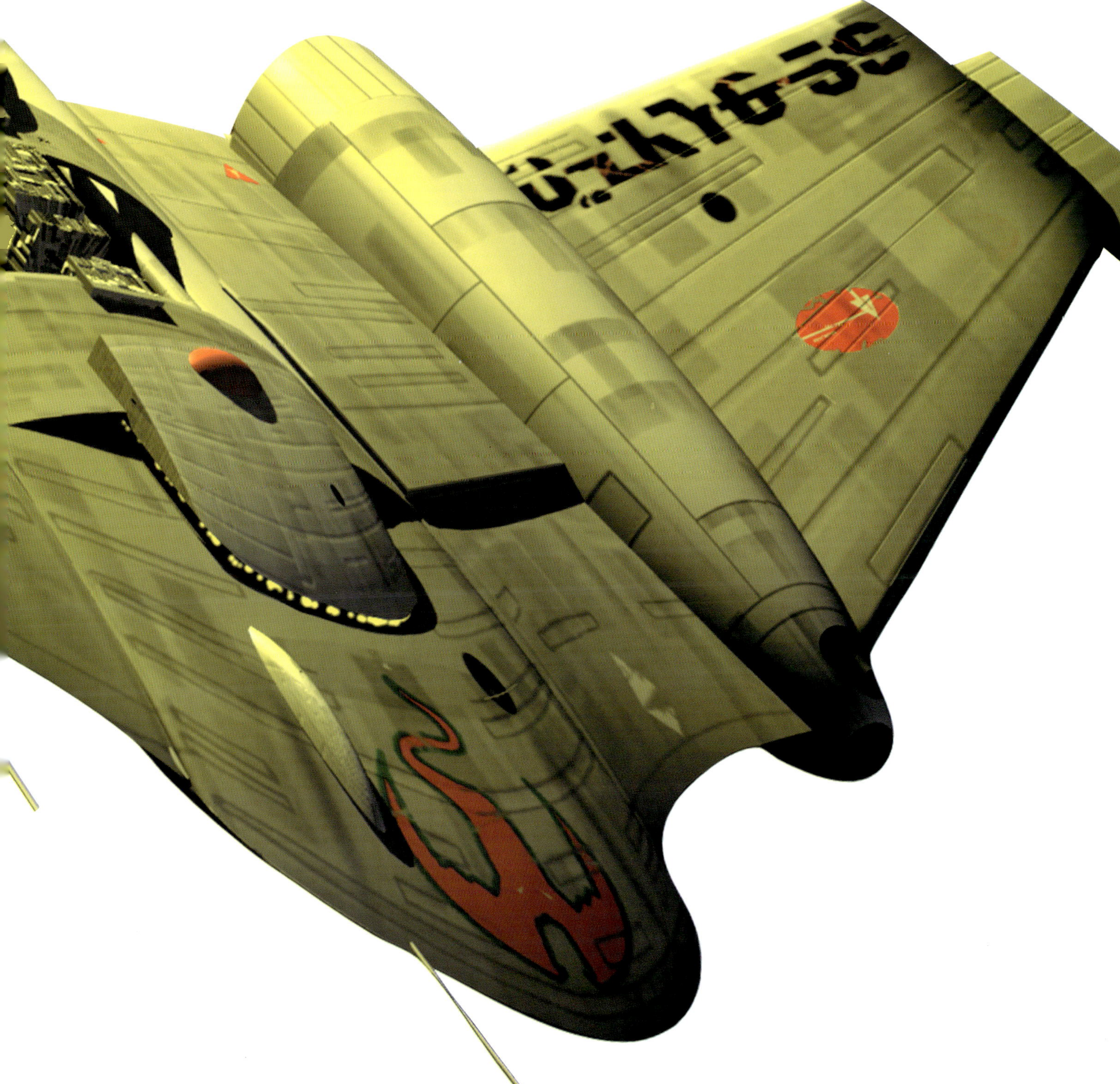

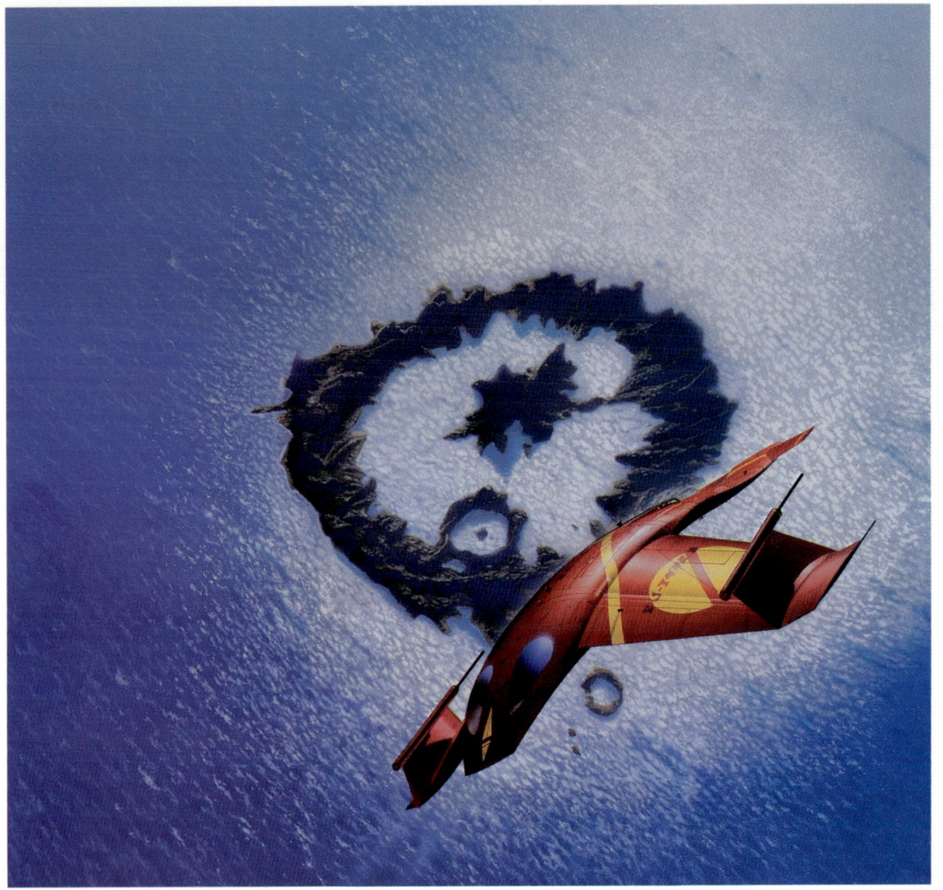

LEFT

BRIGHTNESS REEF

David Brin
Little, Brown UK
Acrylic

I was very pleased when, in the mid-1990s, Little, Brown commissioned me to re-jacket all the David Brin covers, as I had been a long-time fan of his writing. These books included the earlier novels in the Uplift Series, but I also had a manuscript that was to mark the start of a new trilogy.

At the time, pure hardware covers had fallen out of favour, so I did six roughs to try and cover all bases, none of them hardware. I rarely do more than one idea, unless my arm is twisted. I was helped in part by the wealth of wonderful visual material always present in Brin's work. I was also, at that time, the tentative owner of a brand new Apple Mac and had some early attempts at spaceship modelling, along with a flooded crater generated in Bryce, sitting on the hard drive. The crater looked a bit reef like, surrounded by bright water.

I included the rough almost as an afterthought, simply to make up the numbers, so I was surprised when they chose it, so setting the theme for all the other covers.

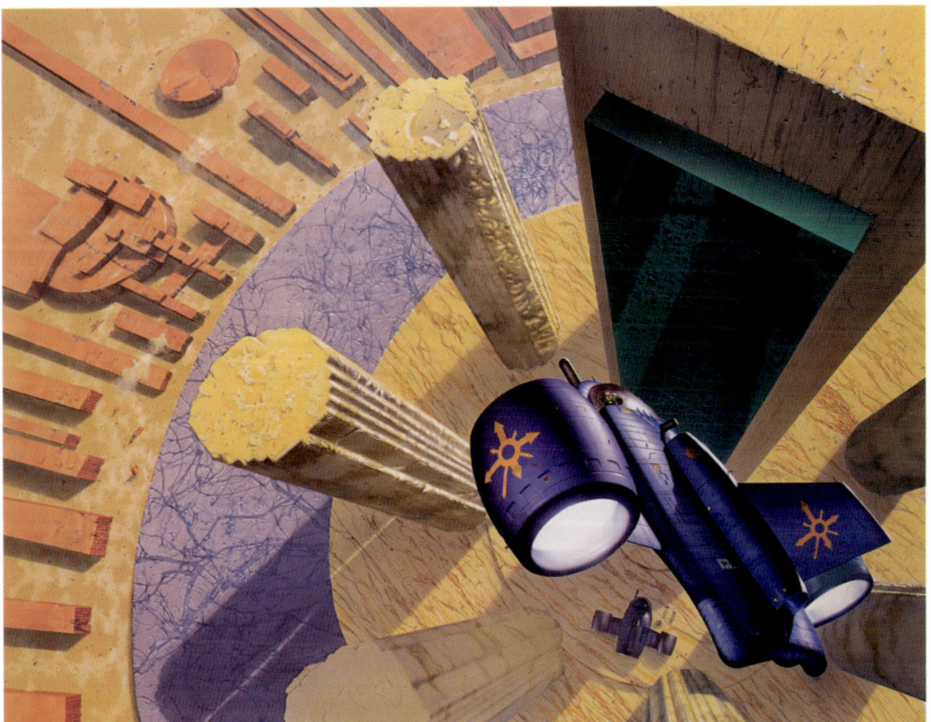

LEFT

THE RIVER OF TIME

David Brin
Little, Brown UK
Acrylic

The textures in this painting were achieved by a variety of spatter techniques. The blue texture, for example, was a result of deliberately flooding the art board with paint from the airbrush and then chasing the wet paint around with air. Once I had a texture that appealed to me, I went to work on it with a small sable brush, until I felt I had achieved the desired effect. The influence of the computer can be seen in the dramatic perspective, something that would be increasingly evident in future images.

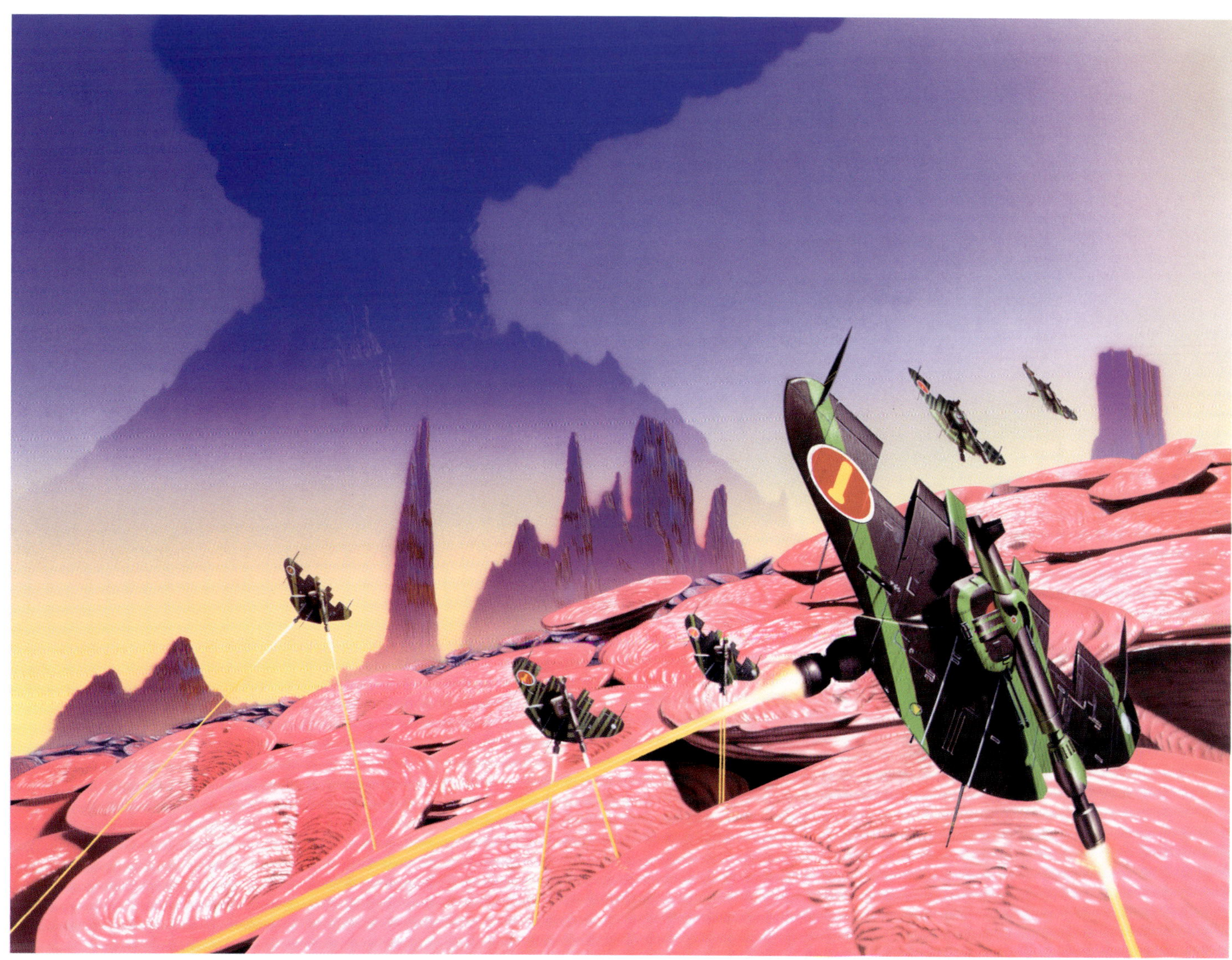

ABOVE

THE UPLIFT WAR

David Brin
Little, Brown UK
Acrylic

After *Brightness Reef*, I turned my attention to the other books in the series, following the same theme. I wasn't convinced that I had yet developed the expertise to create the covers on my Mac. So, instead of my usual practice of building models in the real world and photographing them, I originated my reference in the computer, and then printed it out to use for the final painting. This was a good way to cut my teeth on the Mac and these covers can really be said to be my first computer images. Although this is an acrylic painting, the influence of Bryce on the distant pinnacles can be clearly seen.

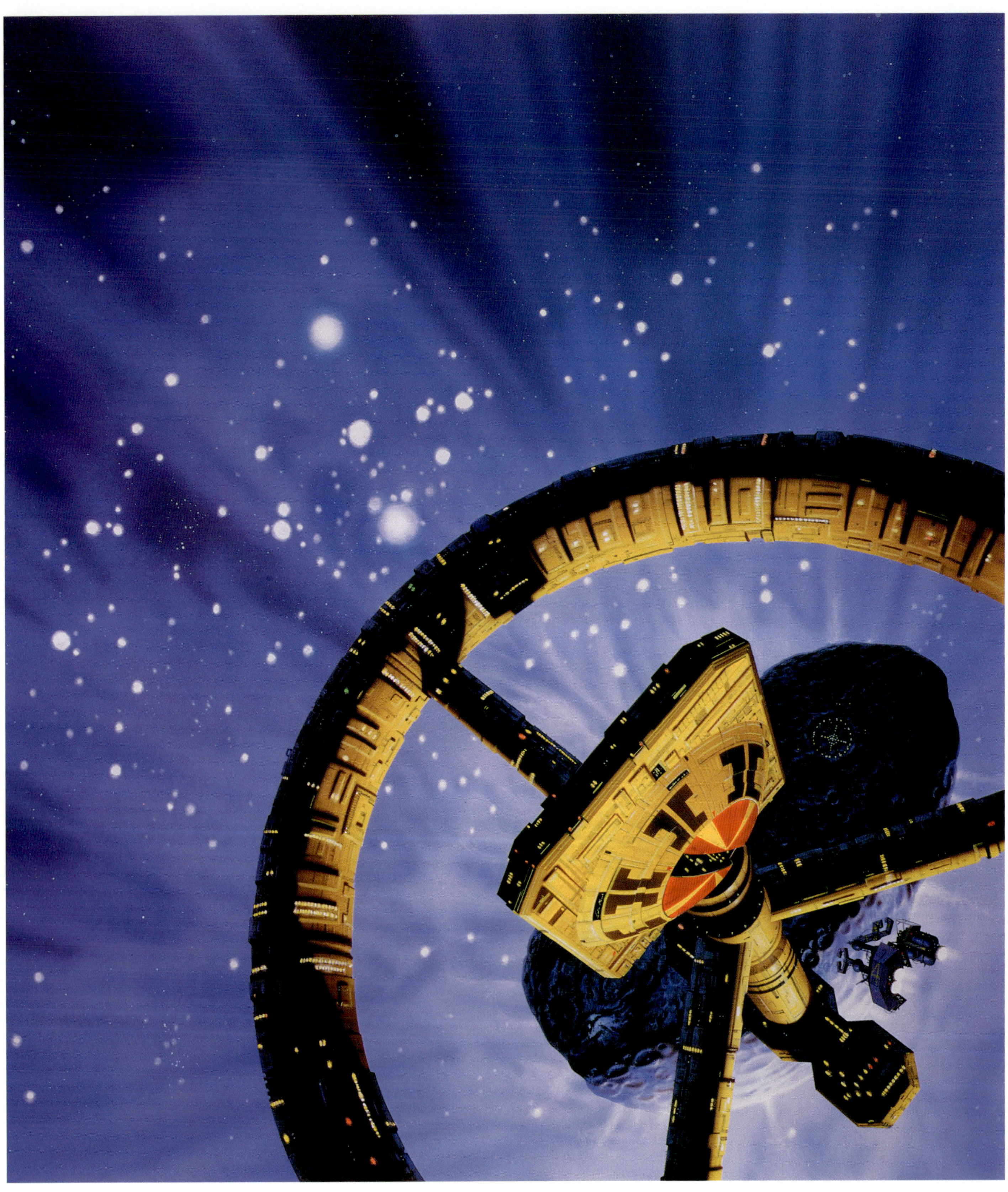

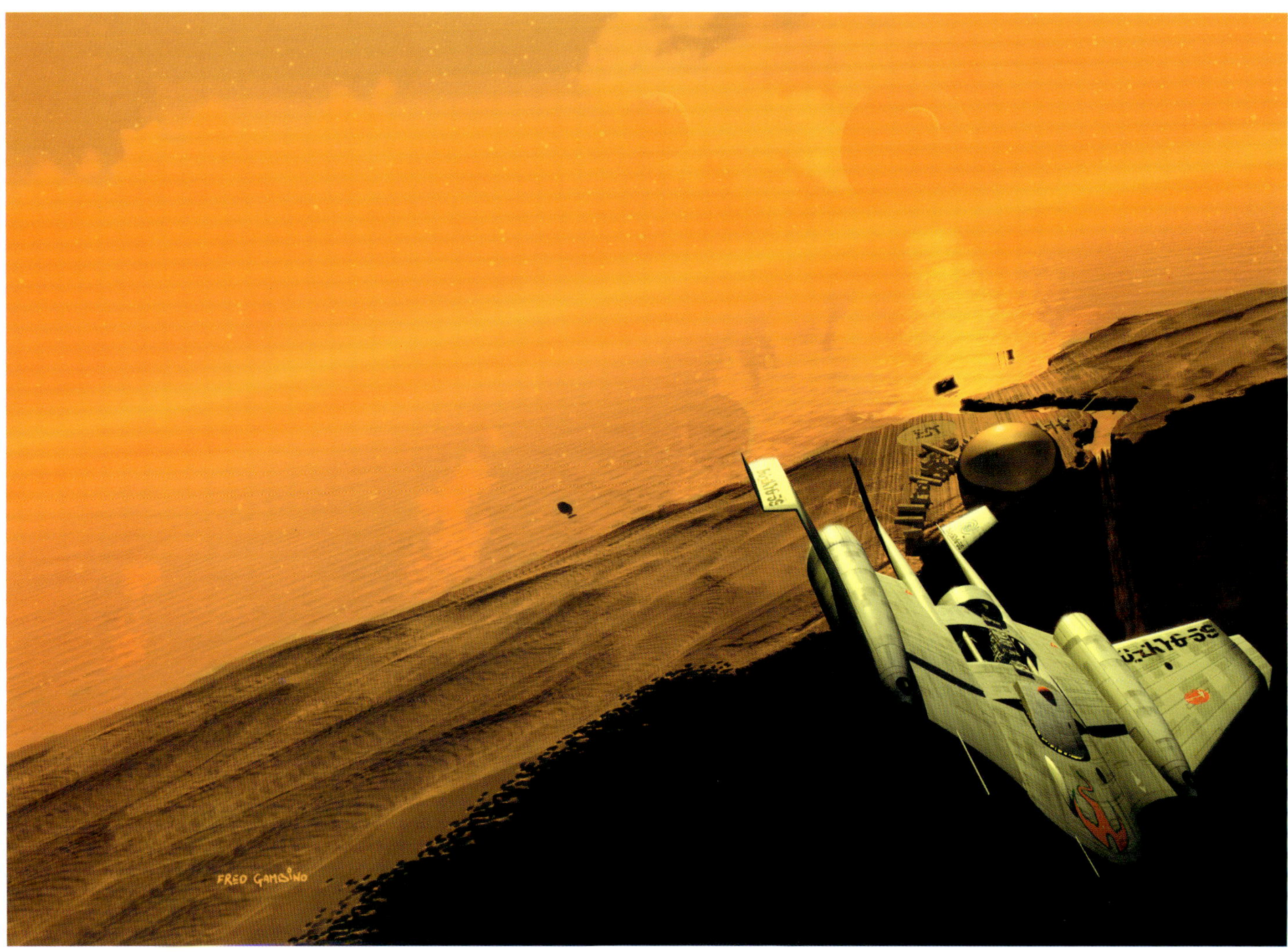

OPPOSITE

HEART OF THE COMET

David Brin and Gregory Benford
Little, Brown UK
Acrylic

This cover probably marks the end of my formative time with the computer and represents the time that I started to produce my images digitally. It had taken a year and it was now clear that my initial investment was going to pay off. Far from being left behind, I was one of the first, certainly in British publishing, to produce this sort of image digitally. There had been people working with the computer before me of course, but I had set out, not to push the illustration envelope in some new way, but to simply carry on doing what I had always done, just using pixels instead of paint.

ABOVE

INFINITY'S SHORE

David Brin
Little, Brown UK
Digital

Peter Cotton, the art director at Little, Brown, was by now sufficiently convinced to allow me to do the rest of the series digitally. Although I had read this manuscript, the truth is that I had the cover in mind as soon as I read the title. A bright reef had gone down well for *Brightness Reef*, so what better than an infinite shore, with water reflecting infinity, for *Infinity Shore*?

The ship, which has a decidedly retro look, was another of my early attempts to get to grips with Alias Sketch, but by now I was sufficiently proficient to take that model and finish it properly.

OVERLEAF

HEAVEN'S REACH

David Brin
Little, Brown UK
Digital

When the manuscript arrived, I was so taken with Brin's wonderful imagery that I felt compelled to break my cardinal rule, and submit more than one rough. It's always a danger, unless specifically asked, to submit more than one visual, as you leave yourself open to being asked to combine them in ways that often dilute the original idea. I was particularly taken with the description of huge spindle structures orbiting a Neutron star. But, sadly, due to email problems, that rough didn't reach the art department in time. I still have it, ready for some future job.

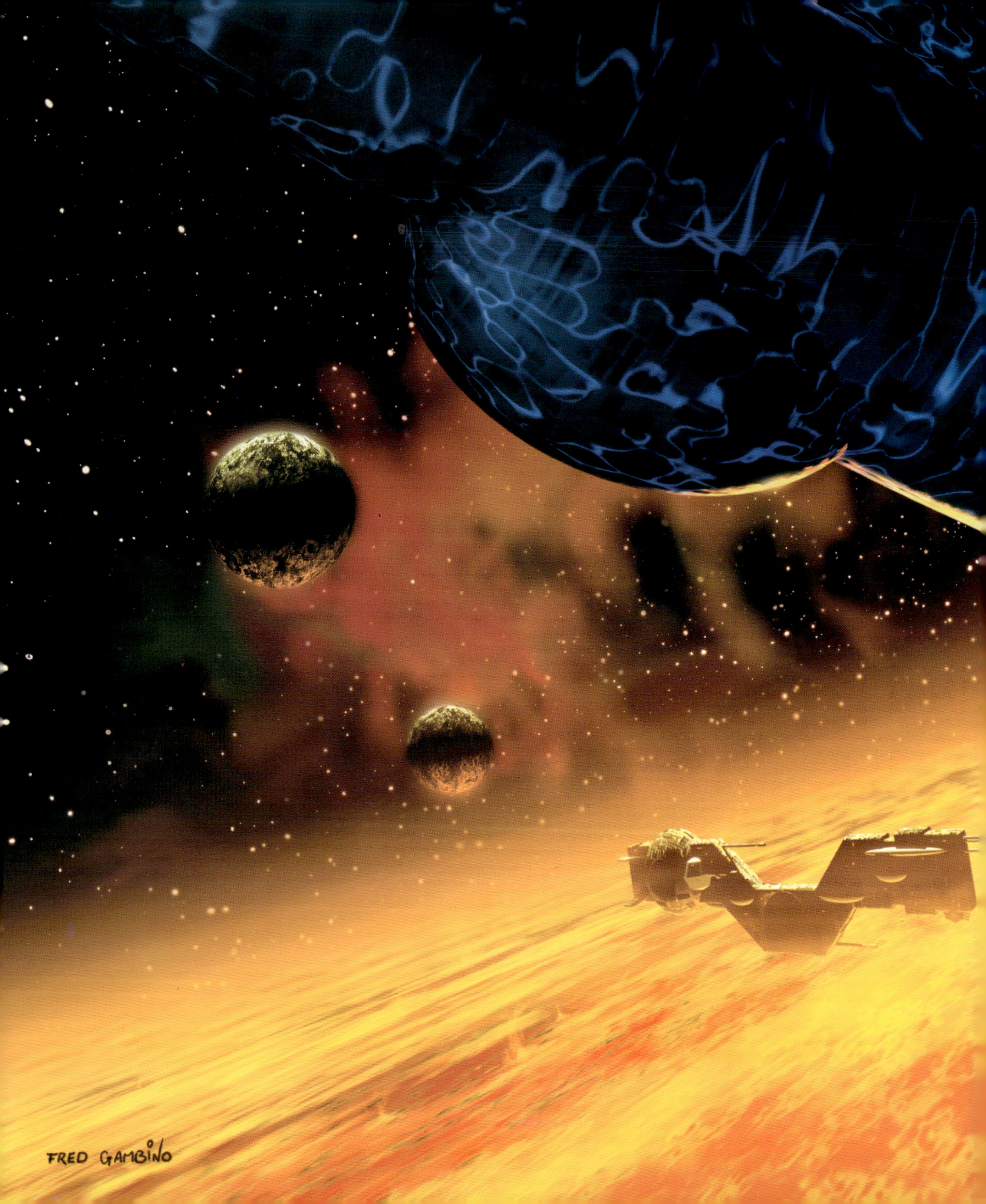
FRED GAMBINO

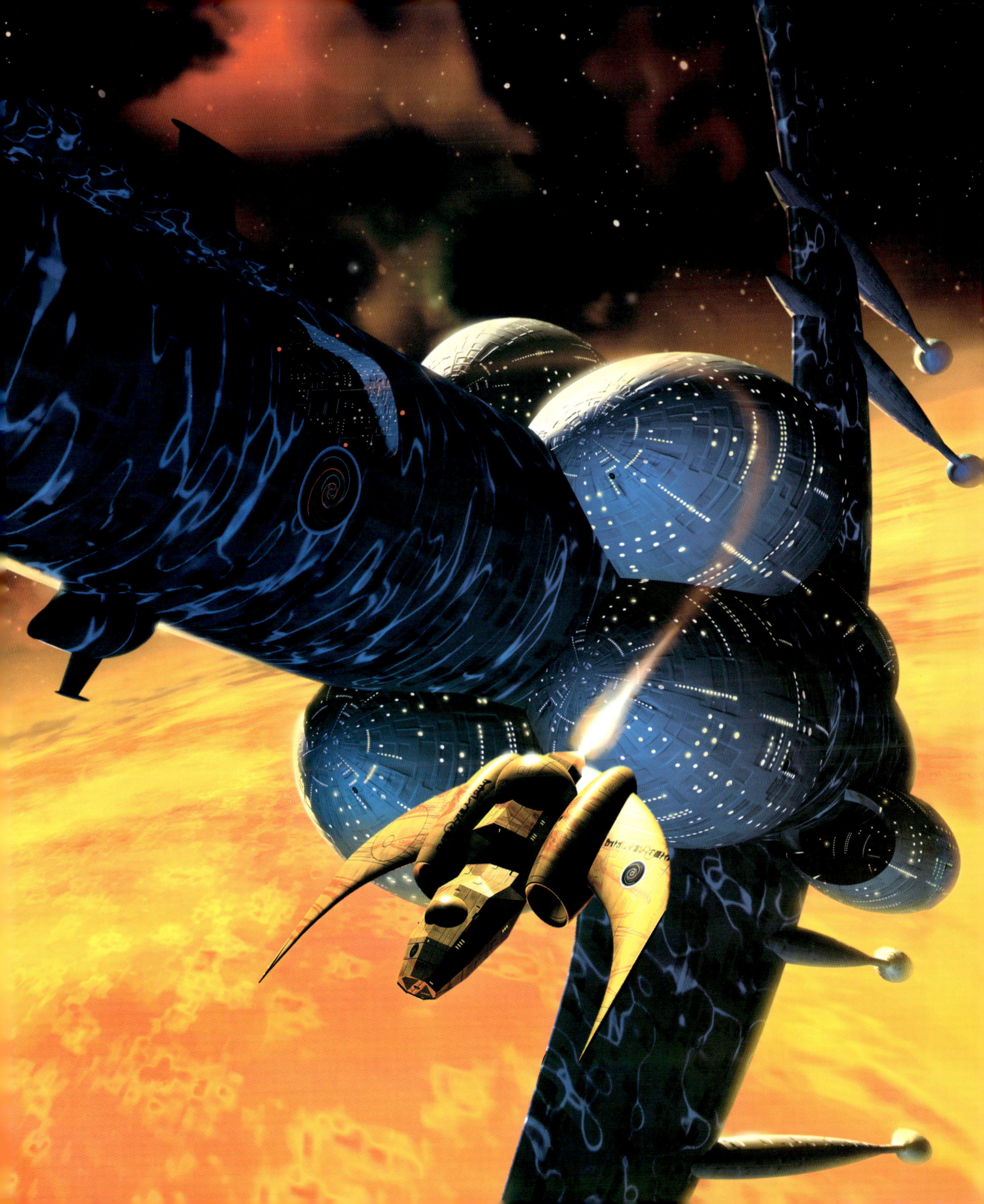

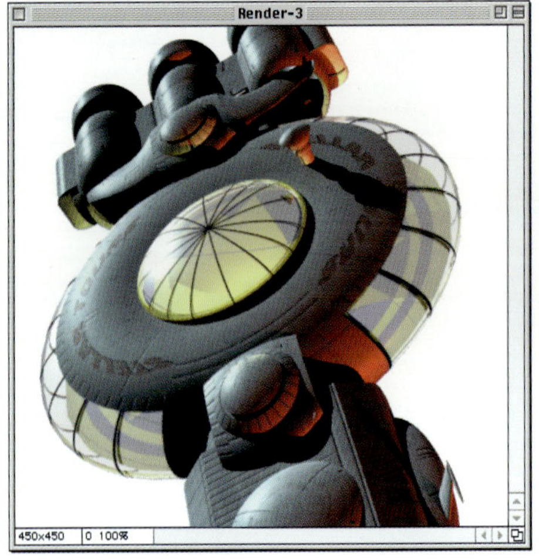

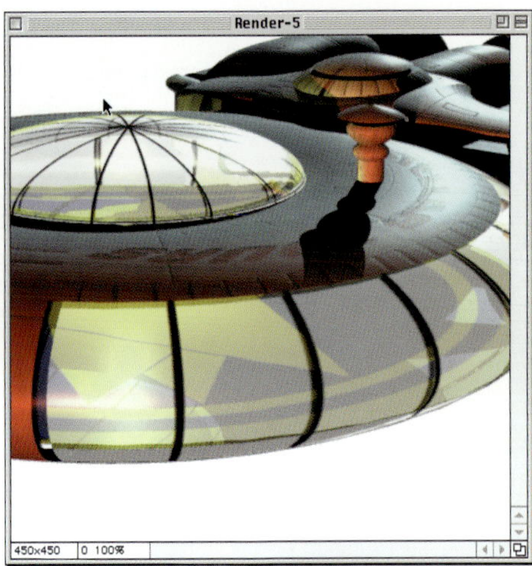

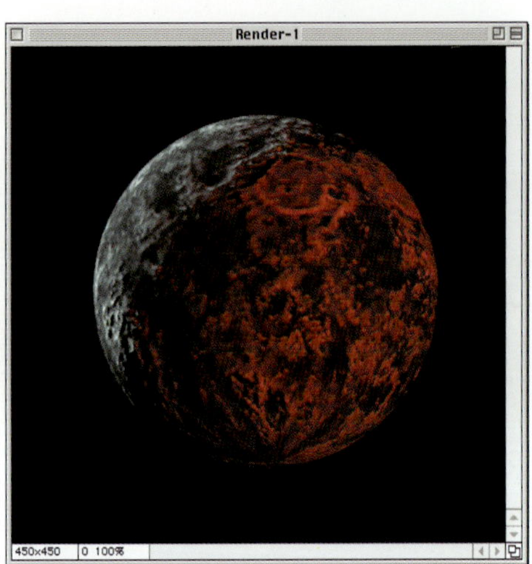

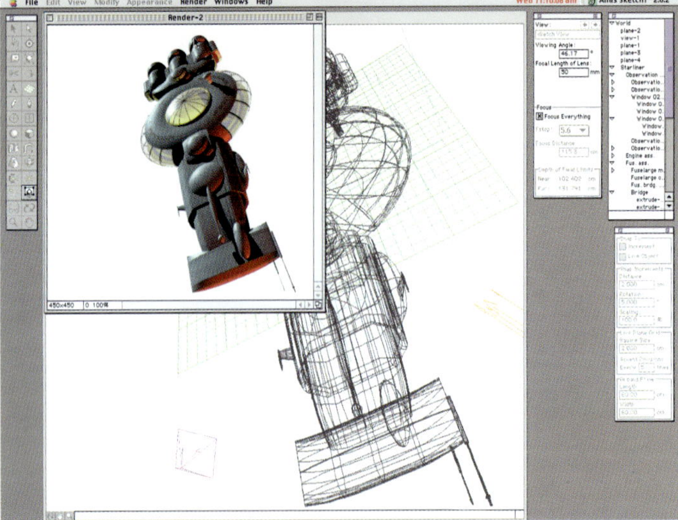

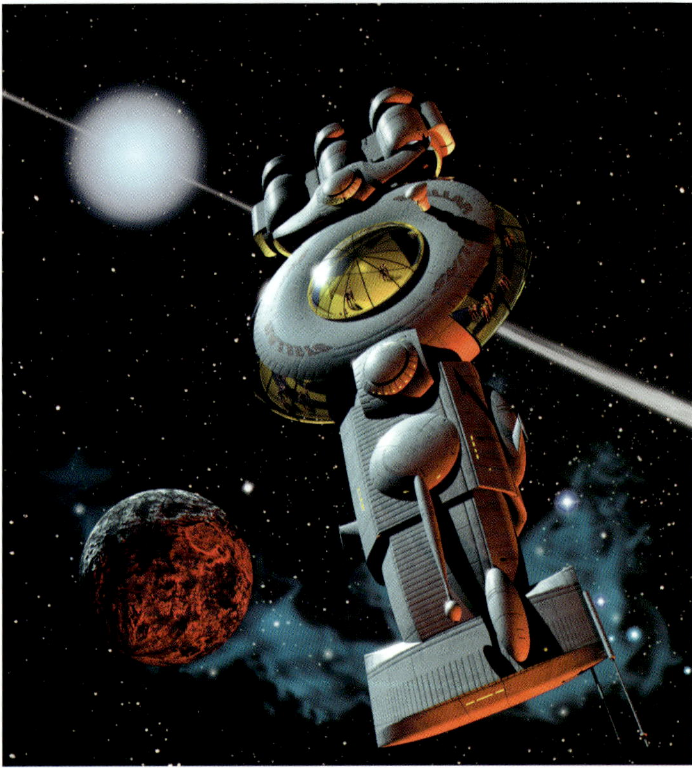

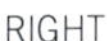
RIGHT

PULSAR

US Postal Service
Digital

In 1998 the US Postal Service produced a series of stamps commemorating the space program. To coincide with this, they published a children's story recounting the adventures of two children in space.This image features the passenger ship on which most of the action takes place, as it passes a pulsar. The whole thing, including the pulsar, was modelled and rendered in Alias Sketch, with the nebula and space background painted in Photoshop.

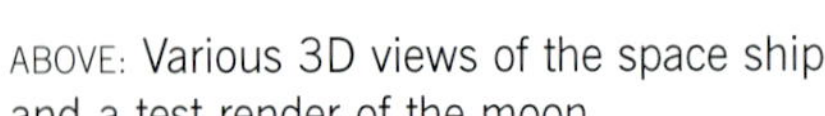
ABOVE: Various 3D views of the space ship and a test render of the moon.

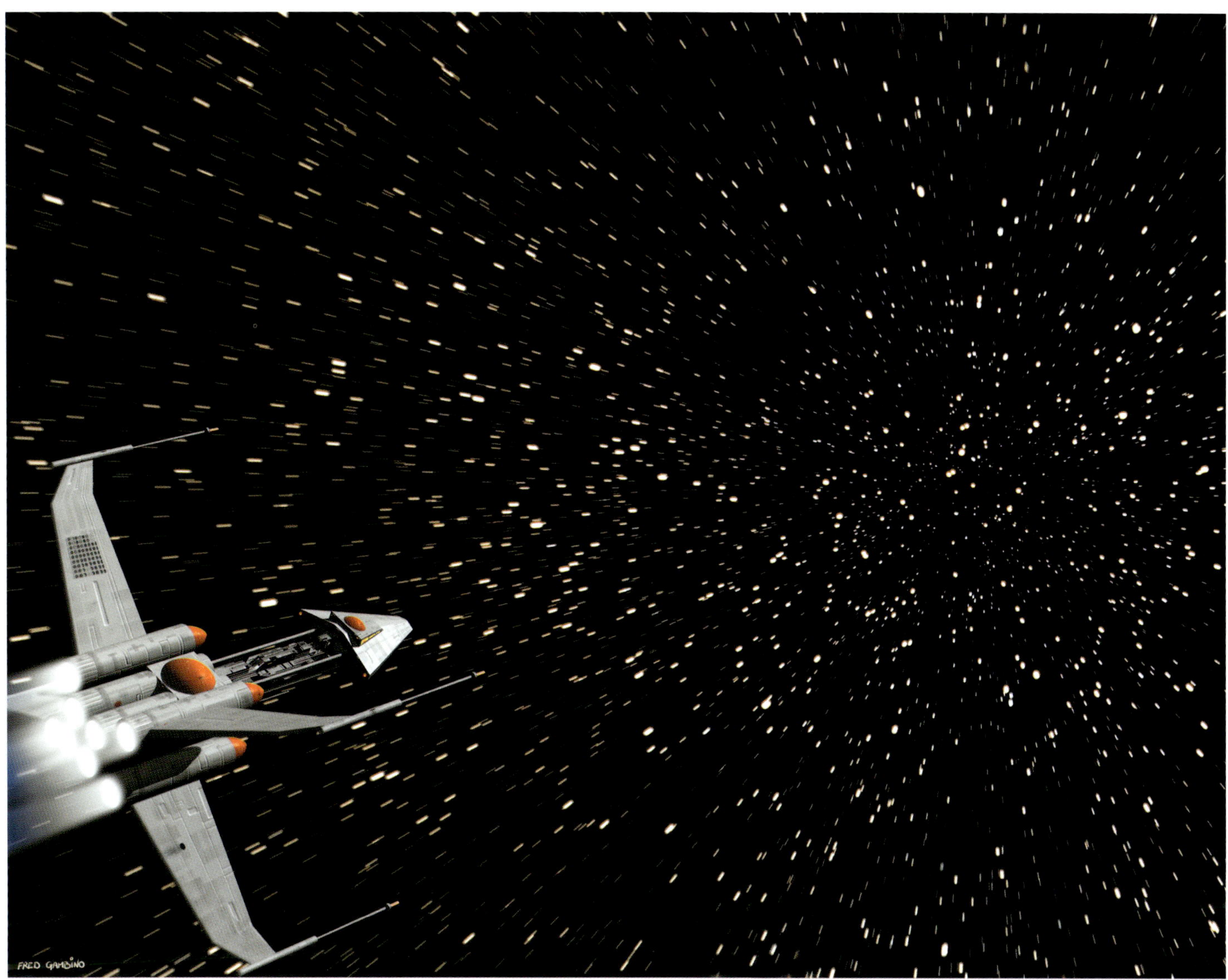

ABOVE

EMPIRE BUILDING

Garry Jenkins
Simon & Schuster
Digital

This was the cover for the unofficial biography of *Star Wars*. The publisher couldn't use imagery from the film so the brief was to come up with a spacecraft, on the back cover, that looked like it had come from the *Star Wars* universe. I thought it might work well to blur the star field in imitation of the ship's going into warp drive. When the art director saw it, he commented on what a good idea it had been to have a different perspective for the stars than that for the ship, giving the impression that the viewer was travelling at warp speed and was overtaking the other craft. If only I had thought of that.

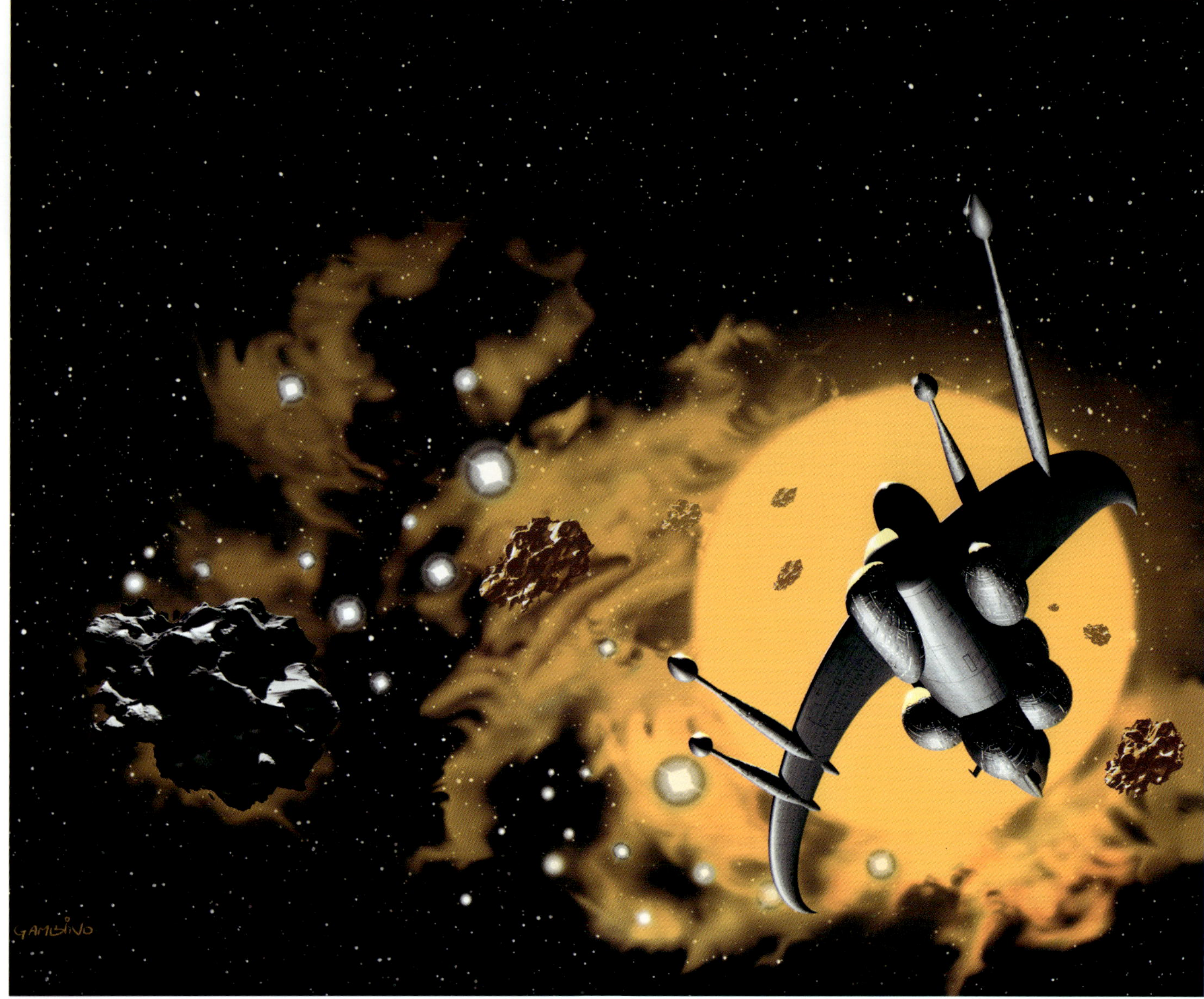

THE GAP SERIES

In 1998, HarperCollins commissioned me to re-jacket the five books in Stephen Donaldson's science fiction epic, the Gap Series. These books had to be good – they had two titles each. They feature one of the most repugnant anti-heroes in science fiction, Angus Thermopyle, who starts out as a depraved villain, but by the end of the series gains the reader's sympathy and becomes the hero. I found myself hooked from the beginning and, somewhat unusually for me, read them all from cover to cover before I started work.

I hope I did them justice, but there were some constraints placed upon me. The publishers decided that the images should be almost monochromatic, with one dominant colour overall, and that the hardware should be in black and white.

Since I had read all the books before I began, I set out to give them a cohesive look from the start. All the alien Amnion technology has a textured look, rather than the more orthodox panelled look of the terrestrial spaceships, but the Earth craft do share an overall design feel, so we know that they come from the same universe.

ABOVE

THE REAL STORY
The Gap Into Conflict

Stephen Donaldson
HarperCollins UK
Digital

The first cover features the space ship from which Angus Thermopyle kidnaps Morn Hyland, the main female character, who is the catalyst for the events which follow. Apart from the asteroids, the background was painted in Photoshop. I wanted this first image to be simple, with lots of impact.

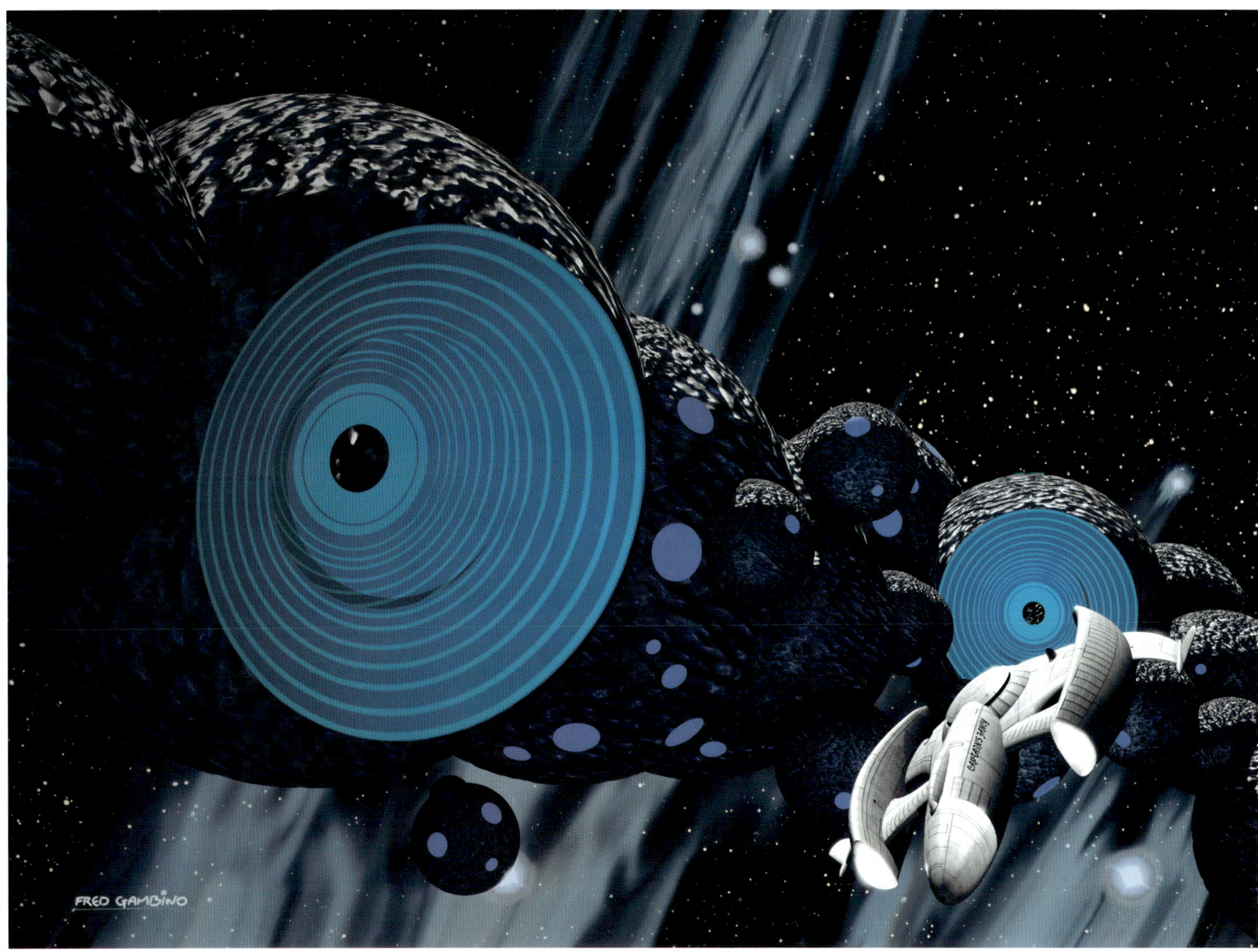

ABOVE

FORBIDDEN KNOWLEDGE
The Gap Into Vision

Stephen Donaldson
HarperCollins UK
Digital

This cover shows Nick Succorso's ship, *The Captain's Fancy*, about to dock with a space station of the mysterious aliens, the Amnions. When I received the final copy of this, I compared it to the artwork I'd sent in. Something was awry, the ship was at a different angle and the name had been removed. In this age of digital artwork, it has become increasingly common for people in the art department to fiddle with the image, simply because they can. Thankfully this hasn't happened to me much, but to change the angle of the ship, that would be unprecedented, if not extremely difficult. It dawned on me that, whether through error or not, they'd used the rough. The rough was generated at half the resolution of the finished artwork, yet there is no appreciable difference in the printed quality.

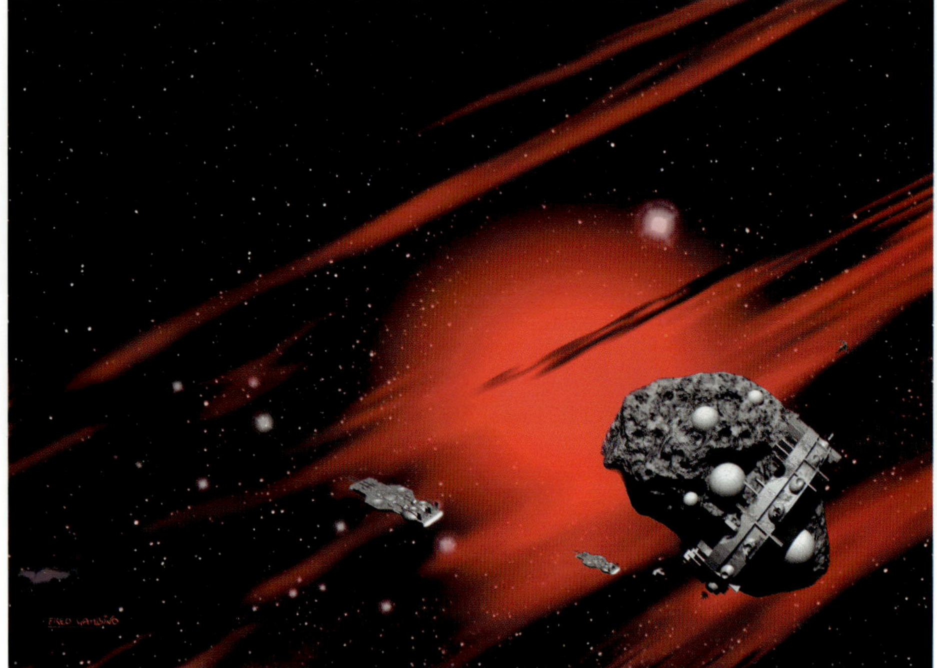

LEFT

A DARK AND HUNGRY GOD ARISES
The Gap Into Power

Stephen Donaldson
HarperCollins UK
Digital

The main focus is the bootleg shipyard of Thanatos Minor. I was taken with the author's description of this asteroid, with its concrete docking collar and domed structures. These were modelled in Amapi. I like this program for its quirky yet intuitive interface, but it is only a modeller and the geometry needs to be exported elsewhere to be rendered.

If you look carefully you can see Nick Succorso's ship, *The Captain's Fancy*, about to dock bottom left, while the ship that is to feature in the next cover, *The Trumpet*, is slightly above it. The alien Amnion ship that appears on the last cover also makes a first appearance.

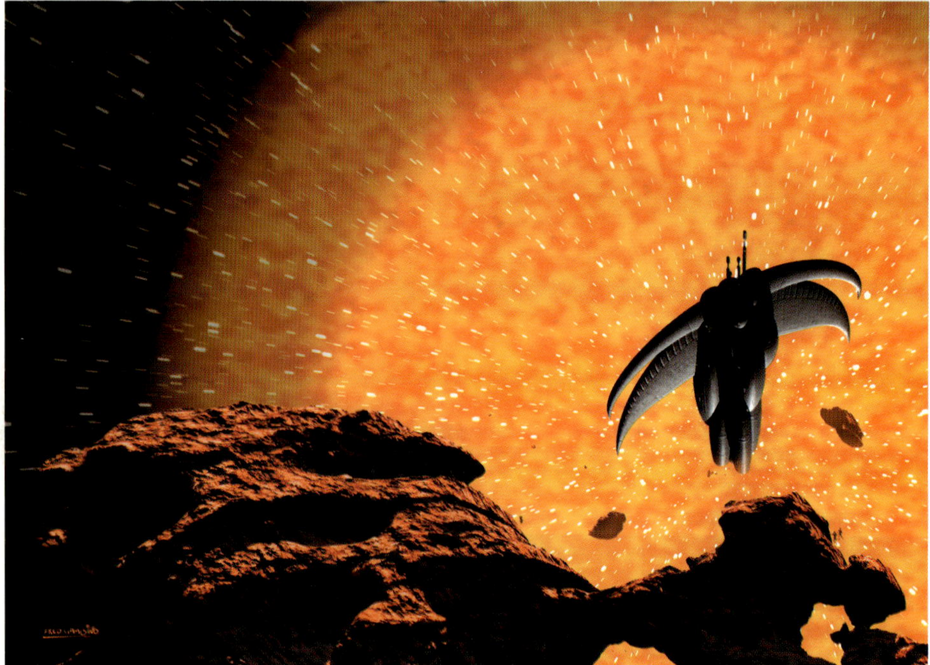

LEFT

CHAOS AND ORDER
The Gap Into Madness

Stephen Donaldson
HarperCollins UK
Digital

The spaceship *The Trumpet* hurtles away from the huge explosion that marks the passing of Thanatos Minor. Two small space-suited figures wait in the shadow of the asteroid in an attempt to sneak aboard and sabotage it. Again, there is an extensive use of Bryce in the background. The explosion texture and asteroid were also rendered in Bryce. Then, in Photoshop, I applied a zoom filter to a starfield and laid it over the blast.

The ship has a similar design to the craft on the first cover. I imagined those big winglike structures would actually be heat radiators (wings, of course, would be useless in space). I like to imagine how things might work when I am designing. Sometimes it helps me to come up with a novel concept.

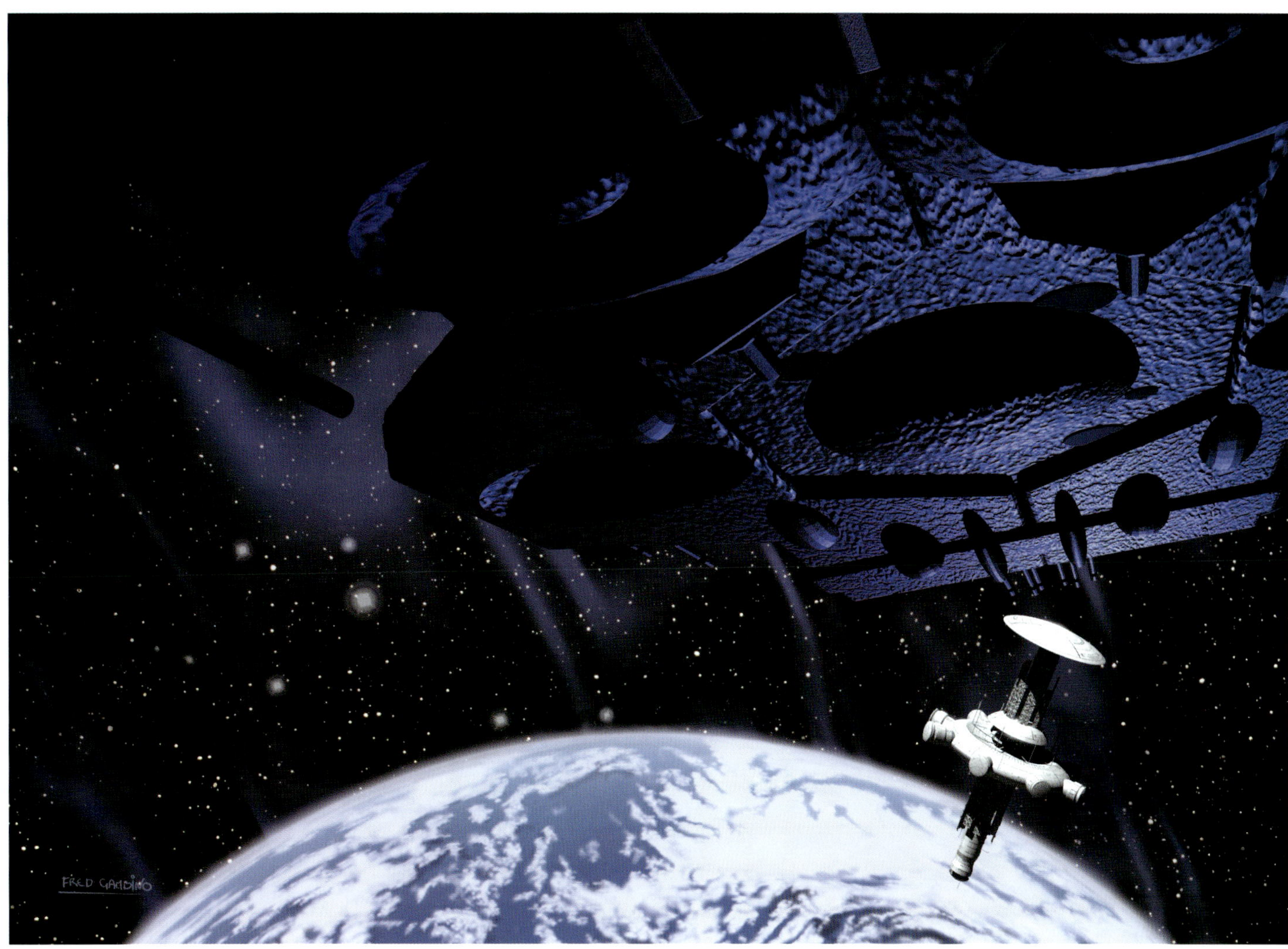

ABOVE

THIS DAY ALL GODS DIE
The Gap Into Ruin

Stephen Donaldson
HarperCollins UK
Digital

The final cover has the huge Amnion ship approaching Earth; the only thing standing between it and the home world is a comparatively small orbital station.

I had been reading about the true texture of shark skin, how it is rough to enable the shark's passage through water. I had this idea in mind when I was designing the alien ships. This ship started life as the craft in the background of *Heaven's Reach* (see pages 38–9). I mirrored it, then turned it on its side; the only new modelling I had to do was to fill in the hexagonal hole left in the middle.

I have a huge collection of ships I have modelled from scratch, and it would be reasonable to assume that I recycle them a lot. In fact I used to, but I rarely dip into them these days. I think it's more important to build shapes that fit the composition in my roughs, rather than the other way round.

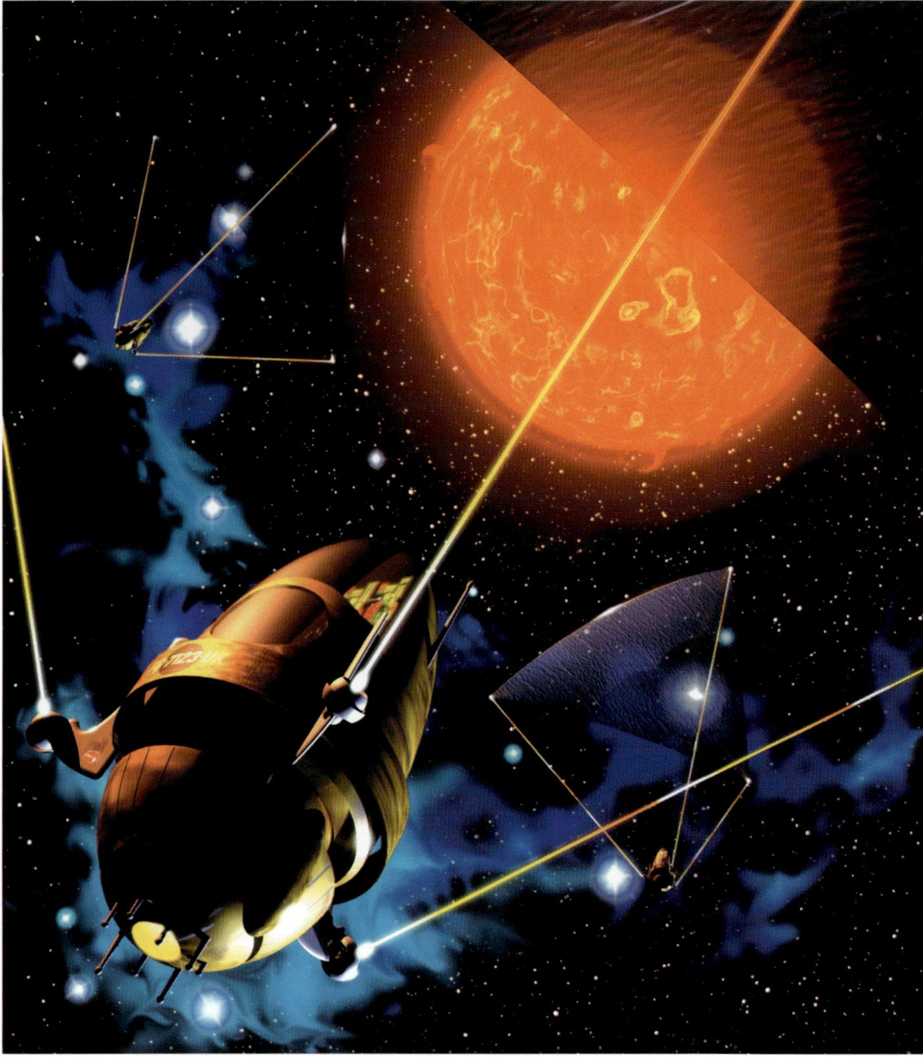

ABOVE

LIGHTSAIL

US Postal Service
Digital

Lightsail has the heroes of the children's story (see page 40) trying out lightsailing in the vicinity of a red giant star.

RIGHT

A GIFT FROM EARTH

Larry Niven
Futura
Acrylic

This features one of those unique Niven planetary environments, with a dense, inhospitable atmosphere and a huge mountainous plateau that rises to where the atmosphere is thin enough to support an Earth-like ecology. It describes one of the characters standing on the edge of the plateau, staring out into the swirling clouds of the void. 'I've just been there,' I thought, 'and what's more, I have a slide to prove it.' The view from Madeira's highest mountain, Pico Riva, fitted the bill perfectly. All that was needed was an appropriate bit of hardware.

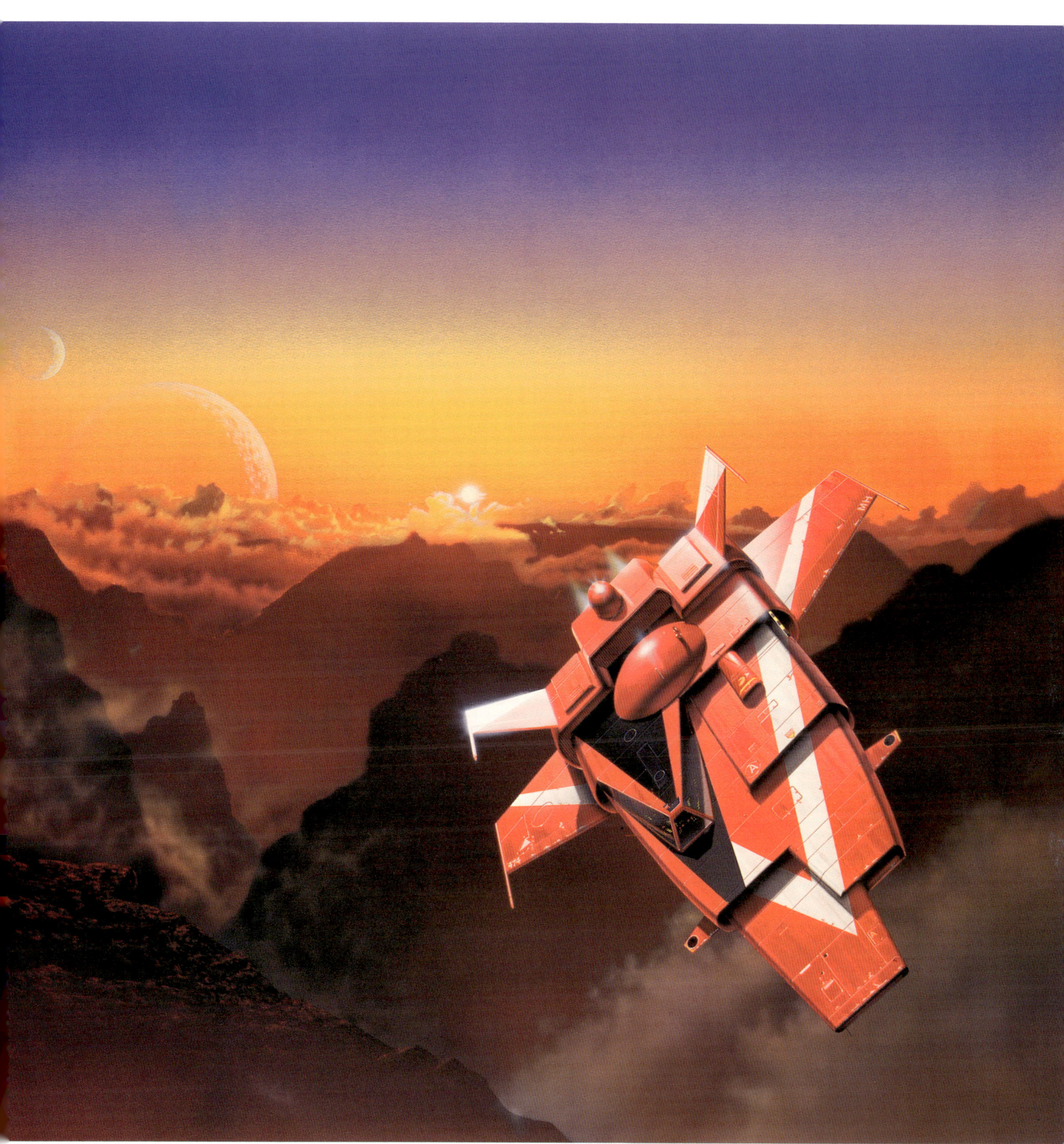

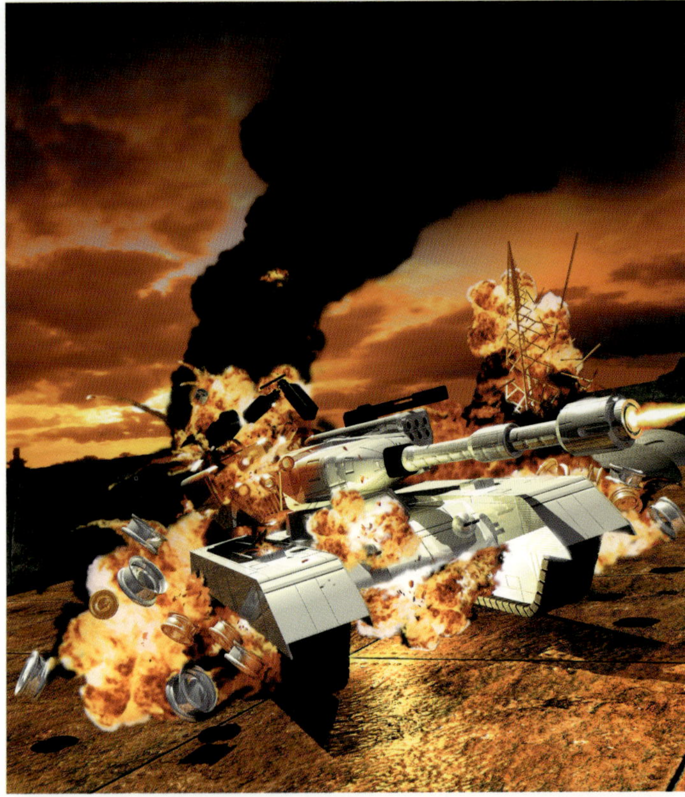

LEFT

RECOIL

Game box for Virgin Interactive
Digital

This image went through three incarnations. Originally, I was asked for a tank in a desert-camouflage colour, with a blast ring, similar to that beloved of Hollywood directors when stars explode. The first thing that was dropped was the blast ring, then the background was changed. Finally they decided that the tank should be made from chrome.

Up until then, the renders had been taking about twenty minutes each. I set about changing the tank material to reflective chrome. This meant that every spinning wheel, every little detail, was going to be reflecting everything else, including the compound that the tank was sitting in. The computer had to calculate all this using a technique called raytracing, the most time-consuming method of rendering an image in 3D. I started this alteration on Friday, the deadline was Monday, but it was Tuesday afternoon before it was finished. This is the longest render that I have ever done and, if I knew then what I know now, I would have found other ways to simulate the reflections.

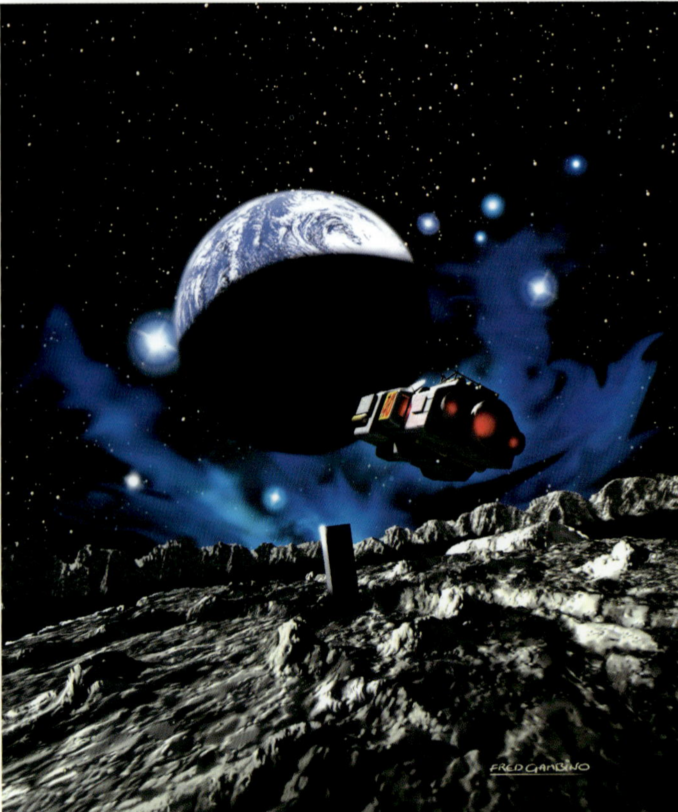

LEFT

EXPEDITION TO EARTH

Arthur C. Clarke
Little, Brown UK
Digital

I originally produced this rough for a different anthology of Arthur C. Clarke stories, which didn't get the go ahead. The story described an astronaut about to abandon a stricken moon shuttle. I had a small figure standing in the airlock of a craft that was supposed to bear a resemblance to the moon buggy in *2001*.

Some time later the art director rang me and asked me if I still had the rough as, with a few alterations, it would do for another Clarke book, *Expedition to Earth*. The resemblance to the *2001* buggy proved fortuitous as this anthology included 'The Sentinel', the short story that the film was based upon. All I had to do was remove the spaceman, add the monolith and we had it.

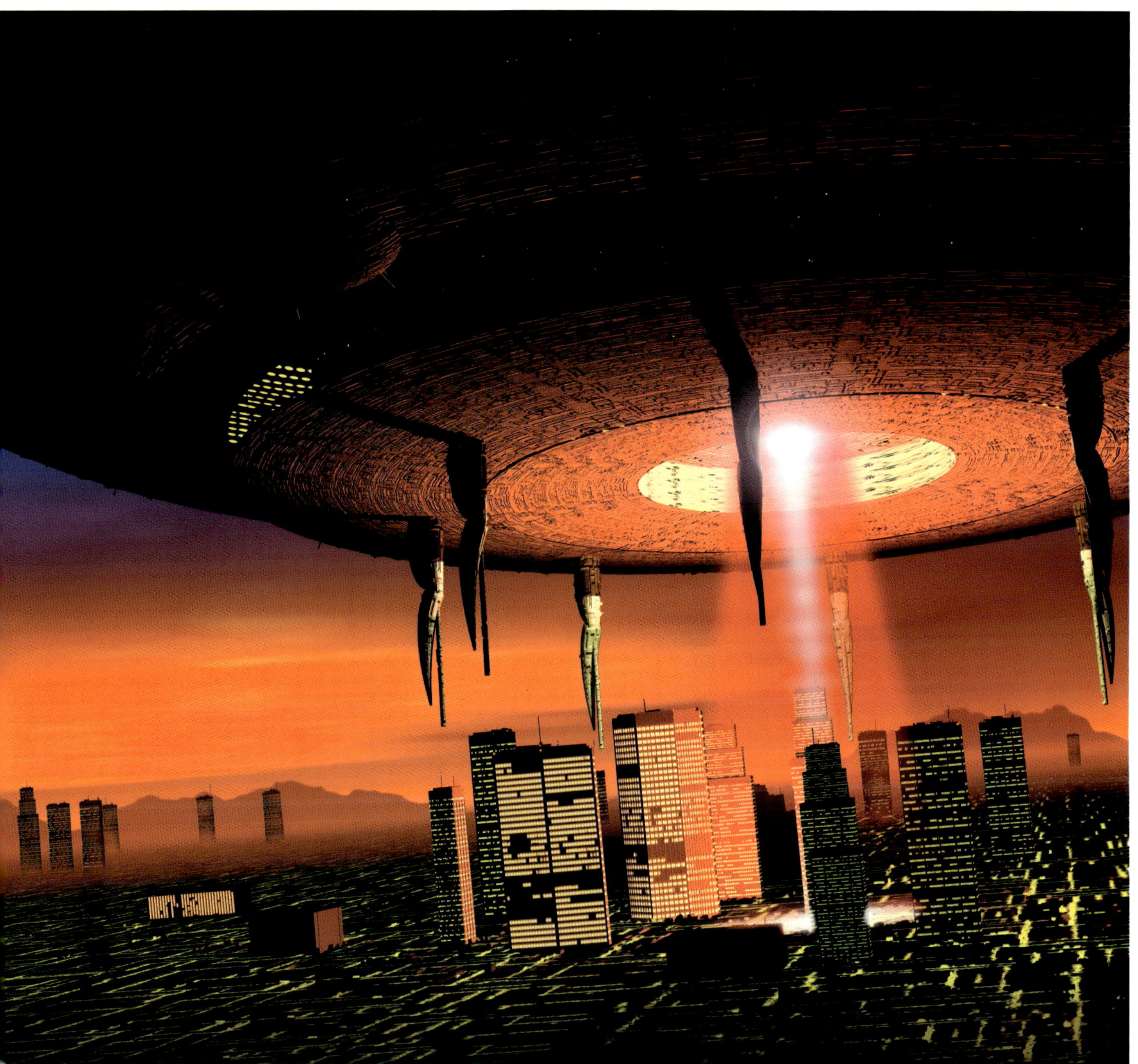

ABOVE

THE ALIEN YEARS

Robert Silverberg
HarperCollins UK
Digital

It will come as no surprise to anyone that this was published the same year that the film *Independence Day* hit the screens. The manuscript arrived, along with the poster from the movie and that age-old art director's cry, 'do something the same, but different'.

I actually had a lot of fun with this, trying to get that sense of scale and the feeling of a huge mass floating impossibly above the city. I had to do a considerable amount of freehand work in Photoshop before I felt that the city had sufficient conviction.

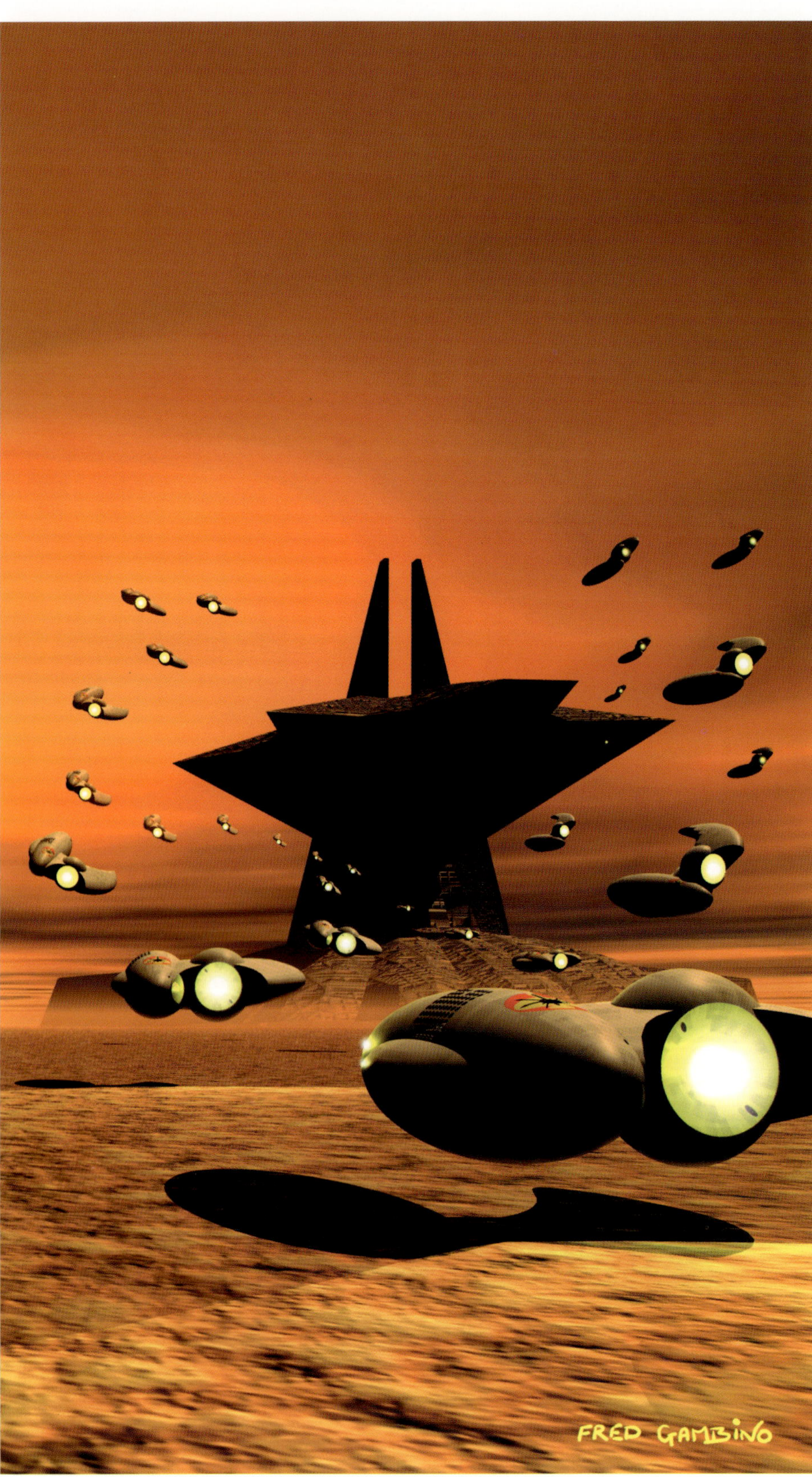

LEFT

ALIEN CITADEL

Douglas Hill
Pan
Digital

This was the final part in a trilogy of children's books for Pan, and, again, an early computer-generated image. As the budget wasn't huge, the art director was happy for me to take short cuts if need be. I find it difficult to cut corners, every job I tackle gets the same attention, because once I get involved I can't help myself. However, I could speed things up by using the same alien ships on each cover, which would be the unifying element that the publishers wanted anyway.

There were three programs used in the execution of this piece, Amapi for the citadel, transferred into Bryce and rendered into a desert scene and Sketch for the ships. I think this is an example of how sometimes very simple shapes can be the most effective.

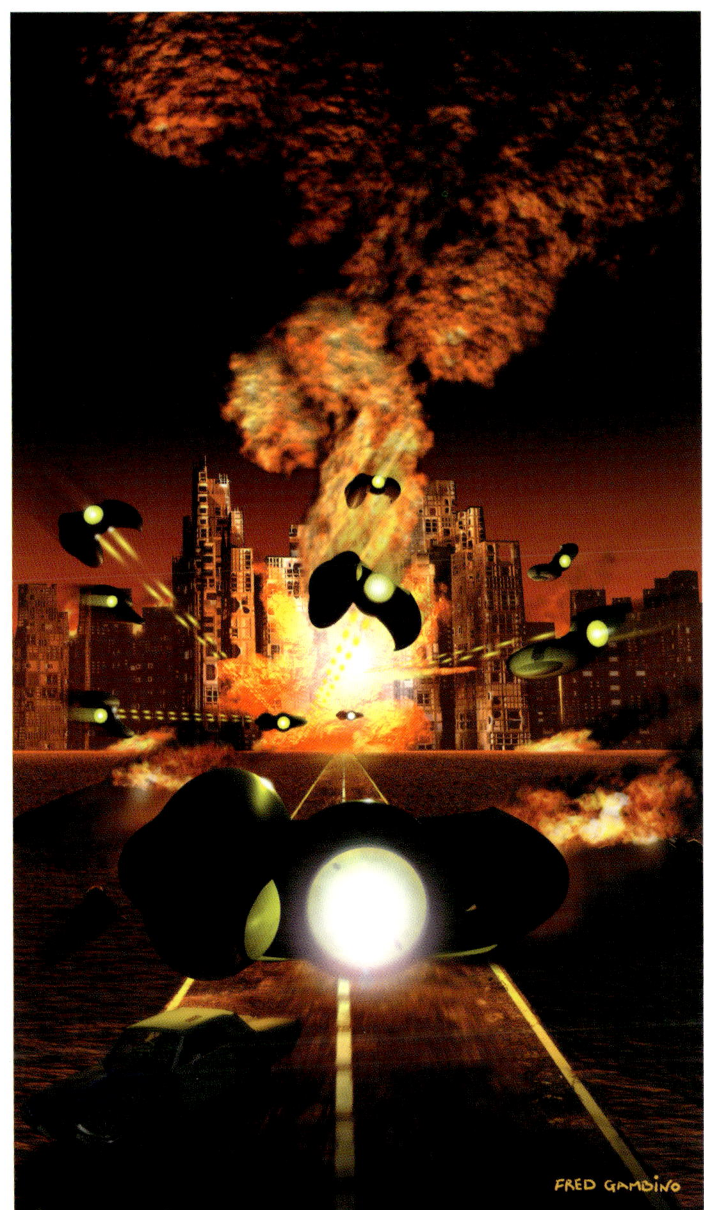

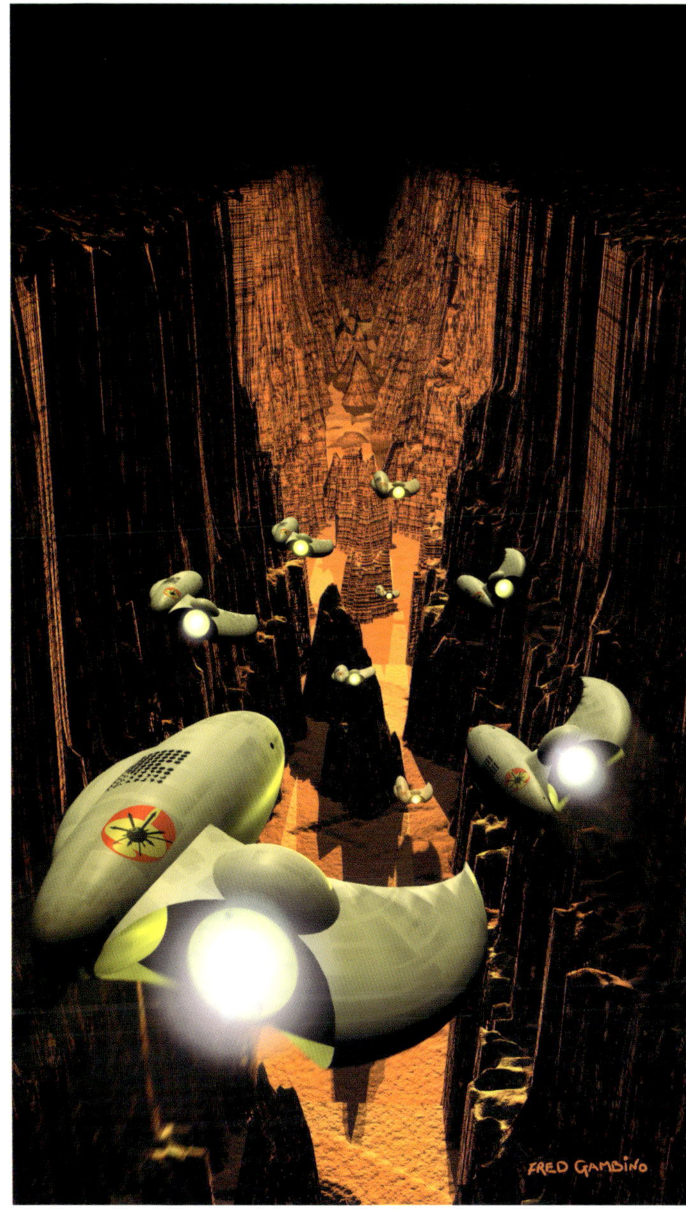

ABOVE
THE HUNTSMAN
Douglas Hill
Pan
Digital

This is the first book in the trilogy. As I was still finding my way with the computer, I was a sucker for anything new and had just discovered Photoshop plug-ins. At the time, I had just acquired one that, amongst other things, produced fire and smoke. I struggled with these, but the best could only be described as mediocre. It took me a while to appreciate that, for something like this, the best kind of filter is the one I carry in my head. It also has the benefit of producing effects that are unique to me.

ABOVE
CREATURES OF THE CLAW
Douglas Hill
Pan
Digital

This is the second in the series and shows a background produced entirely in Bryce.

THE MOTE IN GOD'S EYE

Larry Niven and Jerry Pournelle
Futura
Acrylic

This was the last painting that I completed in the Niven series. I had read the book some years before, while at college, and had thoroughly enjoyed it. There are so many aspects of this book that would make an exciting cover, but I knew from the start what I was going to do – the two Earth warships heading for the Mote, a small star orbiting a red giant.

My normal practice, then and now, is to paint on illustration board that has been primed with gesso primer, but this is one of the few paintings that I airbrushed straight onto the smooth board. Working this way is a lot less forgiving than priming the support first, as the surface is much more delicate, making alterations harder. It also doesn't take a paintbrush as well, lacking the tooth of the primed board. On the other hand, it does stop you overworking the image.

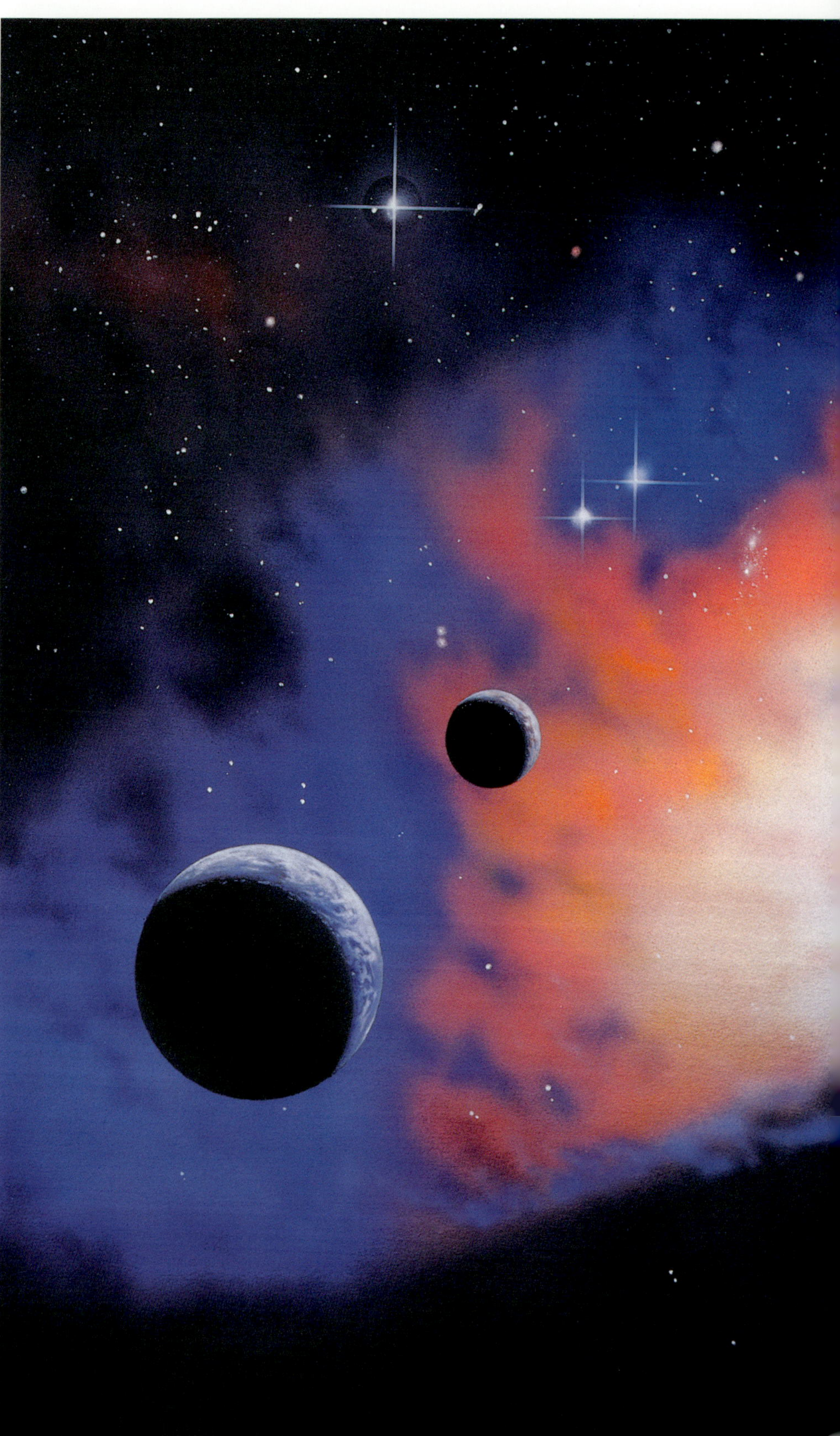

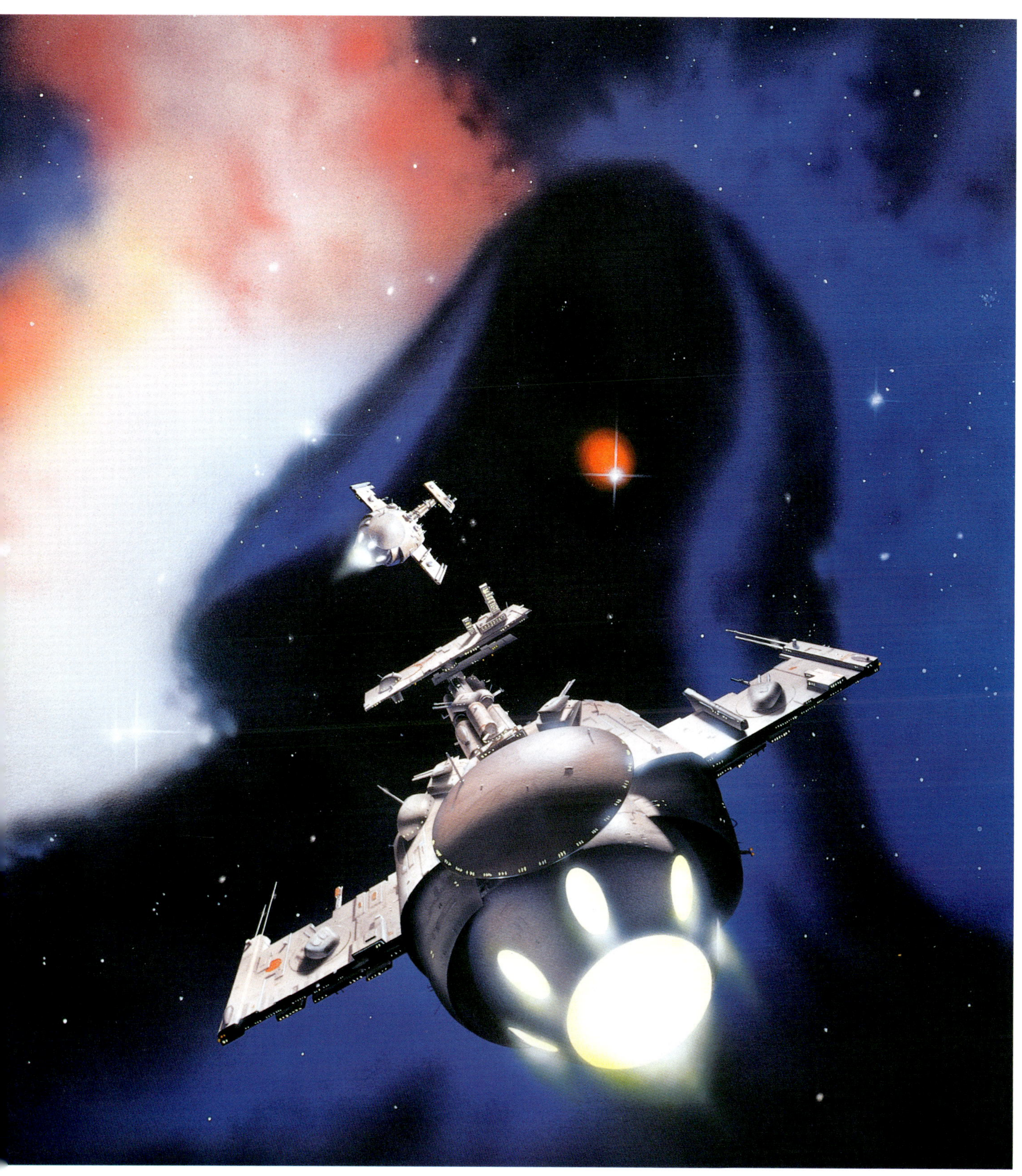

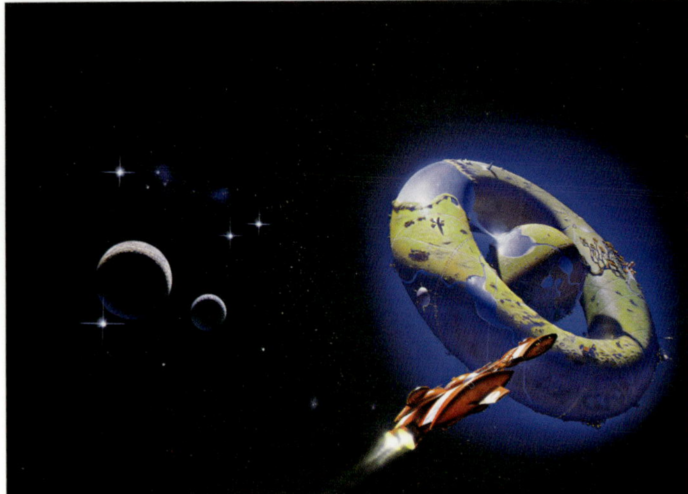

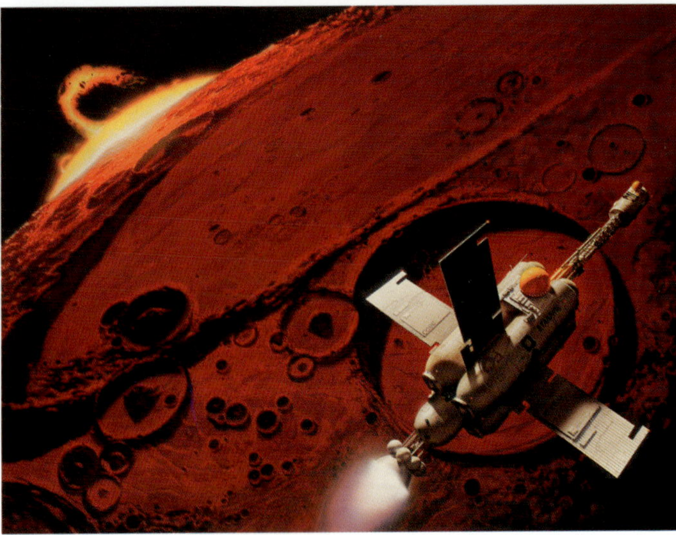

ABOVE

STARFIRE

Paul Preuss
Orbit
Acrylic

This painting was executed when the idea of my using a computer to illustrate was about as likely as my holidaying on the moon. The model for the spaceship was constructed from various household items. As a contact lens wearer, I bought cleaning solutions that came in very useful containers. The four main tanks were saline solution cans, the bridge section was a lens-cleaning solution bottle, whilst the heat radiators were cut from plastic gallon containers. The booster was on old discarded bulb. Nothing went to waste in those days.

LEFT

PROTECTOR

Larry Niven
Futura
Acrylic

It was a lot of fun trying to recreate this bizarre Niven environment that I affectionately dubbed 'doughnut world'. It shows an artefact with variable gravity built by an incredibly advanced alien being. The characters in the story can swim 'down' the 'waterfall' that connects the central globe with the outer torus and arrive upright at either end. The torus has a number of buildings that have various historical architectural styles.

I built the model from an old truck tyre inner tube and used a football for the central globe. I actually went to all the trouble of painting this, making small plasticine buildings and even using pipe cleaners for the tree. I do look back and wonder sometimes.

RIGHT

THE WORLD OF PTAVVS

Larry Niven
Futura
Acrylic

This shows another interesting use of *objets trouves*. The round part of the body was a frisbee, the engine bay a deodorant bottle surmounted by two A10 tank buster engines from a model kit, and the long forward fuselage section two deodorant bottles glued together.

I was never quite happy with this illustration. The ship just didn't seem to stand out from the background enough. In the version for the book cover, the asteroid is peppered with large domed cities, similar to the ones on the asteroid in the background. When I looked at the painting again, some years later, it was suddenly obvious that these were the problem. They just detracted too much from the ship. So, for this book, I painted them out.

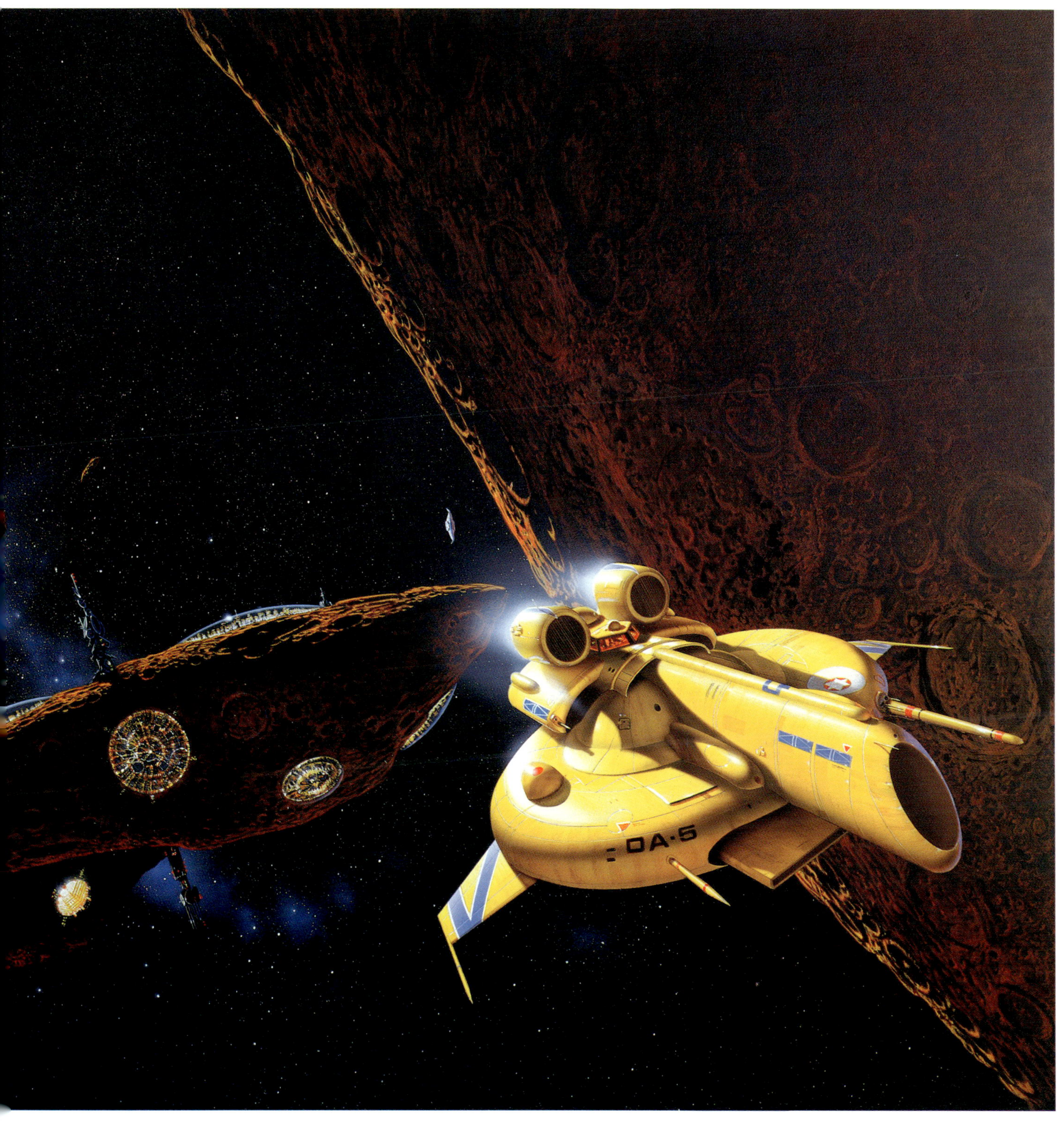
DA·5

Alien Realms

By Robert J. Sawyer

Can a single image convey an entire dimension?

Fred Gambino understands alien worlds better than anyone else painting science-fiction covers today; he manages to illustrate books that others find difficult to capture in a single image. There have been over a dozen different covers worldwide for my 1995 Nebula Award-winner *The Terminal Experiment*, but, of them all, only Fred's managed to encapsulate this story of a man who made three computerized copies of his own brain. I knew the moment I saw his painting that I had to own the original, whatever the price; it now hangs in my living room.

Fred also did the cover for the British version of my *Illegal Alien*, another book with many different editions. Once again, Fred's cover is clearly the best. Not only did he manage to pull off what in other hands might have looked ludicrous – an alien defendant in an earthly witness box – but he also captured just the right tone, with the frightened extraterrestrial peeking over the railing, more terrified of the humans than they are of him.

This kind of brilliance is typical Gambino; he combines the intimacies of character with the grandly cosmic. There are many fine artists in the SF field painting astronomical vistas; many more producing SF portraiture. But being able to mix the beauty of the heavens with realistic – even hyper-realistic – people is a talent unique to Fred.

Fred's spaceships are particularly eye-catching. Whether it resembles a shark at

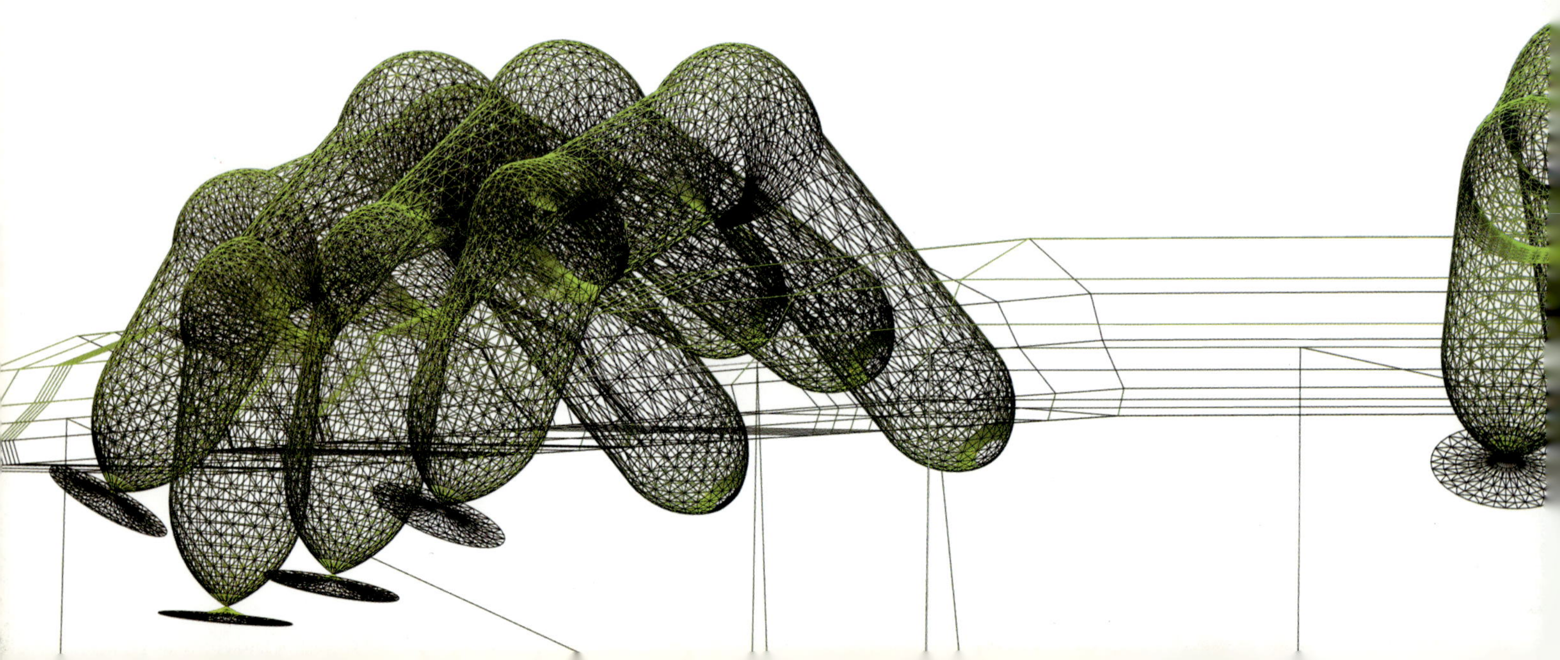

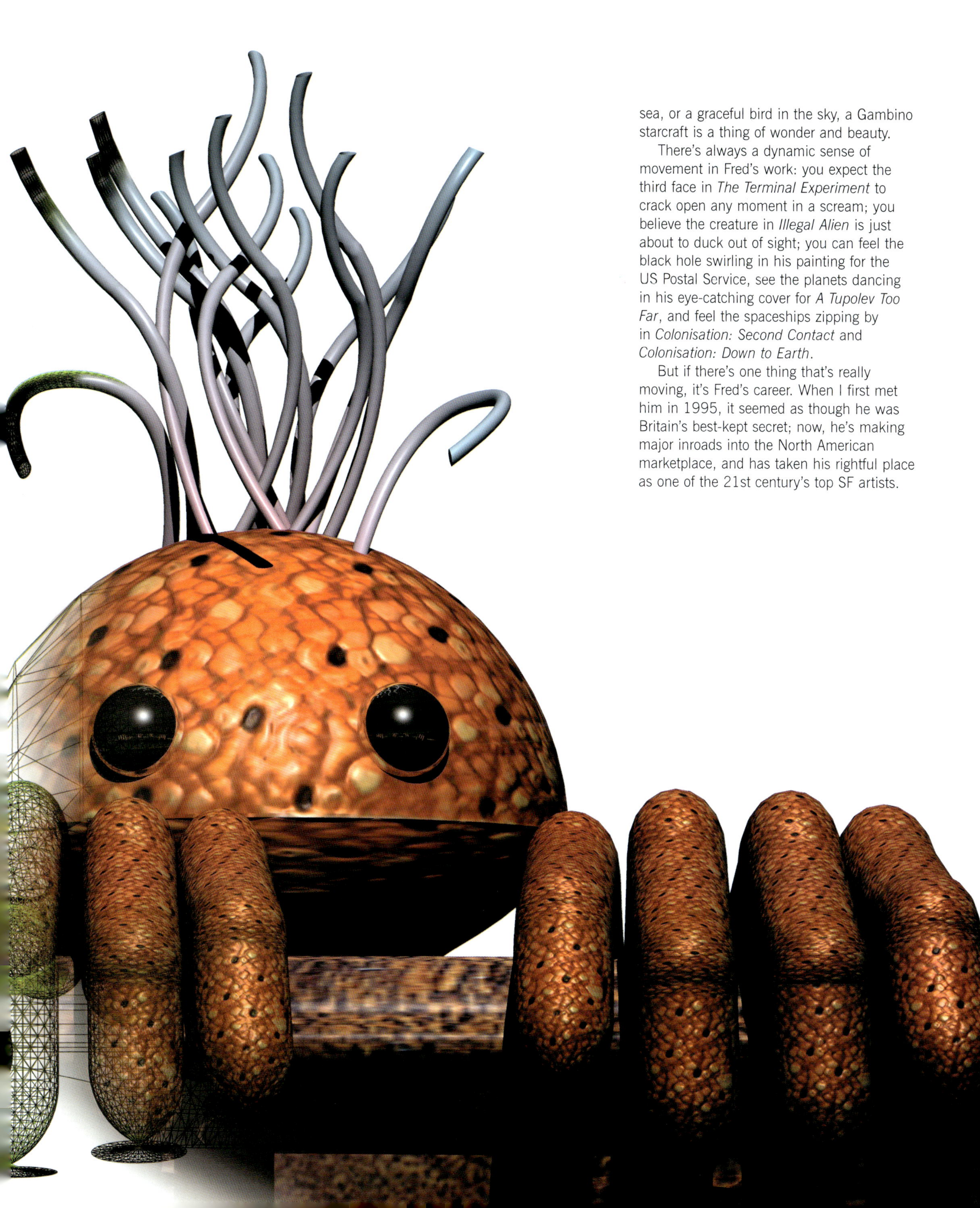

sea, or a graceful bird in the sky, a Gambino starcraft is a thing of wonder and beauty.

There's always a dynamic sense of movement in Fred's work: you expect the third face in *The Terminal Experiment* to crack open any moment in a scream; you believe the creature in *Illegal Alien* is just about to duck out of sight; you can feel the black hole swirling in his painting for the US Postal Service, see the planets dancing in his eye-catching cover for *A Tupolev Too Far*, and feel the spaceships zipping by in *Colonisation: Second Contact* and *Colonisation: Down to Earth*.

But if there's one thing that's really moving, it's Fred's career. When I first met him in 1995, it seemed as though he was Britain's best-kept secret; now, he's making major inroads into the North American marketplace, and has taken his rightful place as one of the 21st century's top SF artists.

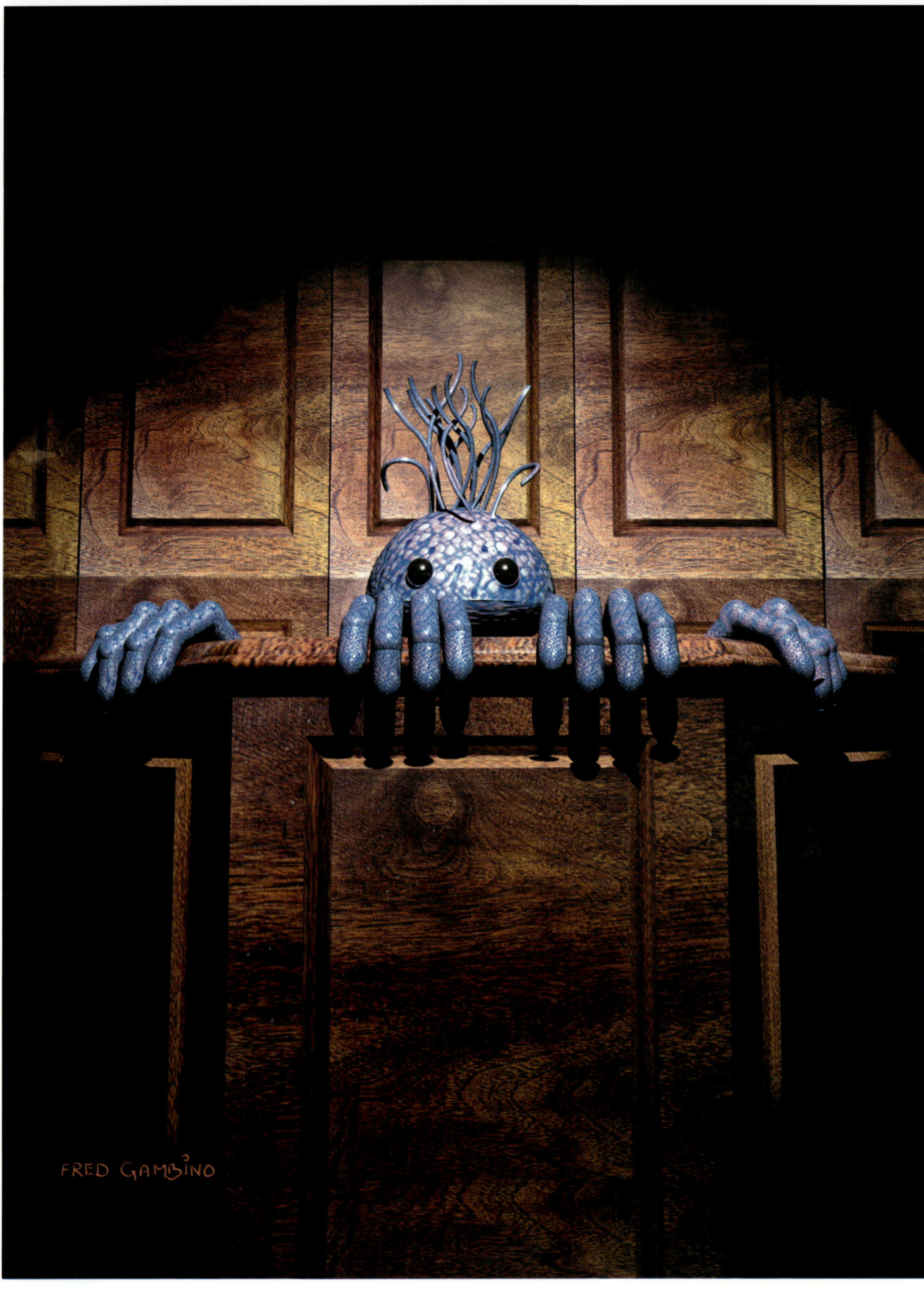
FRED GAMBINO

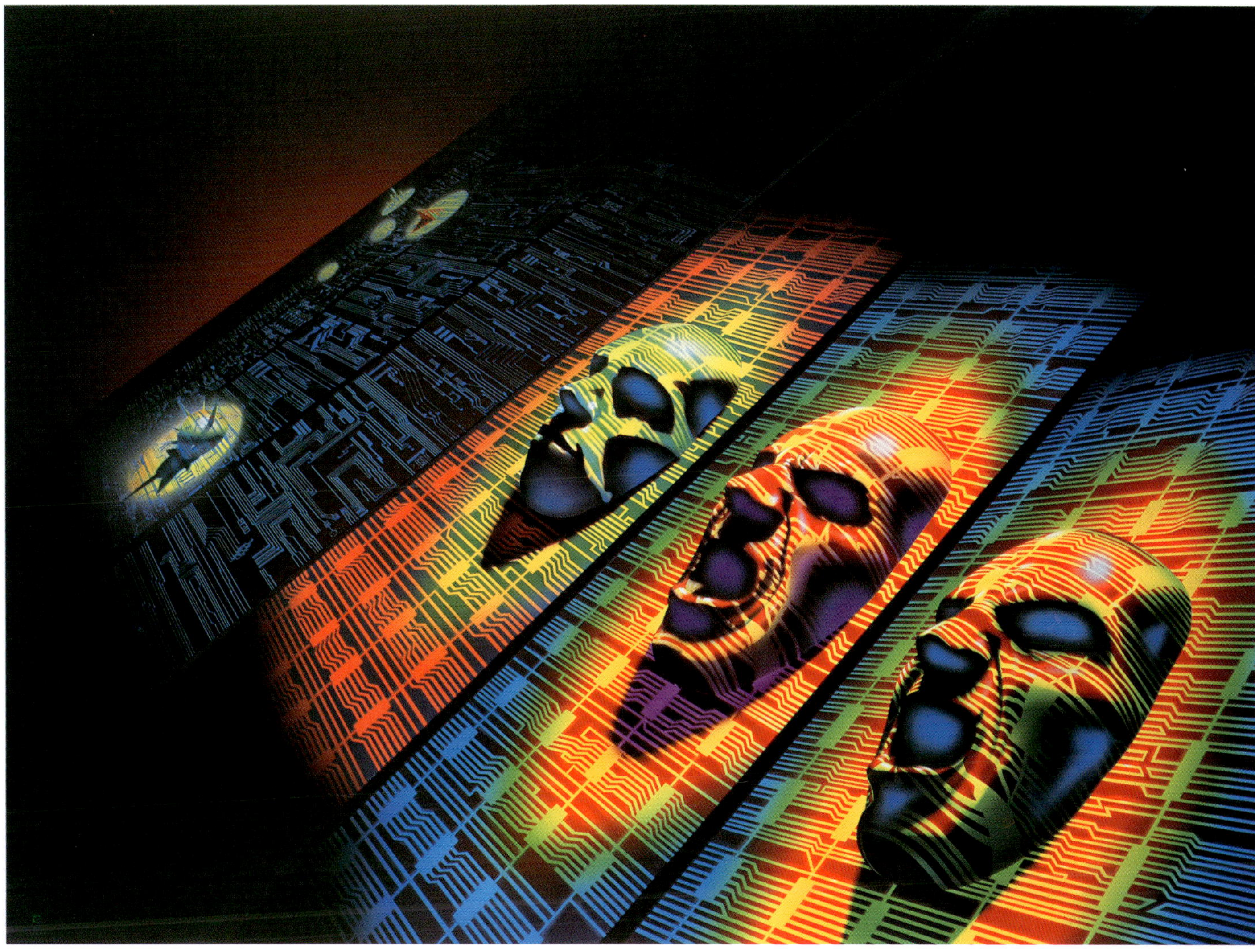

OPPOSITE

ILLEGAL ALIEN

Robert J. Sawyer
HarperCollins UK
Digital

I wasn't given this book to read before I started the job. The art director came up with the idea of one of the aliens peering over the top of a courtroom dock, in the manner of the 'Kilroy was here' cartoon character. A few months later, when I had finished the job, I bought a copy of the book for myself, being a big fan of Robert J. Sawyer's. Much as I like the cover image in itself, I wonder if it wasn't a little too jokey for what turned out to be a fairly serious book. Still, it was a fun image to do.

ABOVE

THE TERMINAL EXPERIMENT

Robert J. Sawyer
Hodder & Stoughton
Acrylic

When it first appeared as a serial in *Analog*, this was titled 'Hobson's Choice'. I thoroughly enjoyed this novel for its mix of entertaining ideas and exciting plot. The brief was to come up with a computer-generated, digital look. This was about a year before I took the digital plunge myself.

In the story Hobson's mind is downloaded into a computer three times, each of these avatars having a different personality emphasis. At the time there was a craze for those 3D images that had hundreds of people staring in glazed stupefaction at what appeared to be an abstract jumble. The image was only visible if you blurred your vision in a particular way.

This gave me the idea of having heads, representing the downloaded personalities, swelling out of the circuitry that made up the computer, each showing a different expression. To achieve the perspective of the circuitry flowing along the contours of the face, I asked a friend to don a bathing cap to hide his hair and put his head through a hole cut into a piece of board. I drew some circuitry onto black card with a silver marker, photographed it and then projected it onto him, re-photographing the whole thing.

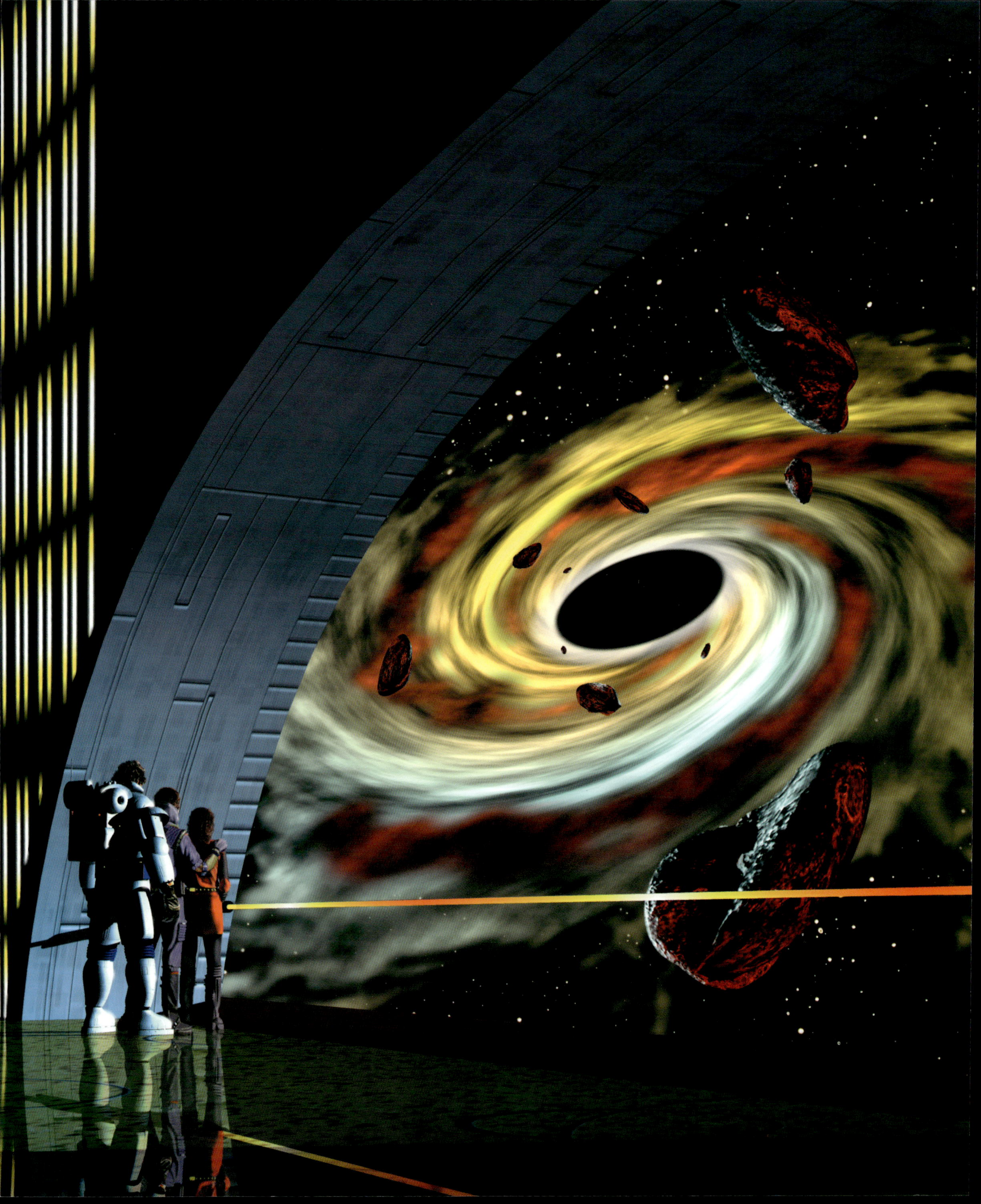

OPPOSITE

BLACK HOLE

US Postal Service
Digital

This was the final picture in the sequence for the US Postal Service (see pages 40, 46, 72 and 82) and shows the two children with their father, gazing at a black hole. The black hole itself was realized in Photoshop, mainly using the cloud and twirl filter, whilst everything else was produced and rendered in Alias Sketch.

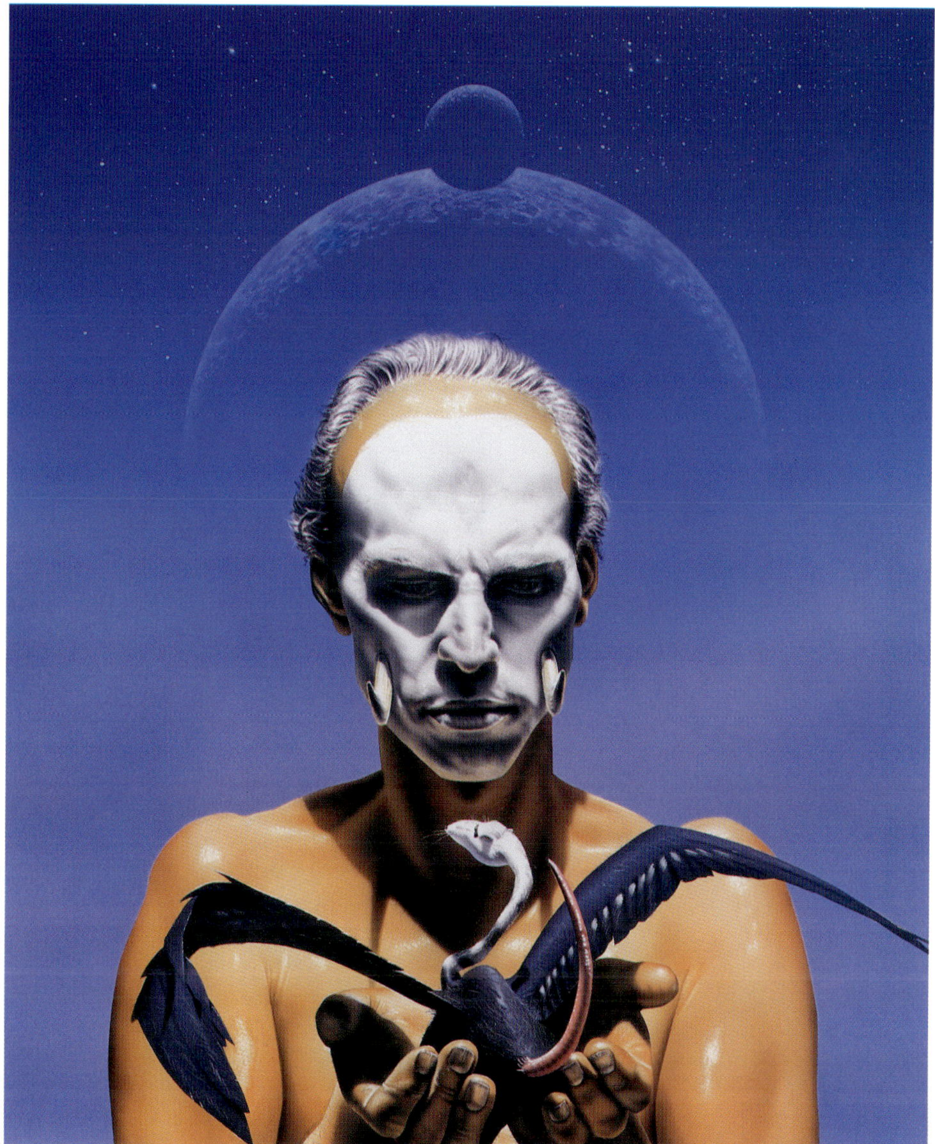

ABOVE

A TUPOLEV TOO FAR

Brian Aldiss
HarperCollins
Acrylic

During the time I rented office space from Adrian Heapy Photography, I found a soulmate in one of the photographers, Nigel Gibson. Nigel spent many hours peering over my shoulder, offering advice, most of it welcome. This almost developed into a partnership, with Nigel becoming an unpaid consultant. Not content with this, he also became a character actor and appears on numerous covers. He can be seen screaming hideously in *Blood Net*, stepping down imperiously in *Ringing the Changes*, adopting three different expressions in *The Terminal Experiment* and communing with the strange alien bird in *A Tupolev Too Far*.

In the story and in my first rough, this scene takes place in thick jungle, but the marketing people had decreed that this book should be aimed at a science-fiction audience and felt the jungle gave the painting too much of a fantasy feel. Hence its replacement with the space background.

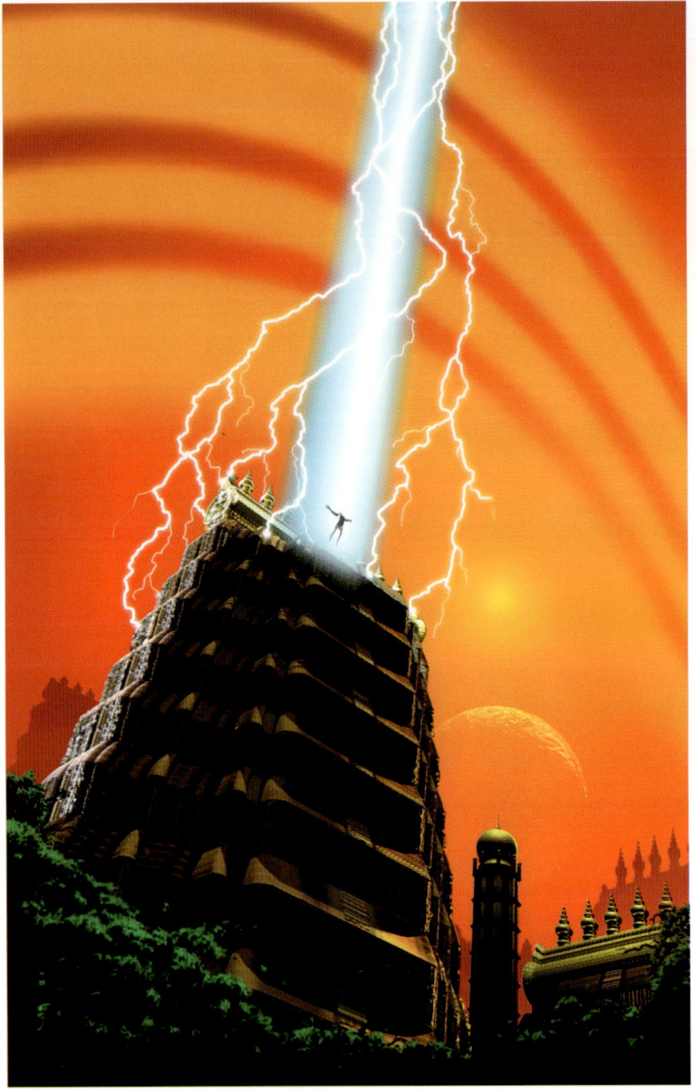

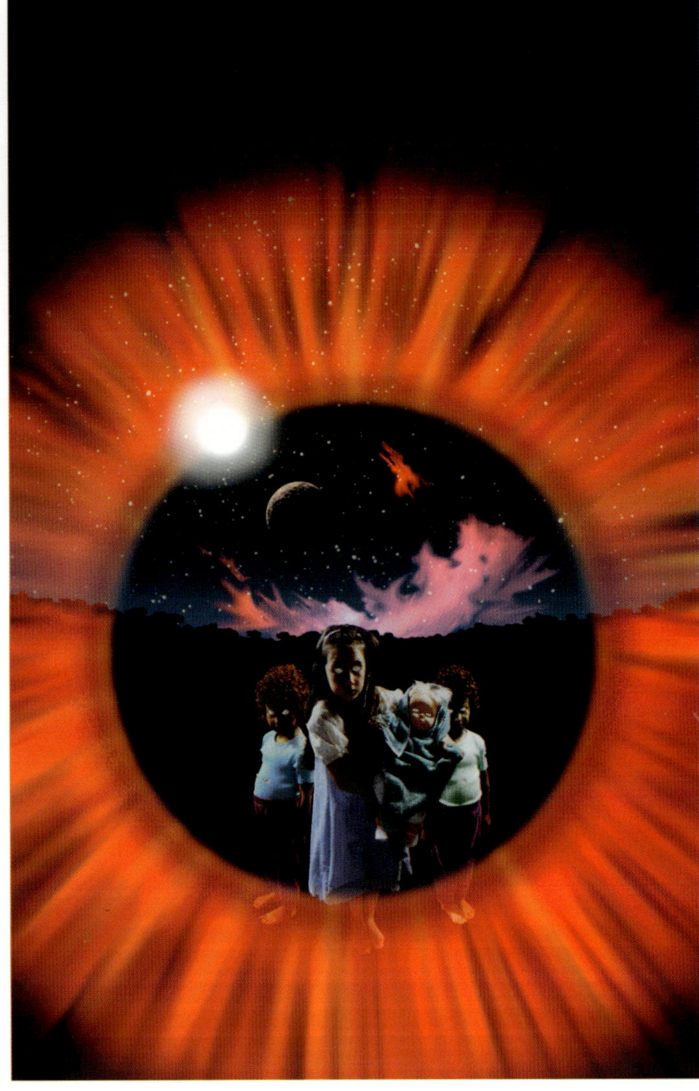

ABOVE

LORD OF LIGHT

Roger Zelazny
Orion
Digital

This was a somewhat tricky proposition – futuristic Hindu temples. This image is a scene lifted virtually straight off the page. The rings in the sky are described in the book and proved to be a useful compositional element. I had several attempts at the lightning strikes, in the end opting to simply paint them in Photoshop. One of the huge advantages of doing something like that in Photoshop is that you can paint white over a background colour, even black, and get it as pure as you wish.

ABOVE RIGHT

MORE THAN HUMAN

Theodore Sturgeon
Orion
Digital

It was difficult trying to realize this idea without making it look like a horror story. The most obvious difference between these mutant children and their mentor and humans is their eyes. I played upon that theme and for good measure had the whole scene reflected in an eyeball. Again, the device of a space background was used to try and give more of a science-fiction feel to the cover.

OPPOSITE

HELLWORLD

Simon R. Green
Gollancz
Acrylic

I first met my partner, Jenny, when I had to find a number of models to pose for a series of romantic novels – the illustrator's equivalent of 'come up and see my etchings', I suppose. She did, in fact, pose for a few other covers after that, but a few years later I was receiving complaints that I hadn't used her for a while. 'Don't worry dear,' I said, 'I'm sure the right job will be along soon.' I'm sure that this wasn't what she had in mind, and the book title is in no way meant to be a reference to our relationship!

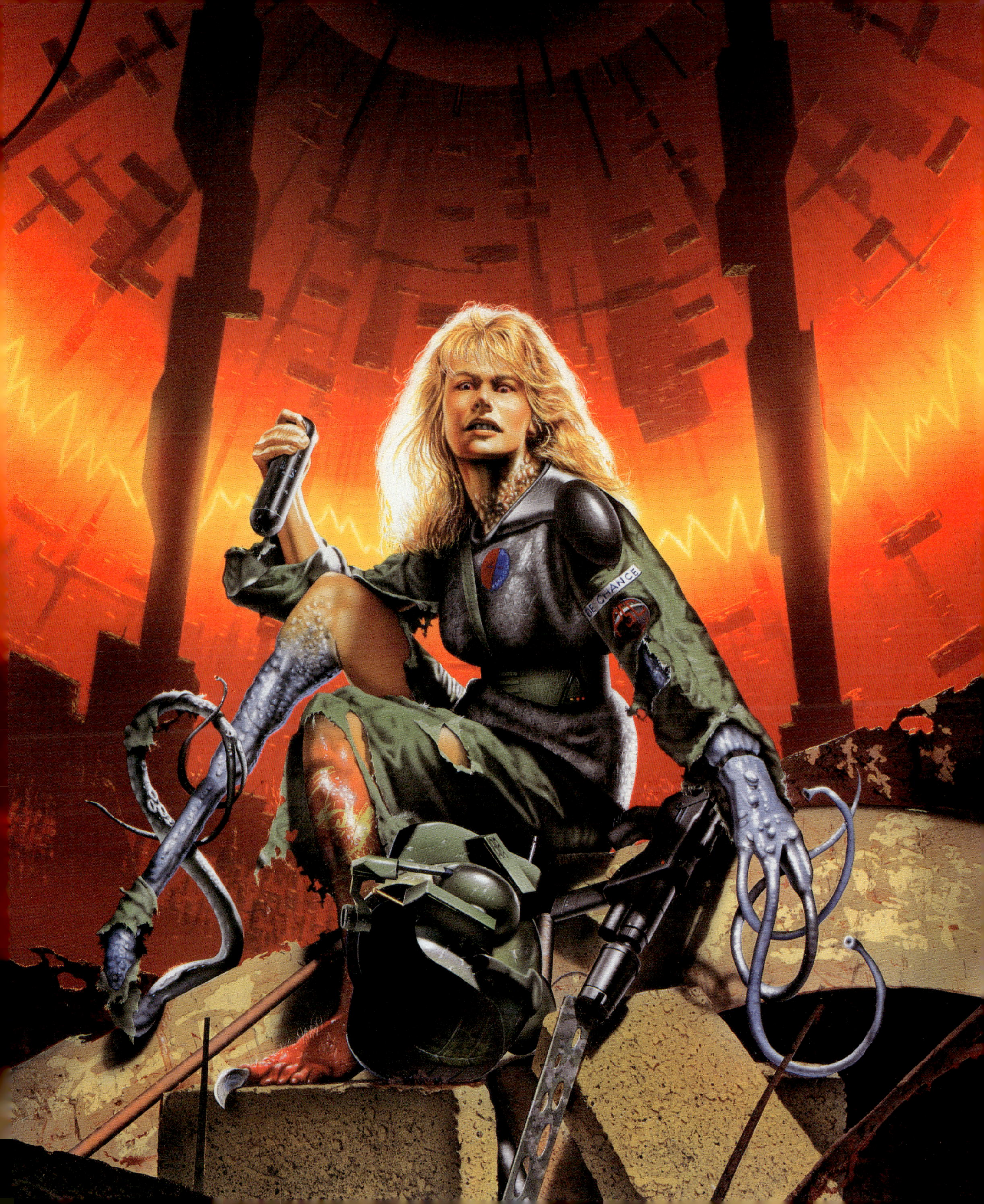
CHANCE

SECOND CONTACT

Harry Turtledove
Hodder & Stoughton
Digital

Trends in SF book covers have tended to change over time, as art directors look for new ways to grab people's attention and the readership becomes more sophisticated. The golden age, in the 1950s, had a predominance of aliens, who were often in pursuit of a hapless female, and a plethora of gun-toting, lantern-jawed heroes. As time passed, images become more sophisticated and, sadly, there seemed to be less room for the old pulp-style covers.

Recently, however, I have had commissions in which I have been able to pay my own homage to those earlier paintings. The covers for Harry Turtledove's sprawling, alternate universe epic *Colonisation*, about a race of invading Lizards, are one such commission.

Covers for the preceding novels, set in the earlier part of the 20th century, had already been done by other artists and I kept some elements of those for continuity's sake. The art director had liked what he called the 'in your face' feel of the Valentine Robot (see page 80) and had wanted something similar, specifically asking for the covers to be done digitally. This presented a few problems, not the least of which was, could I actually build a lizard in Sketch (not the easiest program)? It took over four days just to build my reptilian protagonist, and the rough ended up looking almost like the finished artwork. This wasn't all bad, however, as, when the subsequent commission came in, all the hard work was already done.

There was one other decision to be made. The brief had stipulated that, as lizards generally prefer warm environments, they should be landing somewhere in the world that had a warm climate and would be easily recognizable. A couple of years previously, I had spent three weeks driving around California. What better spot for the lizards to be touching down, I thought, than the place immortalized by John Ford in that other genre of gun-toting adventure and colonisation stories – the Western – than Monument Valley?

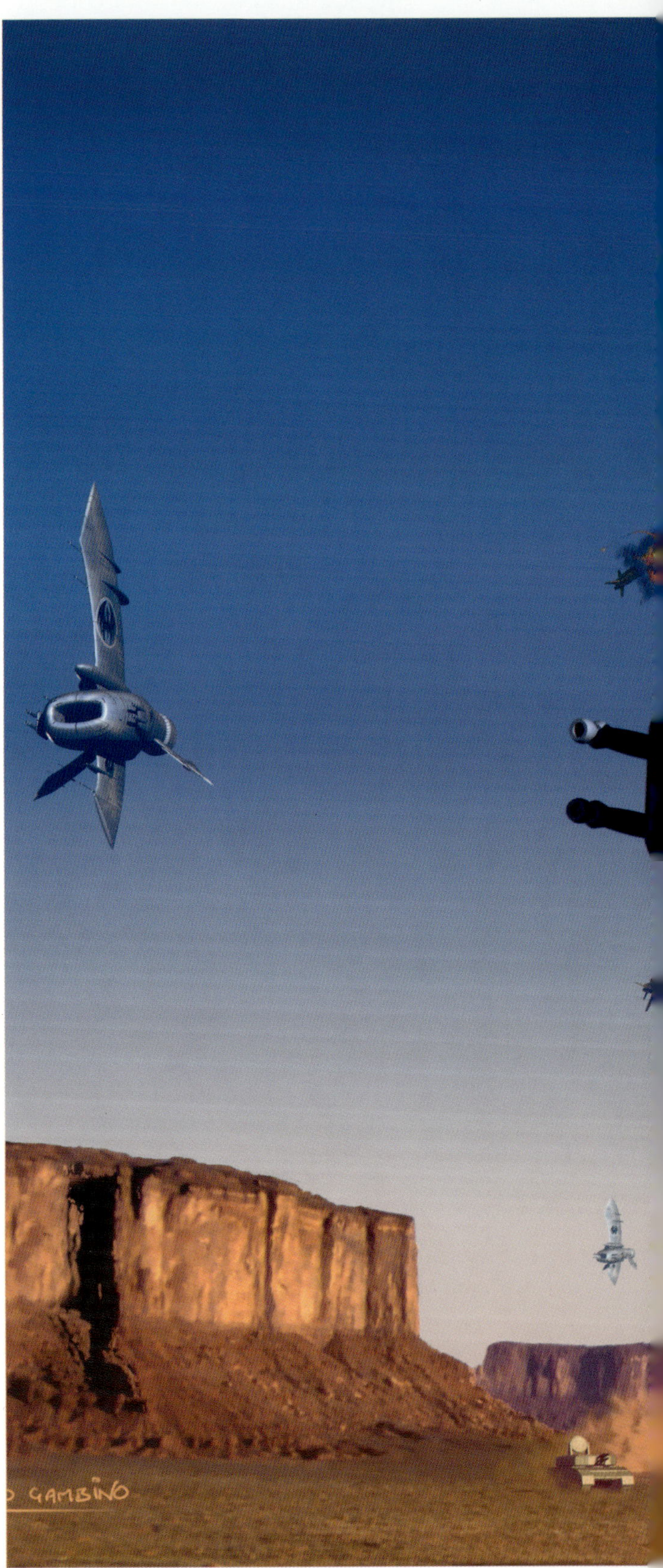

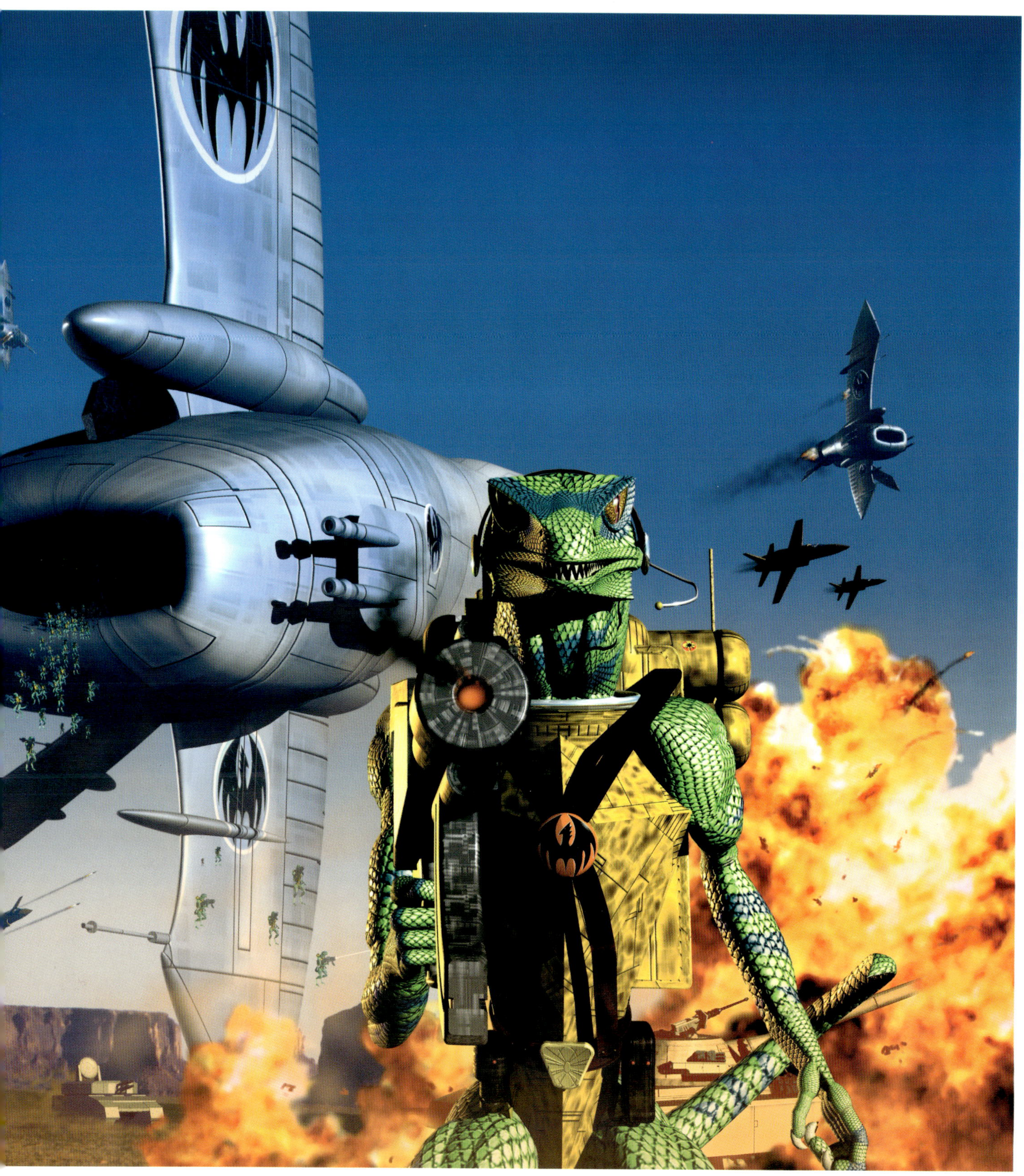

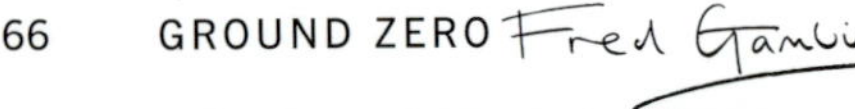

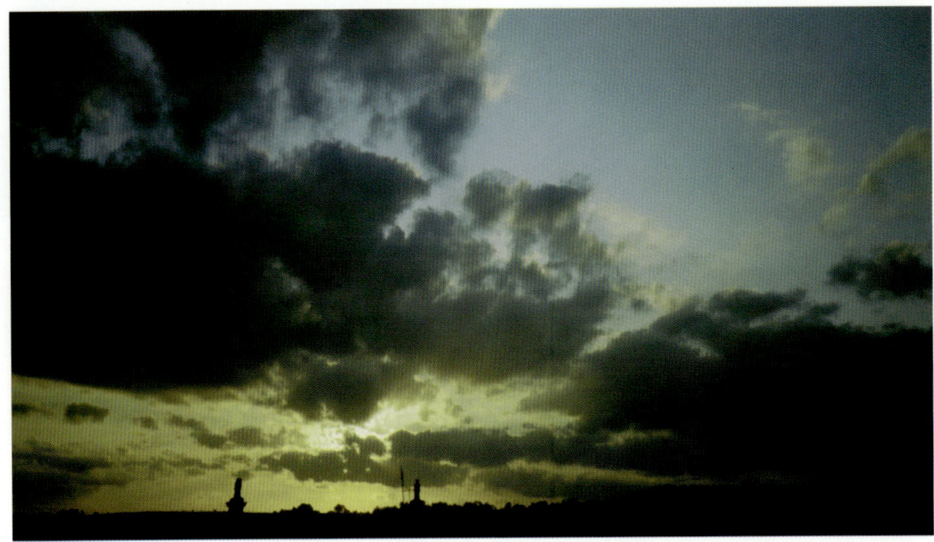

LEFT AND BELOW: Background sky photography and various elements test rendered.

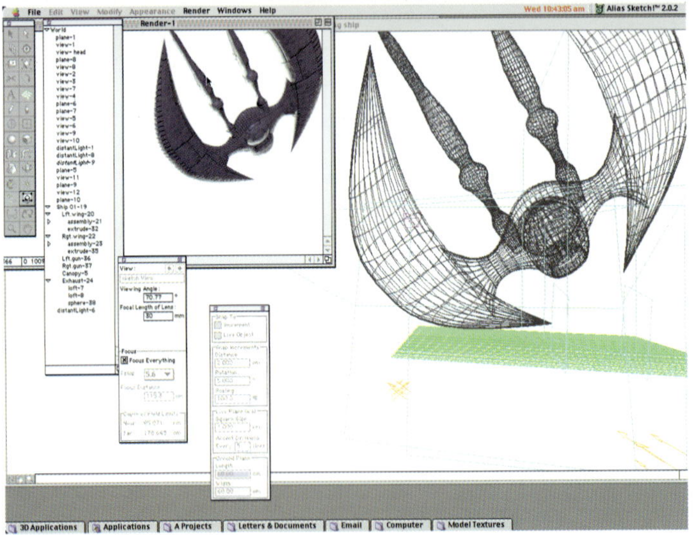

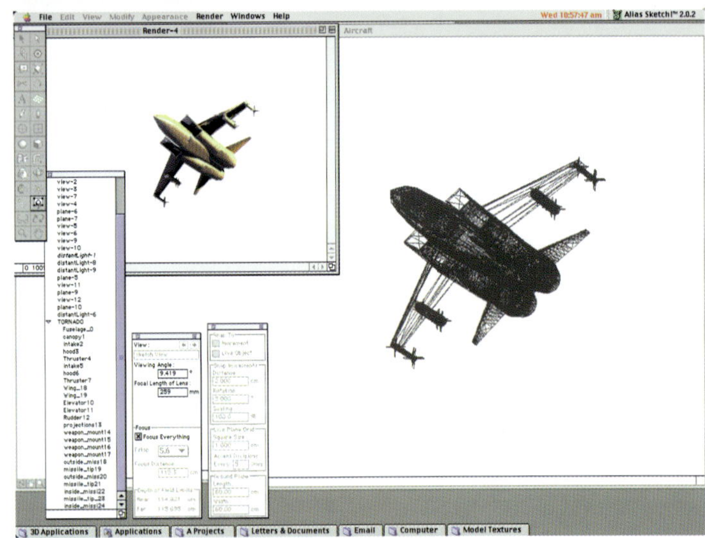

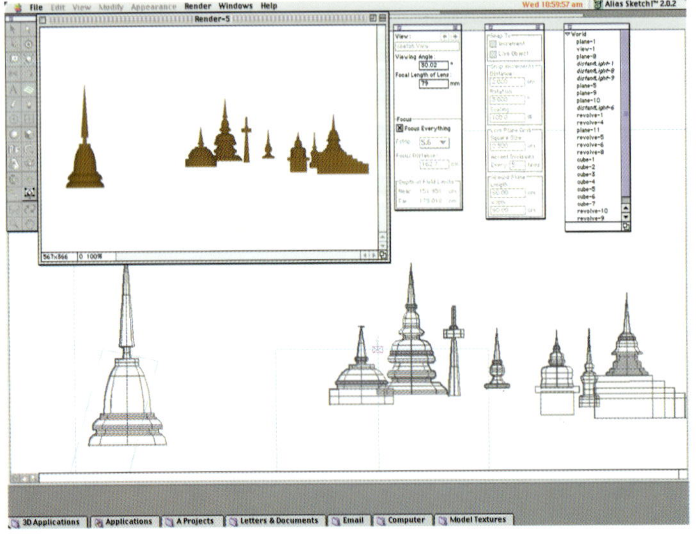

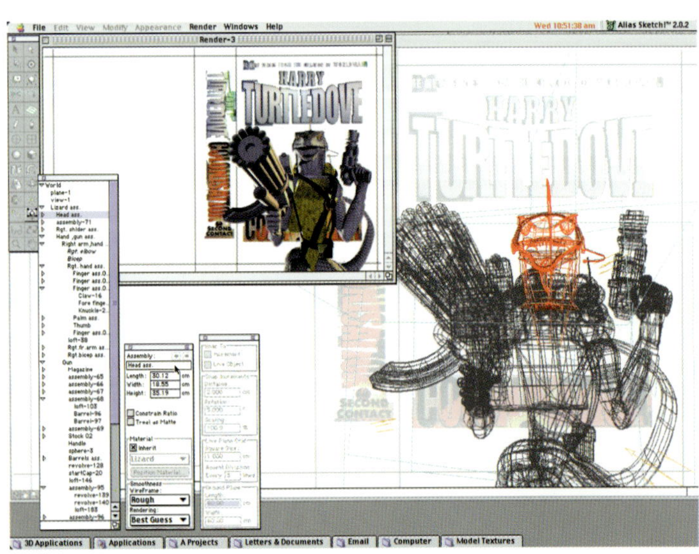

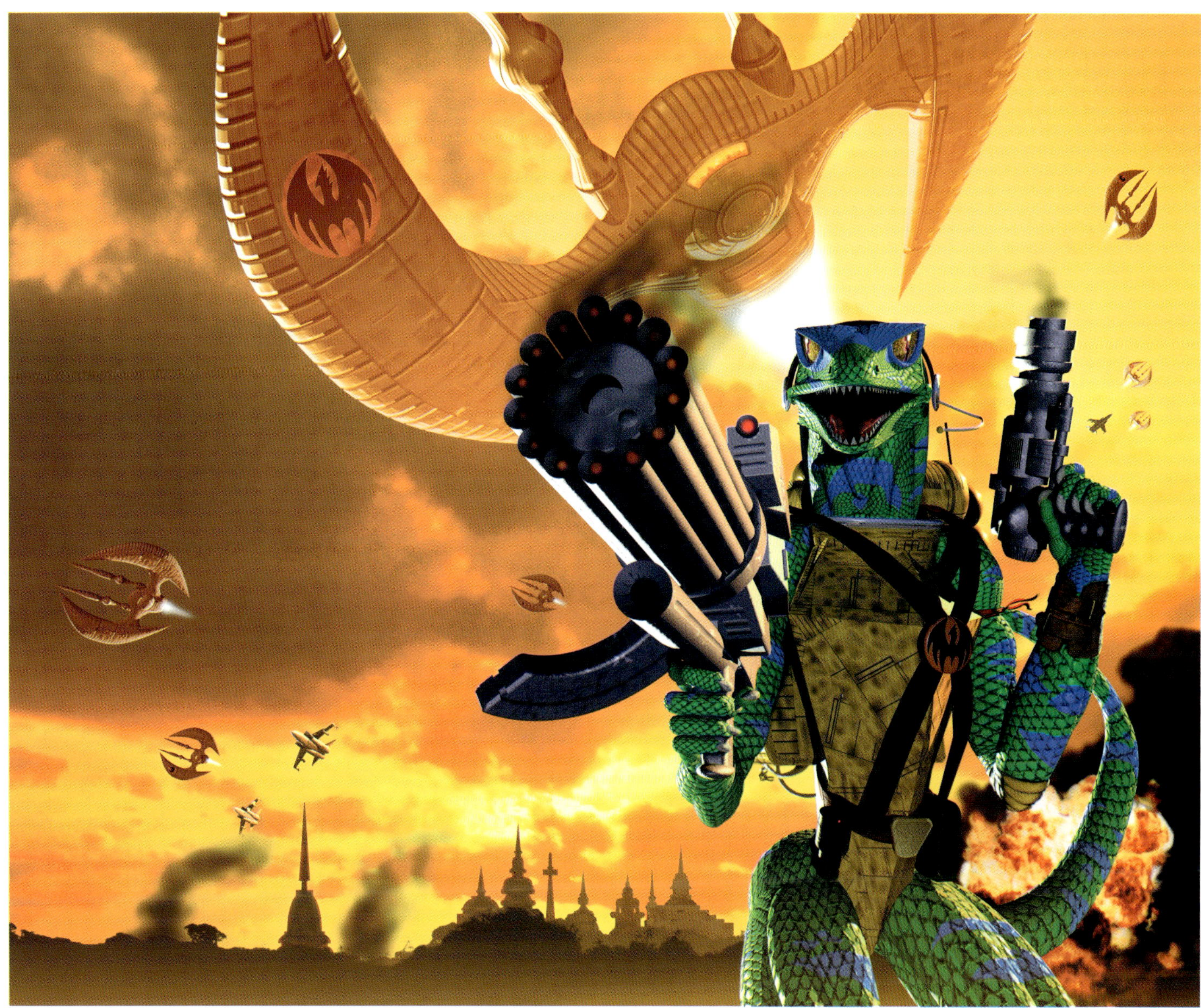

ABOVE

DOWN TO EARTH

Harry Turtledove
Hodder & Stoughton
Digital

This is the second in the Turtledove alternate history, *Colonisation*, in which alien lizards invade Earth, and the second to feature the Arnold Schwarzenegger of the lizard world.

Most of the hard work was done for the first in the series; the only new modelling needed was for the alien craft and the lizards' guns.

I've had something of a mixed reaction to the lizard's expression. To me he looks like he is laughing maniacally as he plunges into battle, but others have expressed the opinion that he looks far too jolly and not nearly mean enough.

OVERLEAF

AFTERSHOCKS

Harry Turtledove
Hodder & Stoughton
Digital

The final image in the *Colonisation* series sees our lizard doing battle in Paris, the Eiffel Tower meeting an untimely demise.

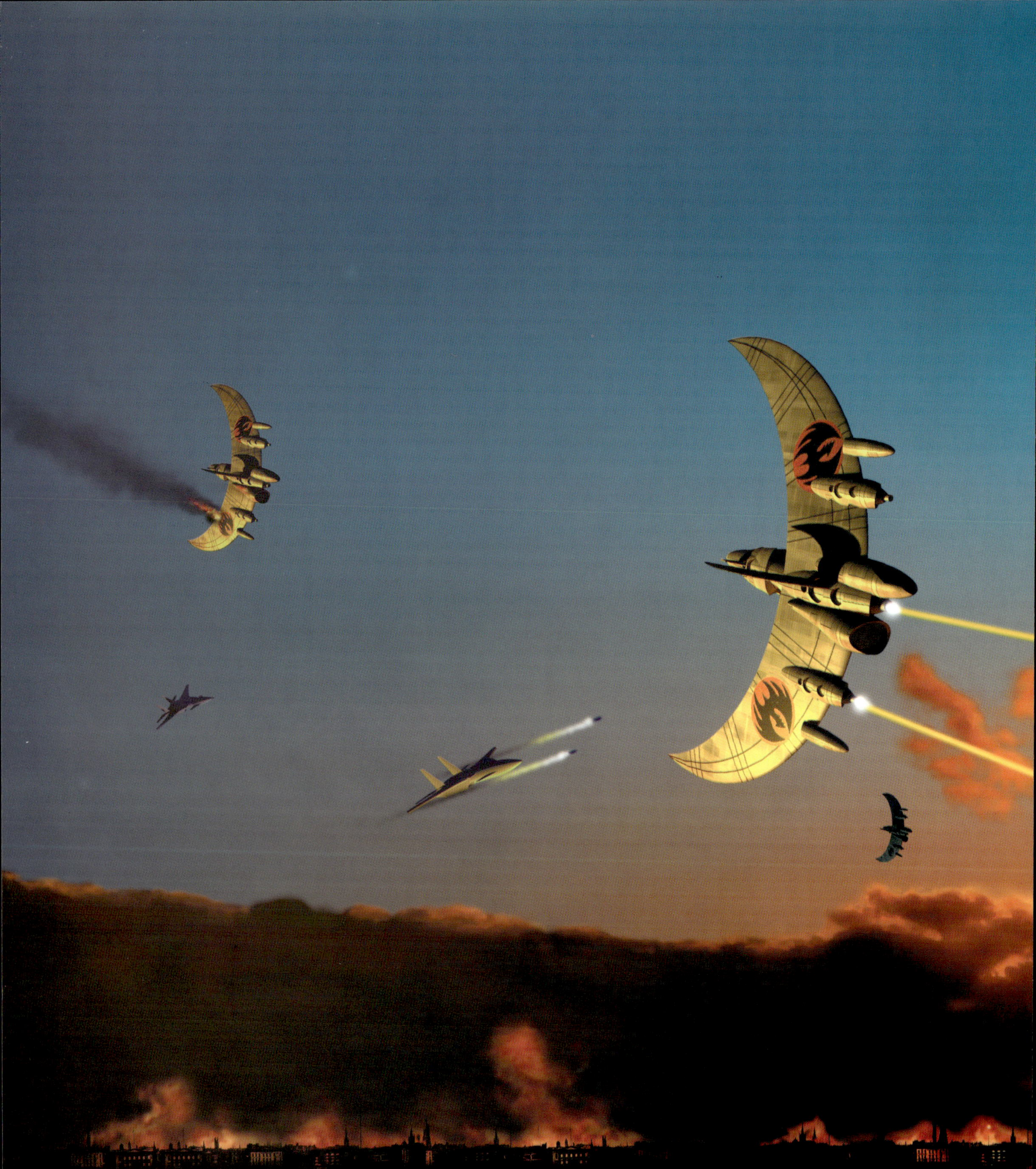

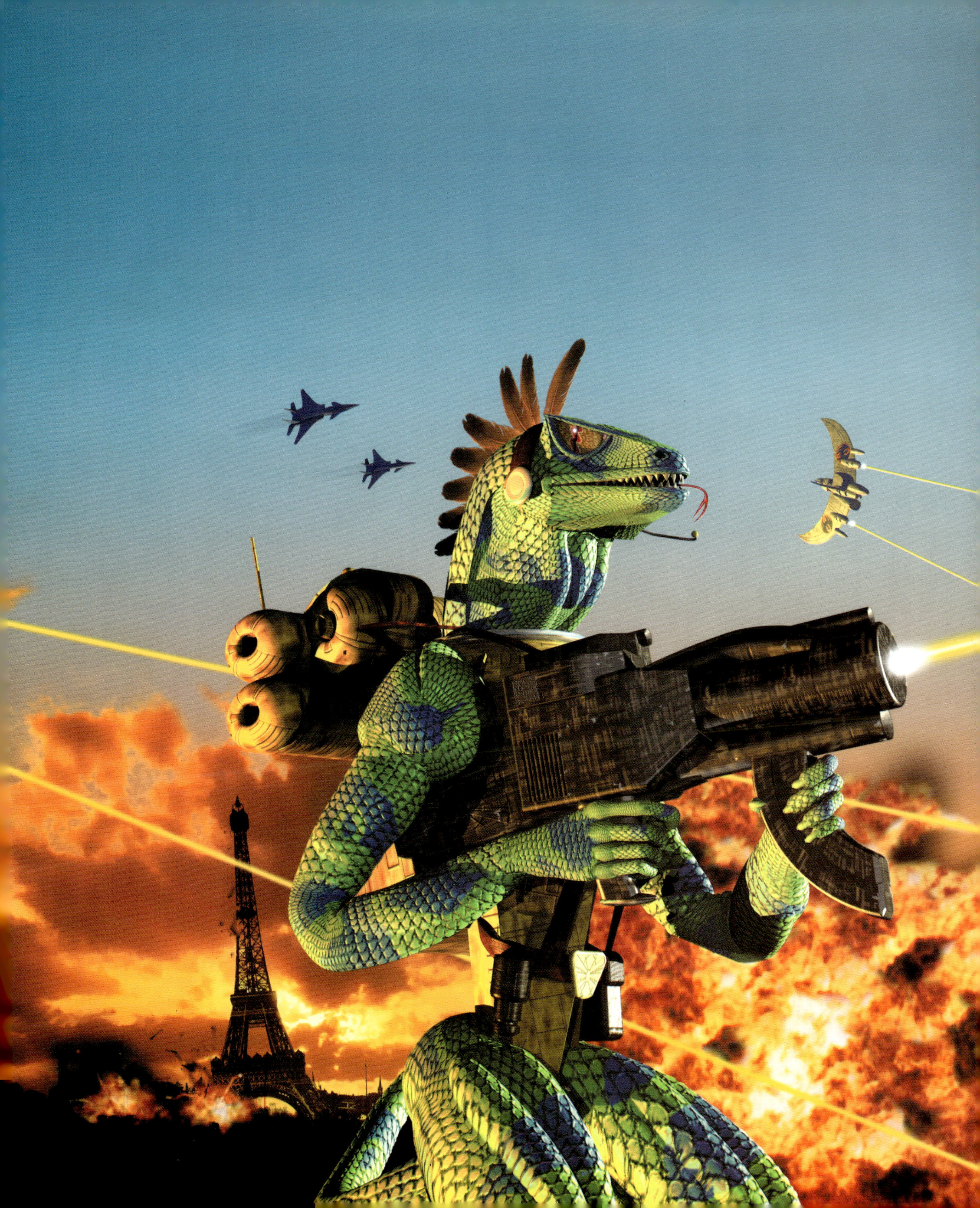

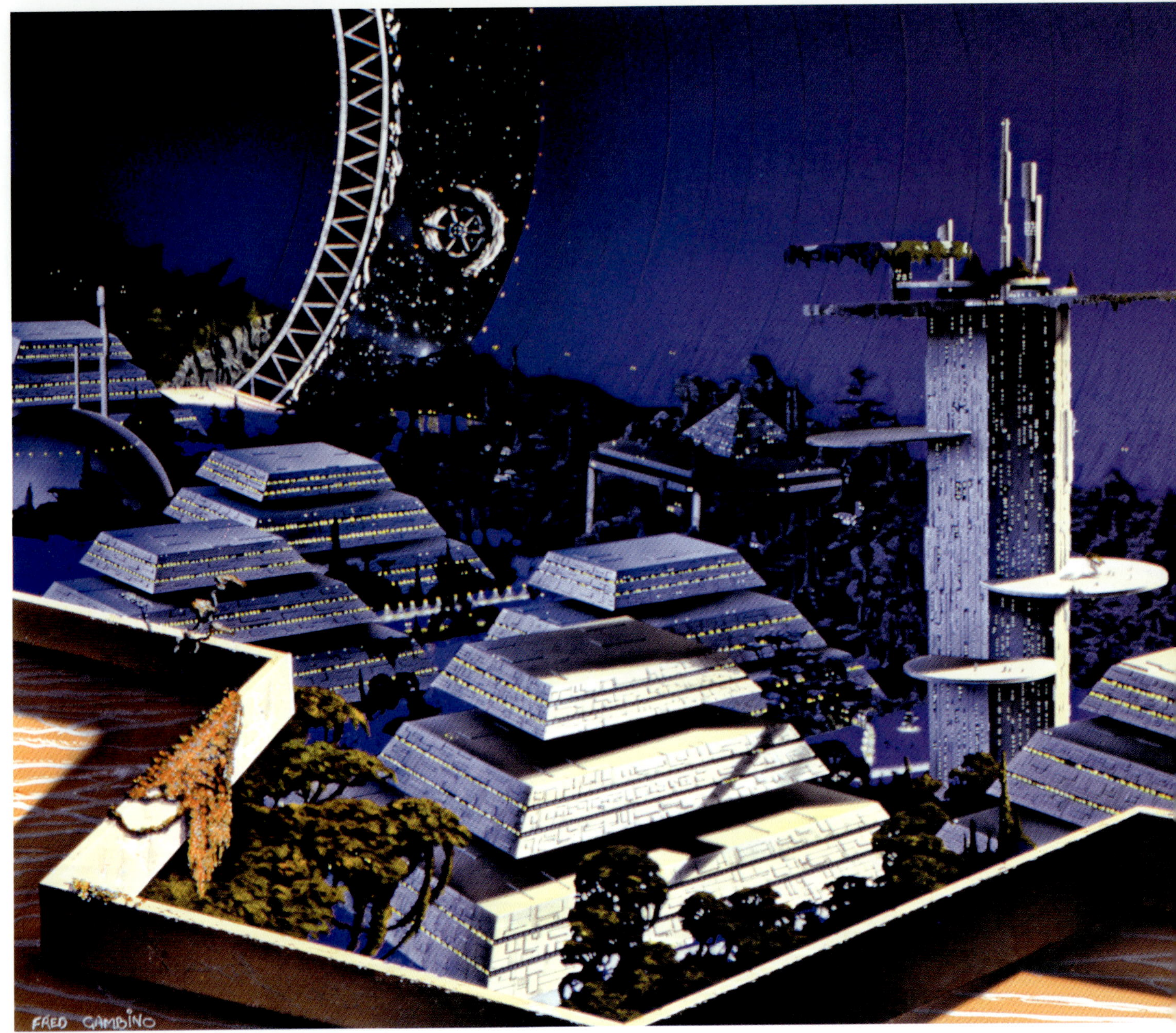

HOT SKY AT MIDNIGHT

Robert Silverberg
HarperCollins UK
Acrylic

For this image I constructed the somewhat Aztec-looking habitat interior out of thin card. The fine line detailing and windows were produced using a technical pen, filled with liquid acrylic. I was very intrigued by the character in the story, who is described as having a sheet of skin stretching over where his eyes should have been, armed with what Silverberg descibes as a 'Spike'.

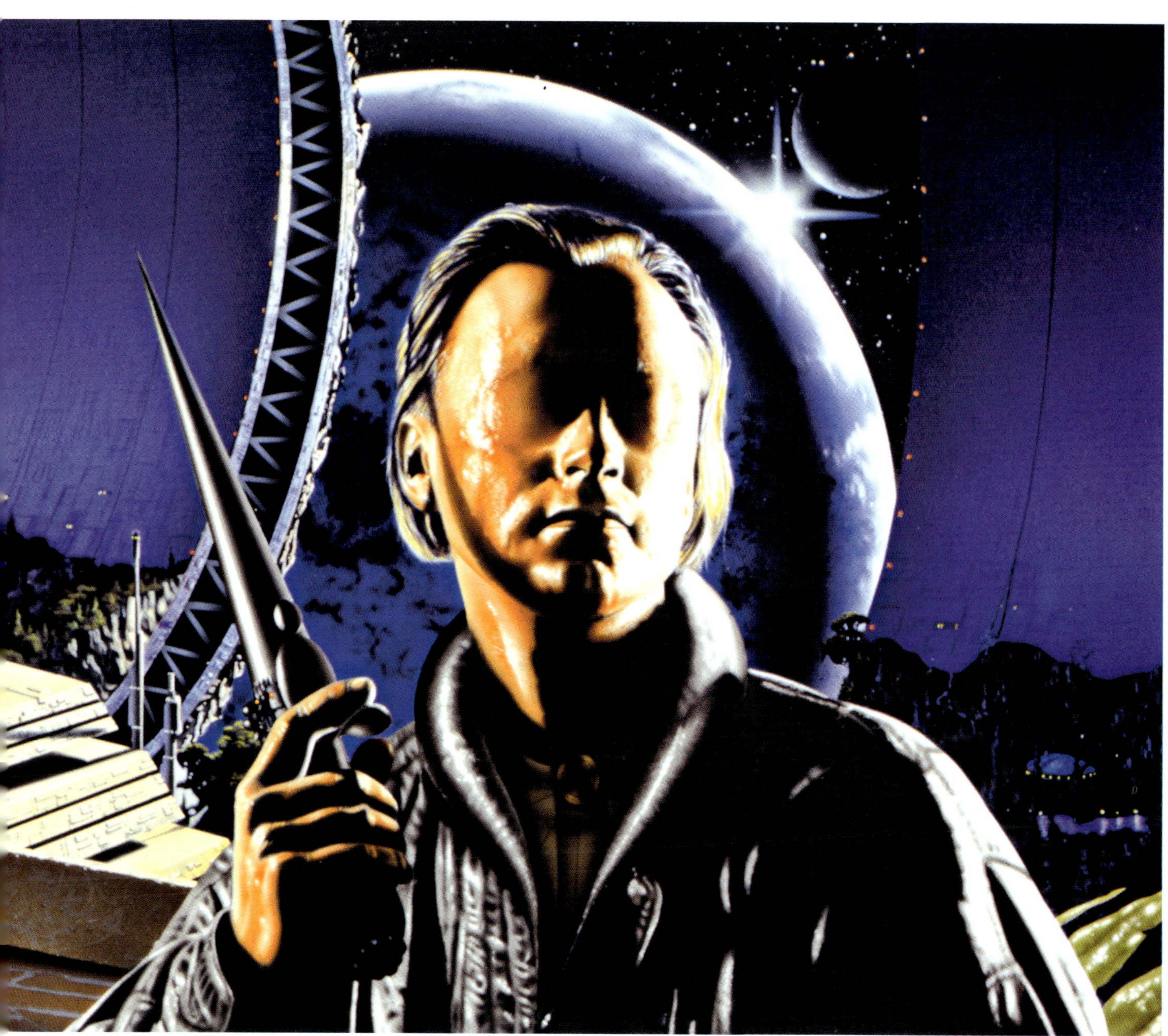

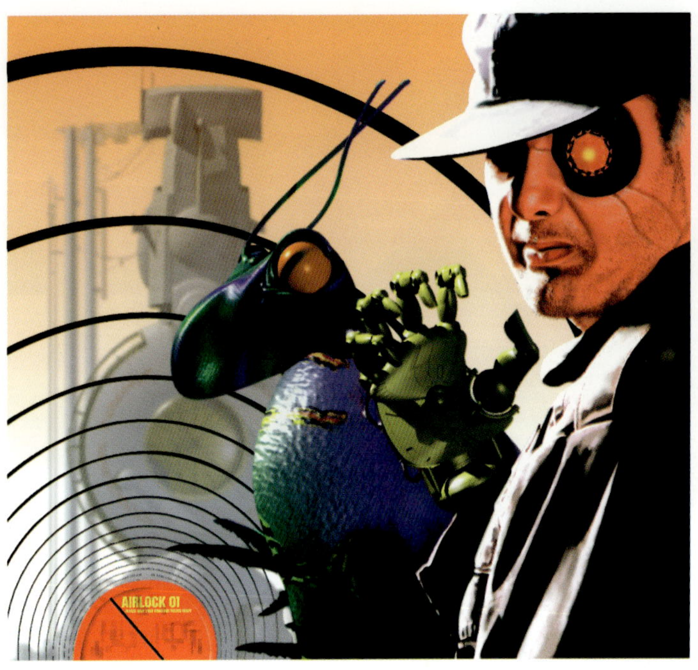

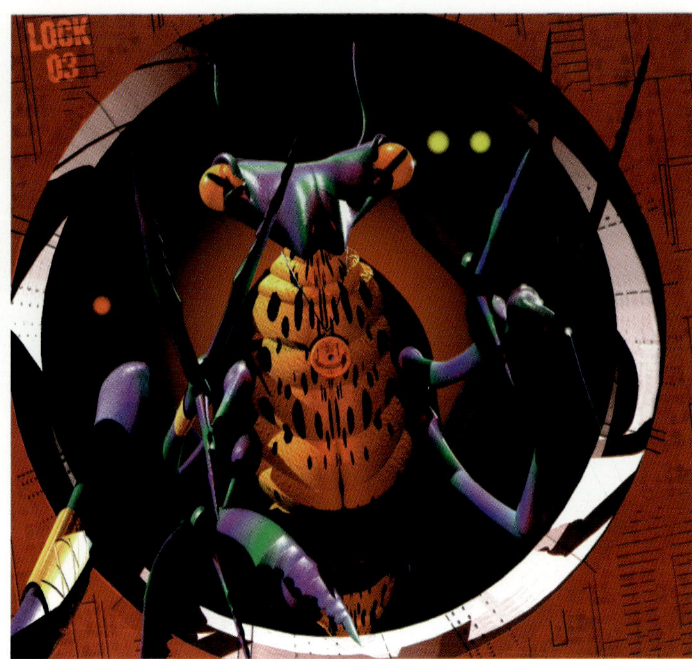

ABOVE

BOARDING

US Postal Service
Digital

This is the only image in the series (see pages 40, 46, 61 and 82) that shows the face of one of the protagonists – the villain of the piece. Who could I find to model who would be cheap and available with sufficiently villainous features at such notice? Myself, of course, wearing a strange bejewelled eye patch. The observant amongst you may also have noticed the hand from *Tek Kill* (see page 86), doubling as an evil-looking prothsetic.

ABOVE RIGHT

BUG

US Postal Service
Digital

I developed quite a soft spot for this bug-like alien. Jane Frank represents me for the sale of originals in the US. Jane, along with her husband Howard, owns one of the most famous and comprehensive collections of science-fiction paintings anywhere, ranging from golden era greats such as Chesley Bonestell to contemporaries like Frank Frazetta. Anyone who knows Jane knows her low opinion of the value of prints, so I was surprised when she expressed an interest in this image. It turns out she collects alien bug pictures. This is the only Gambino in the Frank Collection at present, but I'm ever hopeful.

RIGHT

TITAN'S SKY

US Postal Service
Digital

This was the first in the US Postal Service series to be completed. I originally had Saturn's rings edge-on, as they would be if you could actually see Saturn from Titan. This reduced them to a thin line of light. The client, not surprisingly with hindsight, felt that I should use a bit of artistic licence and tip the ringed planet towards the viewer. He was also concerned that Saturn wasn't totally spherical, thinking it might be some shortcoming of the software, until I pointed out that Saturn actually is this shape due to its low density and rapid spin.

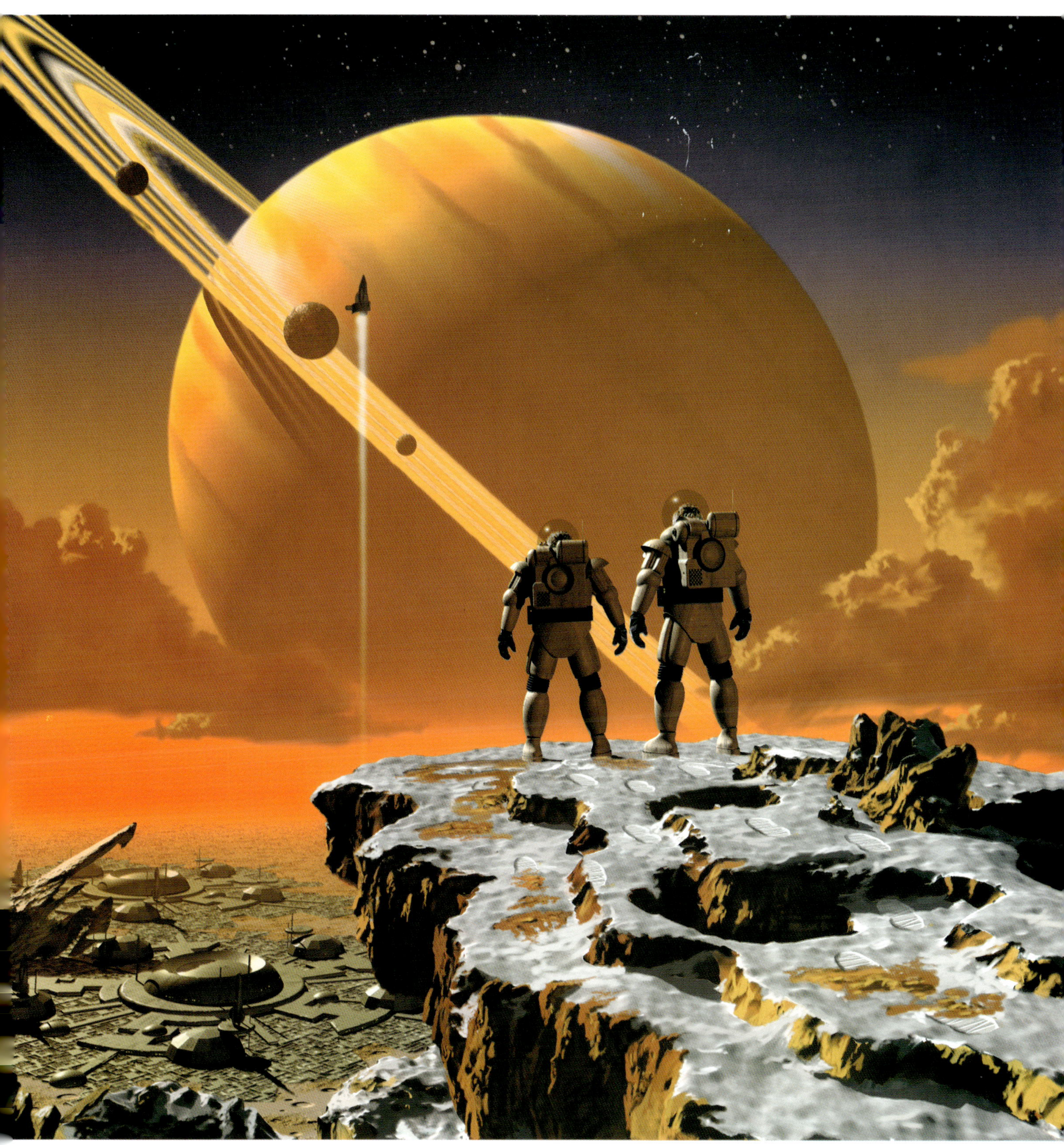

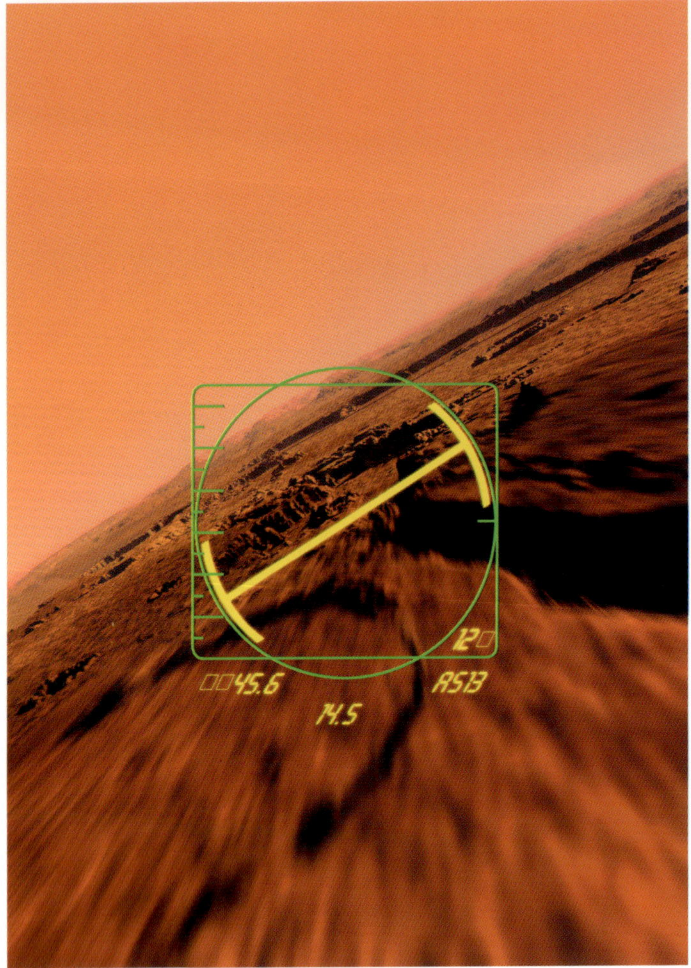

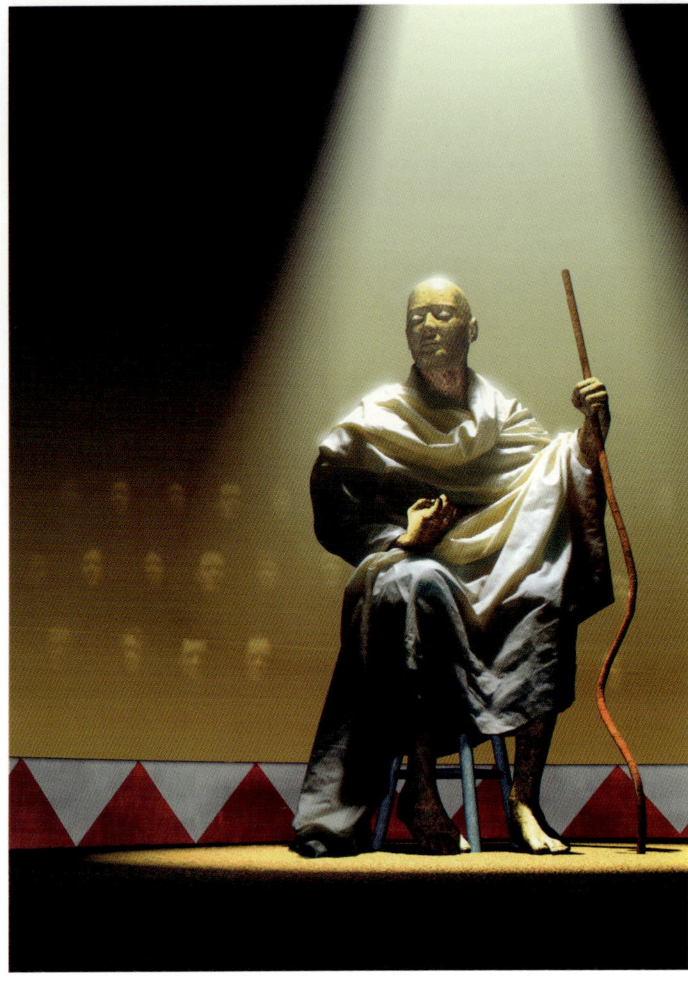

ABOVE

THE MARTIAN RACE

Gregory Benford
Little, Brown UK
Digital

This near-future scenario of man's first visit to Mars is set in a real location on the Red Planet – Gusev Crater. I went to the NASA website and downloaded orbital photographs. I then used these to produce greyscale images that I loaded into the terrain editor in Bryce. This, therefore, is a reasonably accurate depiction of the actual crater. The vertical scale is exaggerated and the distant mountains were added as a device to lend depth to the scene. I don't know if there are any actually there. As a finishing touch I added some speed blur to the foreground, a visual play on the word 'race' in the title.

ABOVE RIGHT

RADIANT GREEN STAR

Asimov's Science Fiction
Digital

This cover for *Asimov's Science Fiction* was realized almost entirely in Electric Image. Something new to me with EI are volumetric lights (lights whose beams can be seen). They can be very effective in some instances. For the toga, I draped myself in a sheet and had my partner, Jenny, photograph me, trying to match the perspective of the cgi image. I had one of my studio lights precariously fixed to a ceiling beam above my head, so as to get the light shining directly down. Often, a dramatic effect easily produced in the computer is very difficult to do when you try repeating it in the real world.

OPPOSITE

BLOOD NET

Game box
Microprose
Acrylic

I painted this image before I had the benefit of a computer. The skyscrapers involved me in a long-winded perspective drawing. I painted them as solid black then replaced the working drawing and retraced the position of the windows and doorframes, painting them in with a sable brush. The figure was airbrushed straight in, without underpainting. I cut a complex set of paper masks, hinged with masking tape, which allowed them to be lifted occasionally in order to give me an overall view. Water droplets were achieved using masking fluid, splattered onto a base colour and then over-sprayed. This produced random splodges to which I added highlights and shadows, giving them a 3D form.

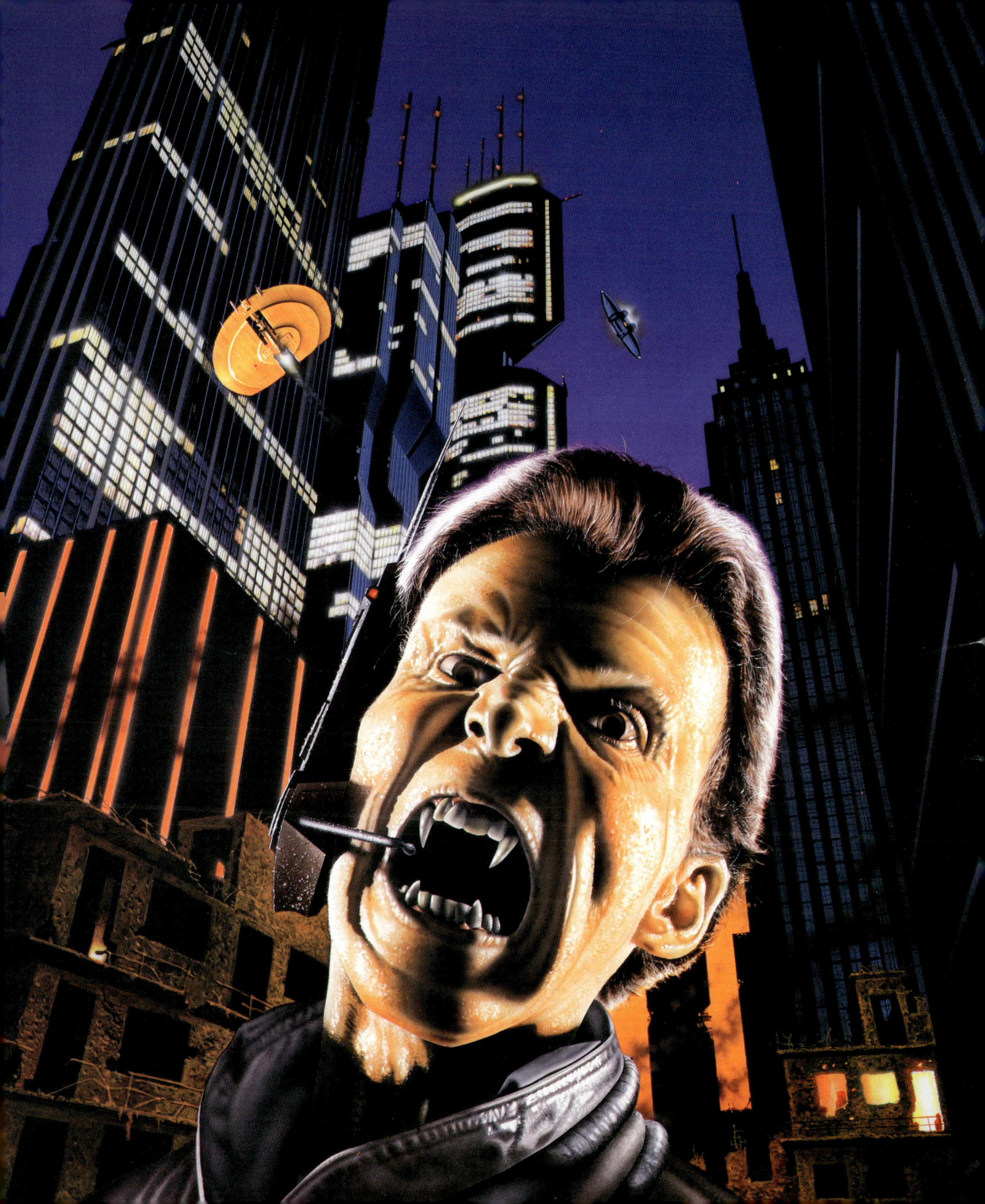

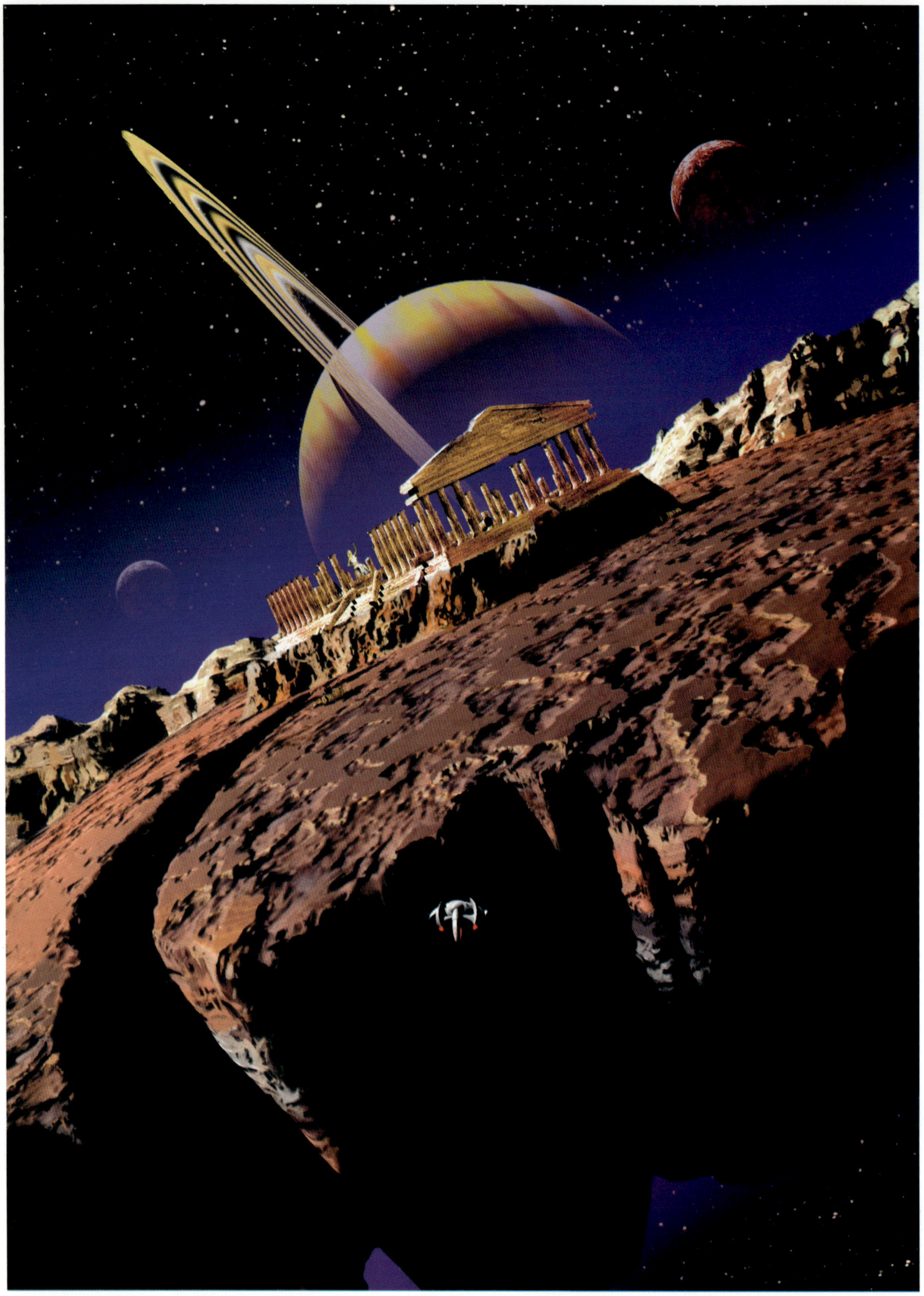

OPPOSITE

TEARS OF THE ORACLE

Justin Richards
Virgin Books
Digital

The brief called for a structure similar to the Parthenon, situated on an asteroid. The oracle in question is a statue of a golden woman dressed in a toga. Those with a powerful magnifying glass should be able to see this statue, complete with golden reflective surface, at the back of the temple.

I modelled the small ship in Sketch, but liked the design so much that I felt it ought to appear more prominently in something else, so it can be seen as *The Captain's Fancy* in the cover illustration for the Stephen Donaldson novel, *Forbidden Knowledge* (page 43).

RIGHT

THE JOY DEVICE

Justin Richards
Virgin Books
Digital

I was given a very descriptive brief for this cover – a building on the edge of a waterfall, a mixture of architectural styles, a ruined city in the background and a winged figure in the foreground, all dominated by a large moon.

A device I often use is that of slanting the horizon, something I picked up from the comics I read as a child. This is an easy way of giving movement to an otherwise static scene. The effect here, however, was to make the building look like it is sliding over the edge. If you look carefully, you will see two figures falling into the void at the bottom, a detail that was almost totally lost on the printed cover.

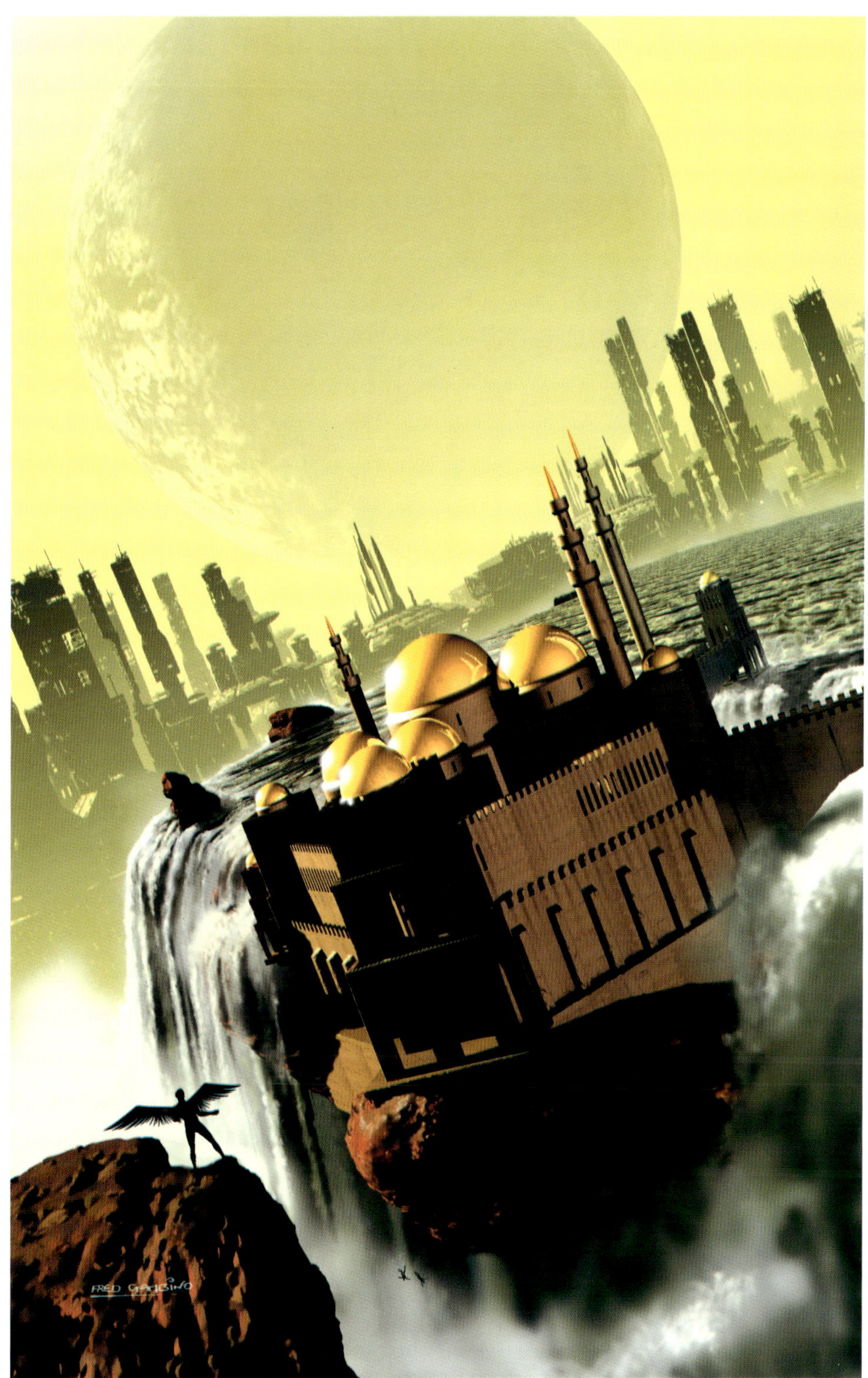

Cyberware

By Jim Burns

Where does the digital future lie?

Each year that passes sees more science-fiction and fantasy art being created digitally, utilizing the mind-boggling capabilities of an array of ultra-capable software now available, in conjunction with the illustrative skills and hyperactive imaginations of the artists who create it. The cutting edge of some of the more inventive uses of this new electronic palette is to be found in the capable hands of a small group of 'fantastical' artists.

Fred Gambino is one of the pre-eminent members of this band of pioneers. He responded to the siren-call of the digital future some time before most of the rest of us and his work has now reached a level of arcane understanding of these magical digital tools that leaves me speechless with admiration. In the hands of less competent artists the 'digital look' has sometimes fallen prey to a kind of sterility of expression, the consequence of over-dependence on the glamorous capabilities of the software itself, and one is left with a nifty inversion of that old adage that 'less is more'. Most certainly it can be the case in digital art that 'more is less'. This is the trap that Fred never, ever falls into. His transition from an extremely talented, traditional wielder of brush and paints to a consummate manipulator of pixels on the screen has been a seamless process and one that I would imagine is the result of deep conviction and scary self-discipline.

And in Fred's embrace of the Mac I detect a bit of a love affair going on with the capabilities of technology and maybe a bit of an infatuation with the future. This is no bad thing: in a cynical time when the future is often depicted as a choice of grim, gritty dystopias of one variety or another, it's encouraging to come upon Fred's shiny, colour-saturated alternatives.

There's wit to be found here in Fred's work, thank God. (There's too much that's po-faced about this genre!) People inhabit Fred's paintings as active part-players in a universe constantly being remoulded by the intelligent intervention of sentience, with humanity maybe as top of the food chain! They live in relaxed counterpoint with their own robotic constructs, servants to a human-ordained future – not as passive or feeble bystanders in a dispassionate, unknowable universe.

Movers and shakers of the times to come!

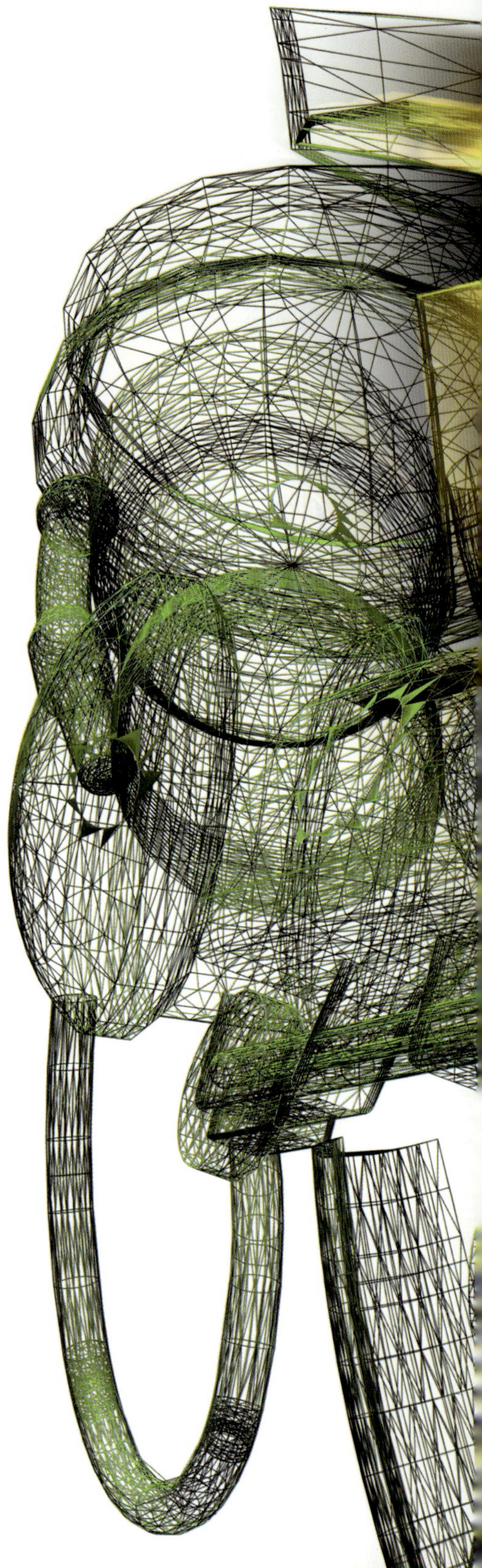

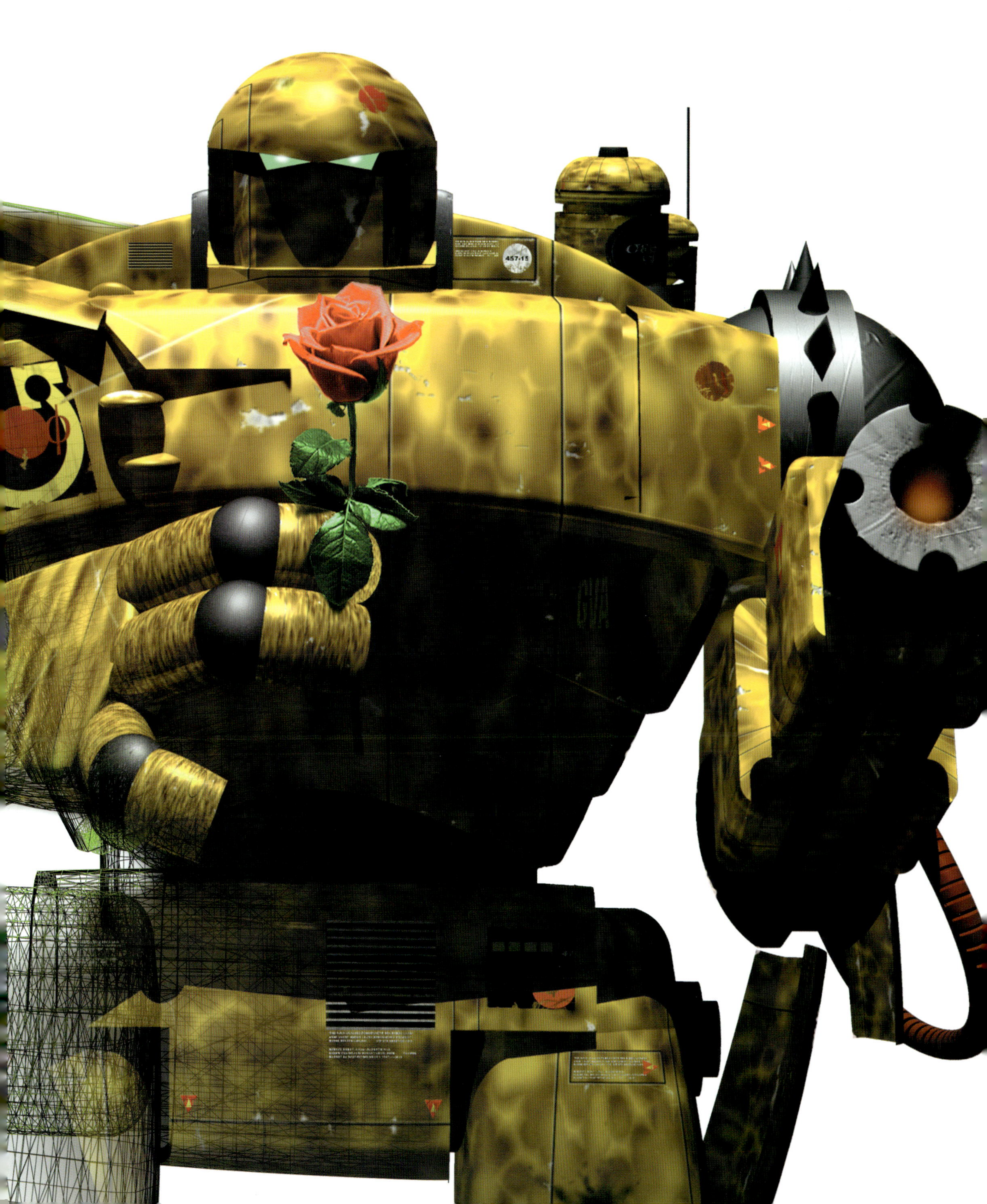

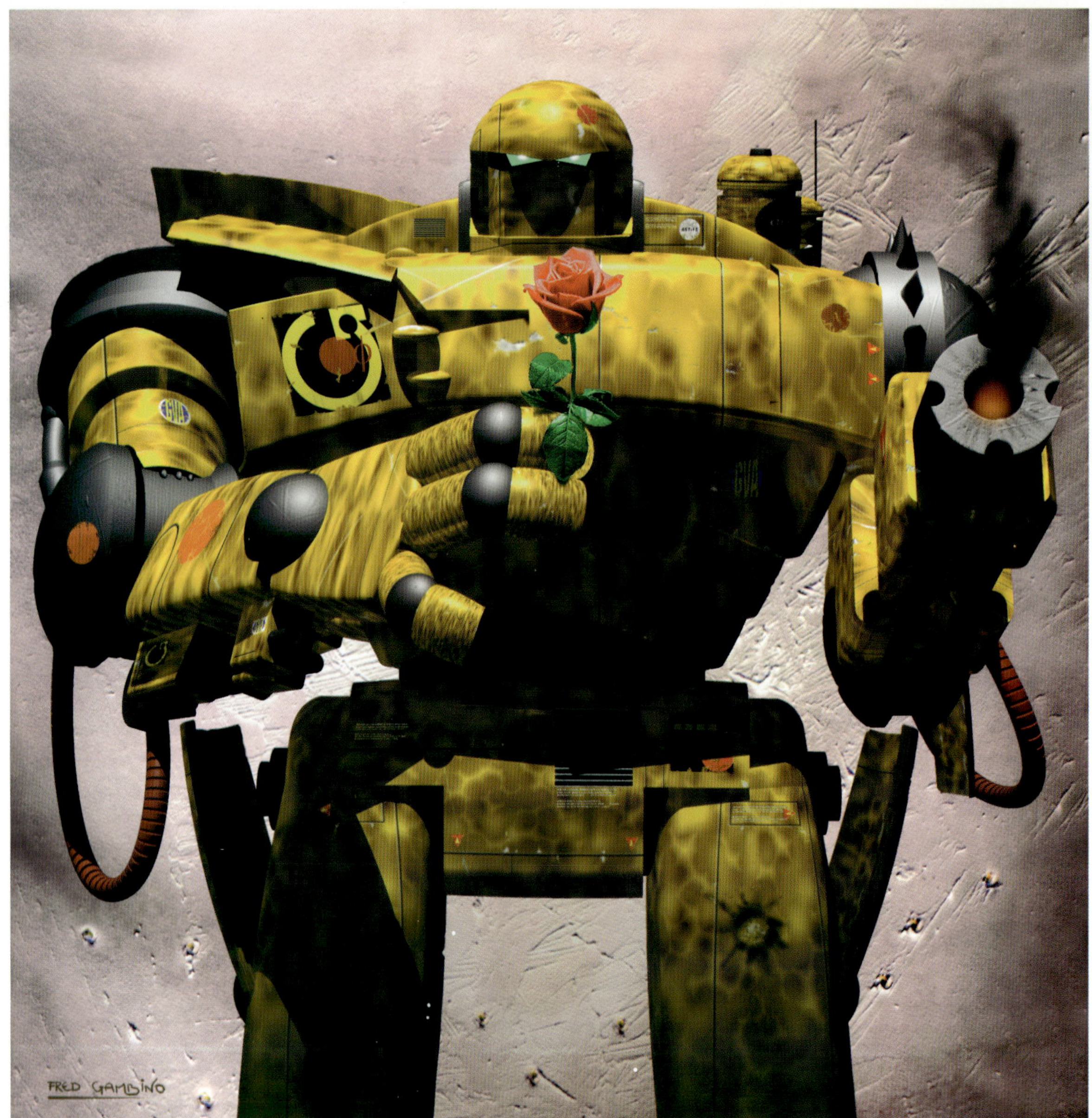

ASIMOV'S VALENTINES

Berkley Books
Digital

This was for a series of themed short story anthologies. The brief was to come up with an image marrying the ideas of science fiction and Valentine's Day. Here was a chance to show off my romantic side, since I have it on good authority that I do not possess a romantic bone in my body.

The background was achieved by building up a texture with acrylic gesso primer on illustration board and then using an airbrush to spray colour at an acute angle, highlighting the pits and bumps. I hammered a screw into the board for the bullet holes and then scanned it into Photoshop, where it was manipulated further. I like to introduce some of my old airbrushing skills into the digital realm where I can. Apart from the satisfaction of using paint, it has the advantage of producing effects that are totally unique to me. The rose was a scanned black-and-white polaroid photograph, coloured in Photoshop.

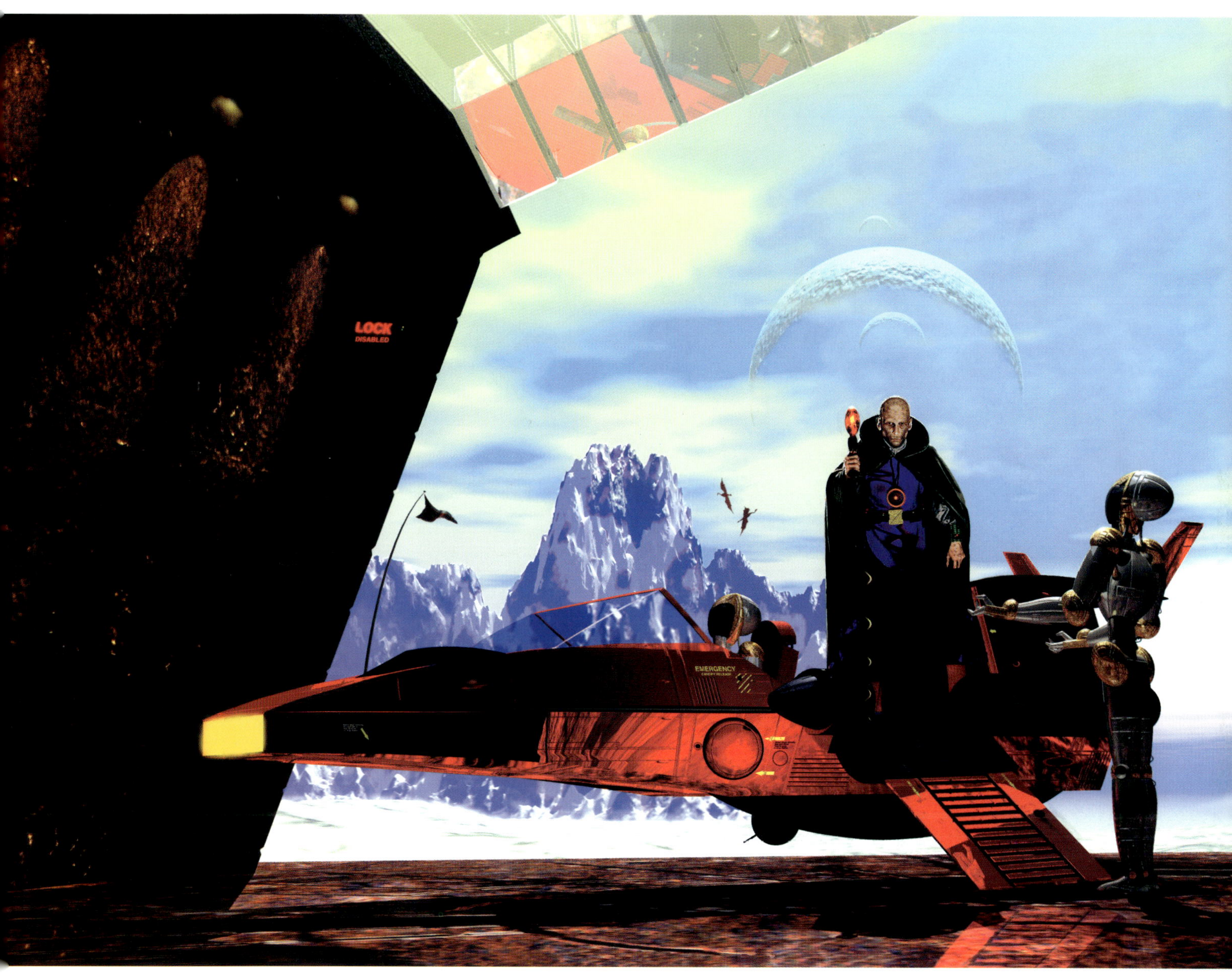

RINGING THE CHANGES

Robert Silverberg
HarperCollins UK
Digital

I love this early stuff, not least because it frequently features those elements of science fiction that you don't often get a chance to illustrate in these more sophisticated days, such as robots and anti-gravity cars.

I was still using my old computer when I did this. This was my first attempt to do the whole thing in one go, necessary because the robots, car and hanger needed to reflect each other. It was touch and go, but the machine just about managed to creak along. I even put the image of the techno wizard into the scene, mapped onto a rectangular surface, so as to get him reflecting into the car. I then substituted a high-resolution version of the figure in Photoshop.

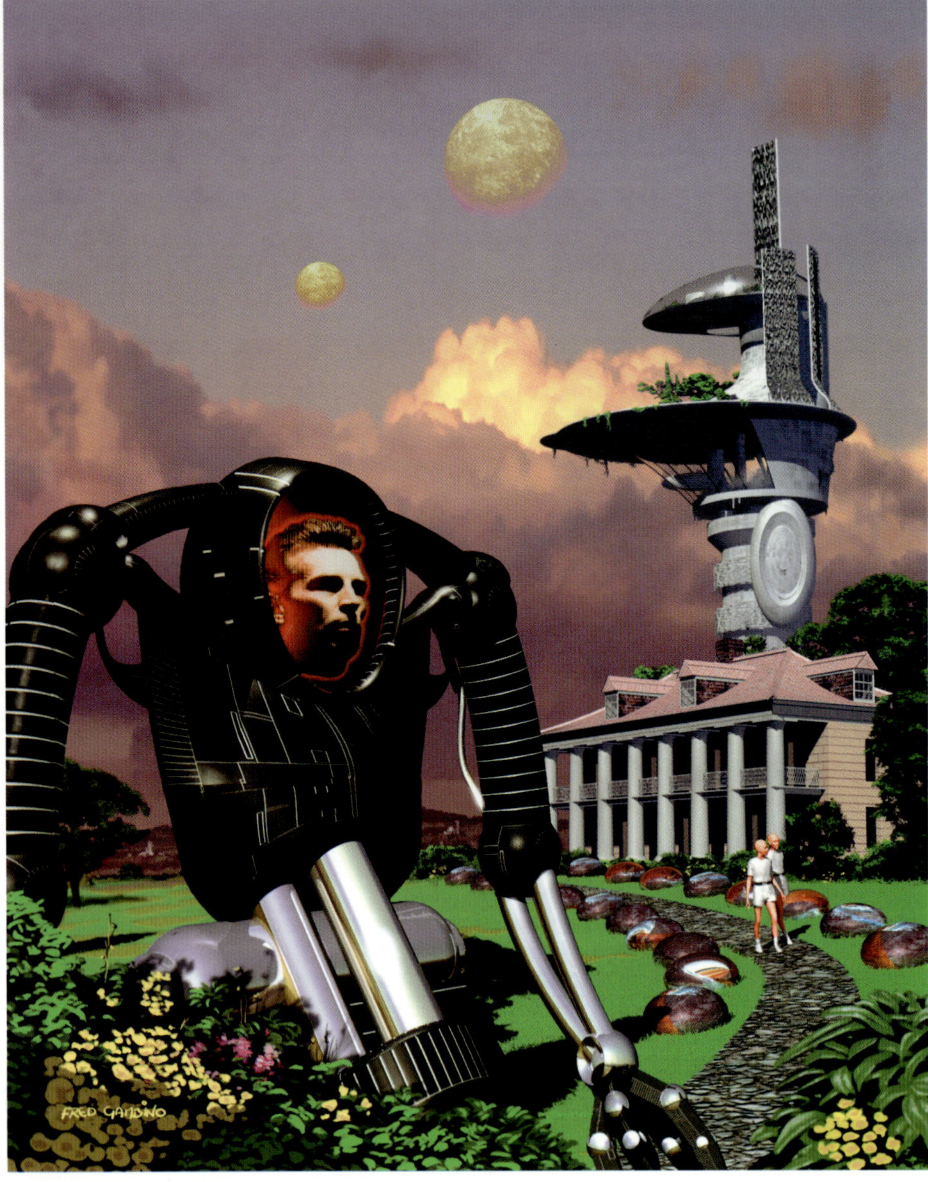

RIGHT

GRAVITY FAILURE

US Postal Service

Digital

For this job I used the interior of the spaceship featured in *Pulsar* (see page 40). Because time was of the essence, I had to cut as many corners as possible. The floating robot valet is the same android seen piloting the air car in *Ringing the Changes* (see page 81) and aficionados of the piste will recognize the 'space boots' as ski boots, with a few 3D modelling attachments.

The weightless globules of liquid escaping the glass in the foreground went through a few transitions. Originally, I made them transparent and reflective. The result was beautiful, each globule reflected each other and the whole of the 3D environment in which they were situated. It took 17 hours to complete, but the result was hopelessly confusing and too distracting from the rest of the image. So, I had to redo them without the reflectivity. An example of how sometimes total reality is not always the best solution in the context of the overall illustration.

ABOVE

THE FIFTH HEAD OF CERBERUS

Gene Wolfe

Orion

Digital

I don't know if it's just me, but I find this image a bit creepy. It has a strange dreamlike, surreal quality, which wasn't what I was striving for at all.

In the story, the robot has a TV screen in place of a head where the childrens' mentor appears, but I thought I might take the liberty of updating the idea somewhat and so changed it into a hologram. That was how the rather unorthodox robot design originated. The two figures in the background were created in Poser and added to the actual artwork – a rarity for me. For once I felt the plastic synthetic look of the computer-generated imagery summed up exactly the look of the cloned androgynous characters in the story.

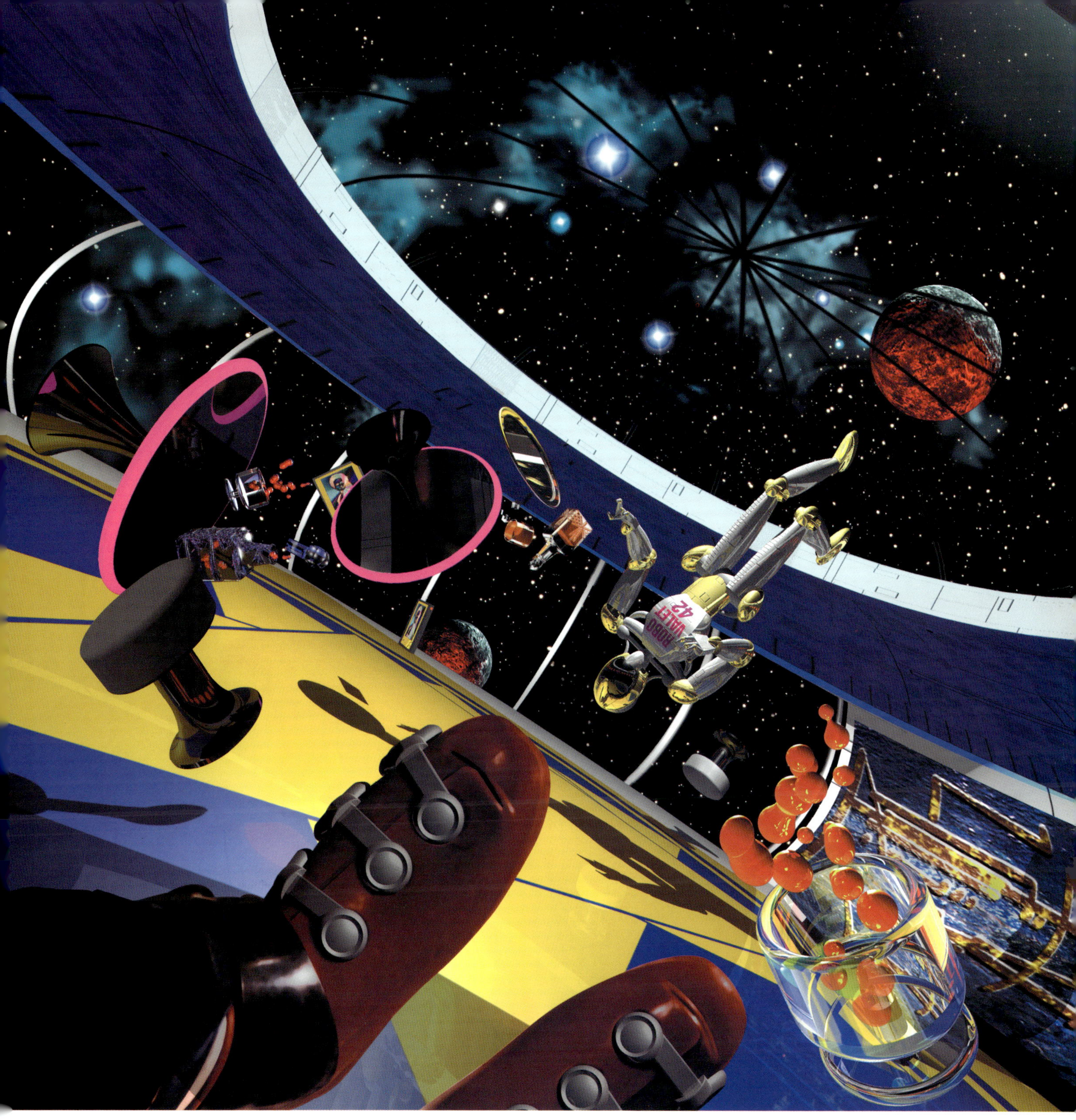
ROBO
VALET
42

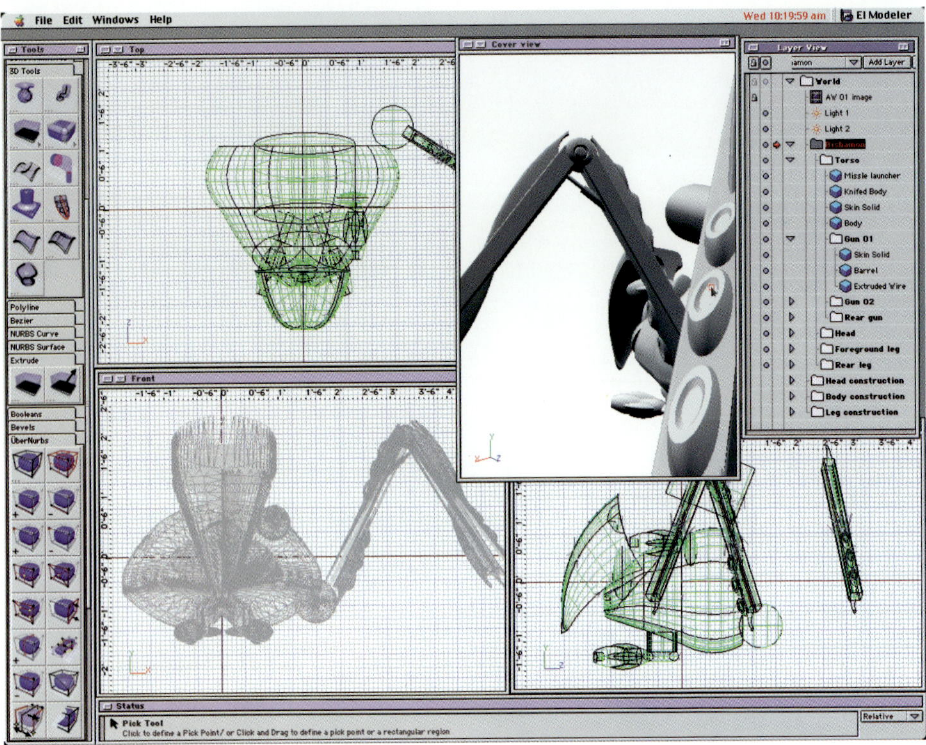

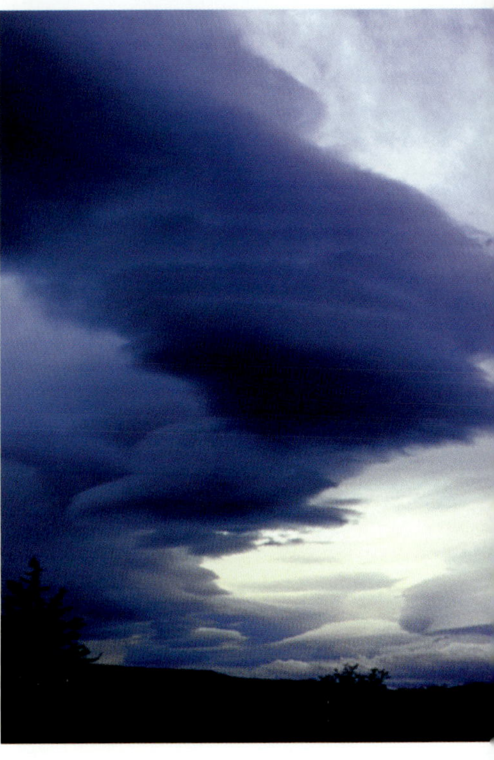

PATH OF GLORY

Randall N. Bills
Penguin–Putnam
Digital

There have been a lot of these covers, all featuring two or more robots either in, or about to engage in, battle. The robot designs are set in stone. I had several sheets showing not only the design but such things as armament, power source, endurance and manufacturing materials.

At the time, I had just returned from a trekking holiday in Patagonia. One morning I had emerged from the tent to witness the most bizarre, alien-looking sky I had ever seen. Needless to say, I grabbed my camera and took loads of photographs, one of which appears in the background here. The desert landscape was modelled in Amorphium and then textured in Electric Image with my patent slate texture.

ABOVE AND BELOW: The Patagonian sky used for the background, and screen dumps from Electric Image and Amorphium showing work in progress.

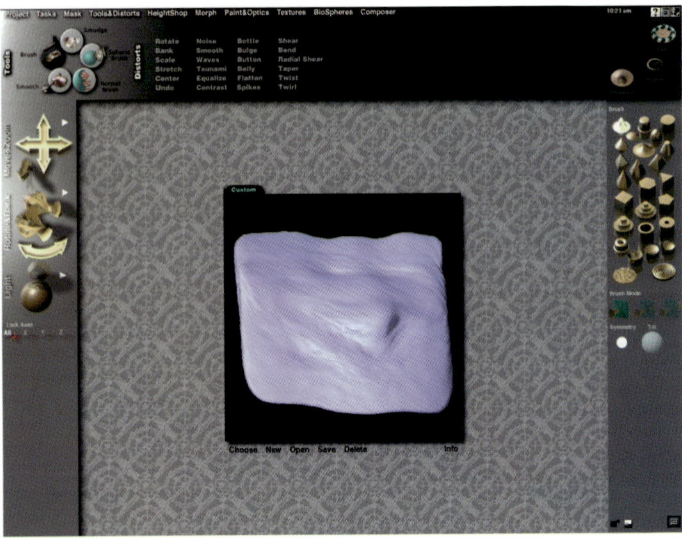

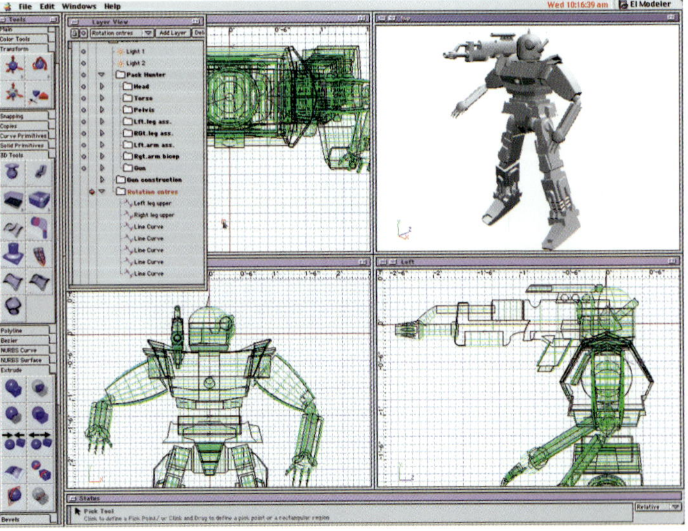

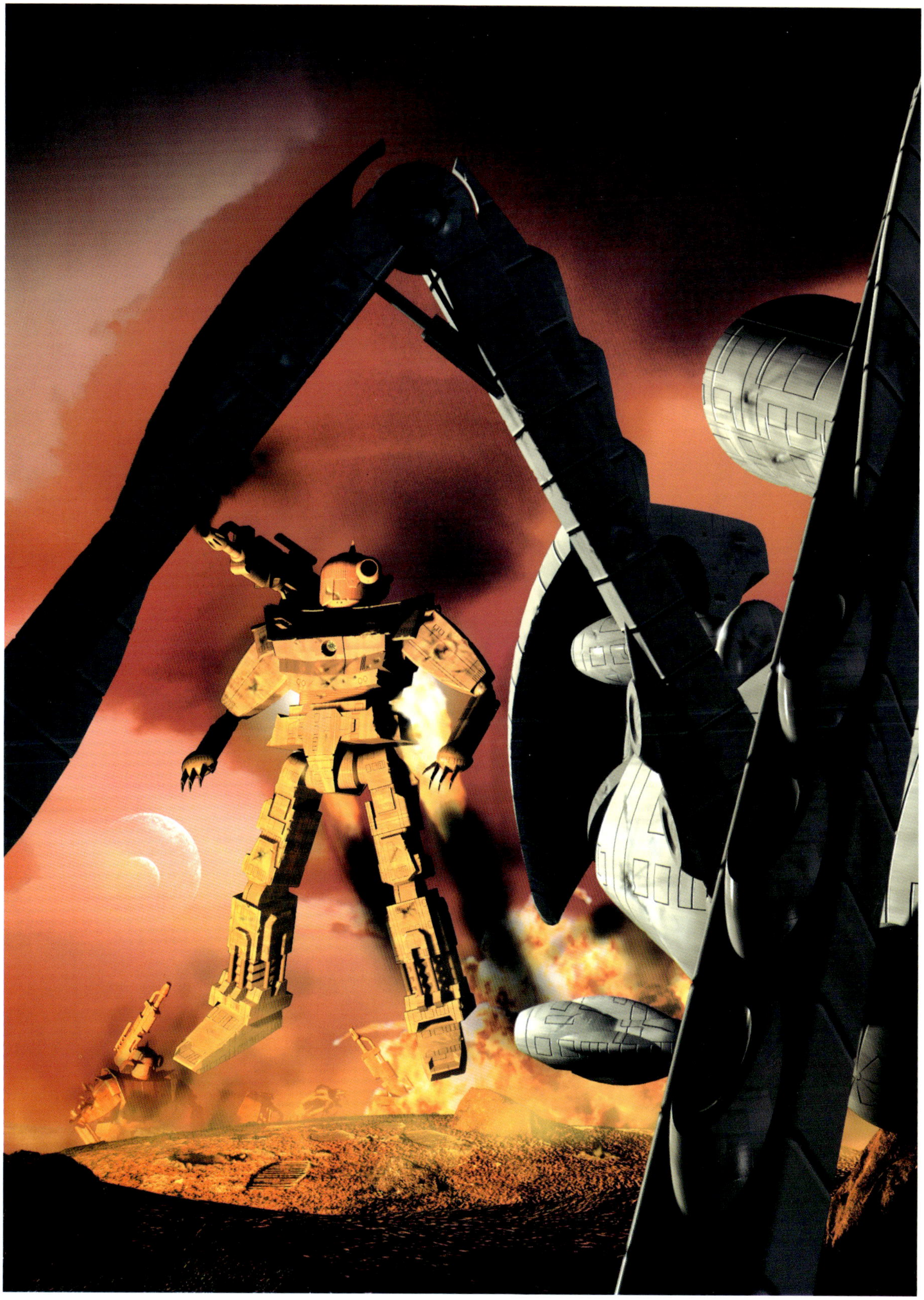

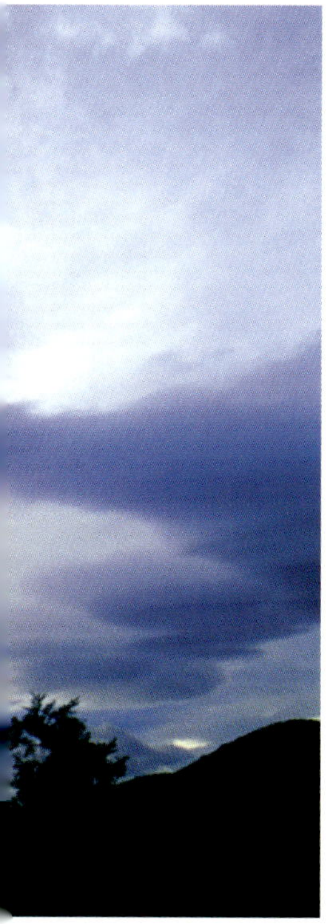

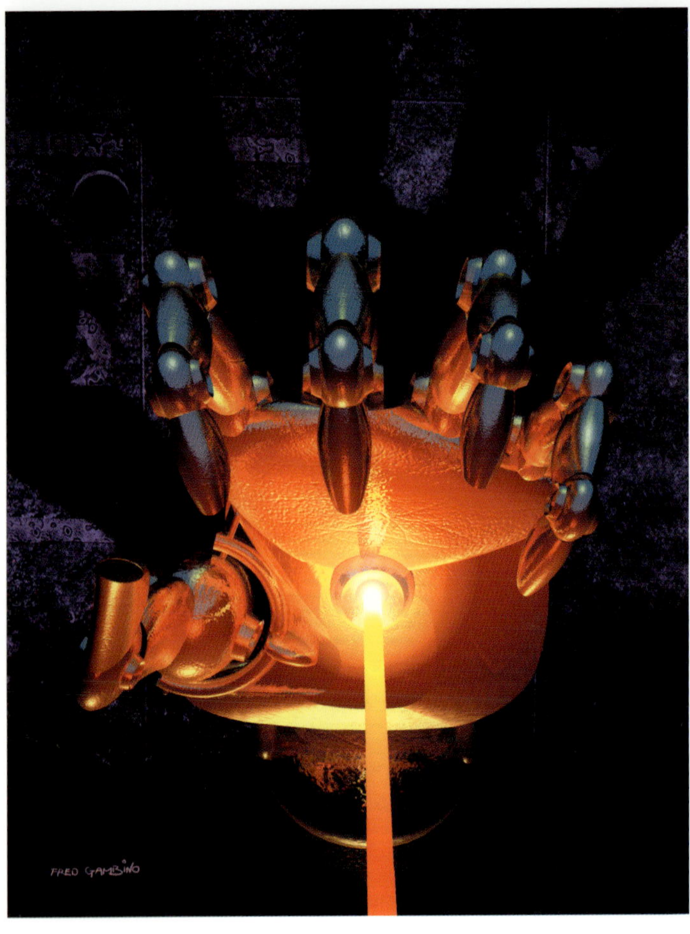

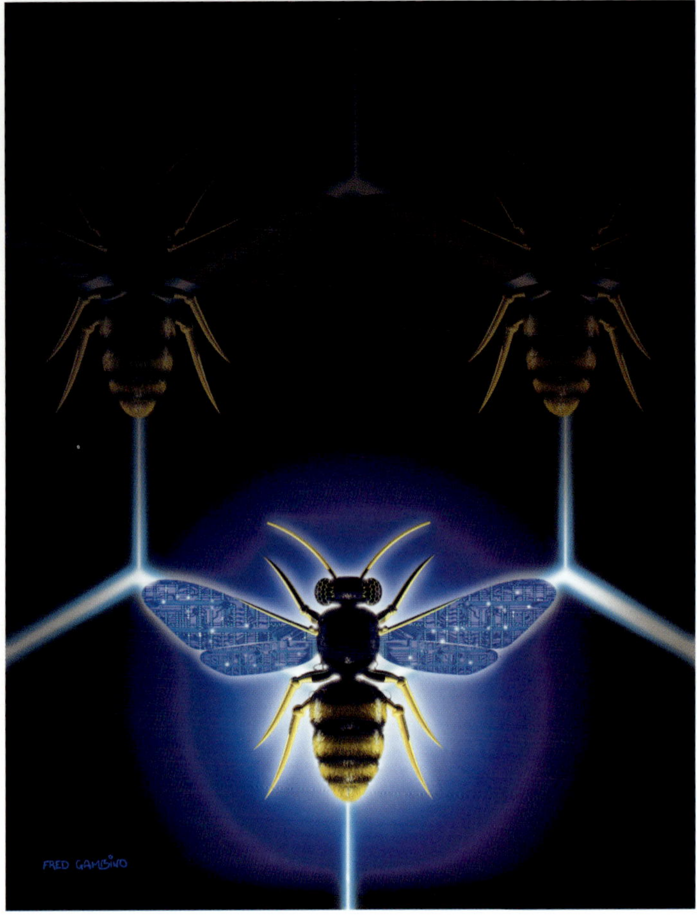

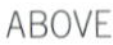
ABOVE

TEK KILL

William Shatner
Simon & Schuster US
Digital

The robots in this book have a nifty, deadly laser in the palm of their hand and, as I read the description, this image just popped into my head. The first version had an orange background, lit as it is by the orange laser. The art director, however, felt that the hand did not stand out from the background sufficiently, so it was changed to blue. Definitely a change for the better.

ABOVE

QUEEN CITY JAZZ

Kathleen Ann Goonan
HarperCollins UK
Digital

For this commission I was asked for something other than a narrative-style illustration – something iconic that would imply nanotechnology. I did two roughs, one showing a nanomachine that was reminiscent of a Swiss Army knife with various appendages and tools, and this one, showing a robot bee (bees feature heavily in the story). I am aware that this doesn't fit the remit of nanotechnology; however, this is the one they chose. I have adopted this image almost as a logo of my own, using it on the front of CDs and as an introduction to my web site.

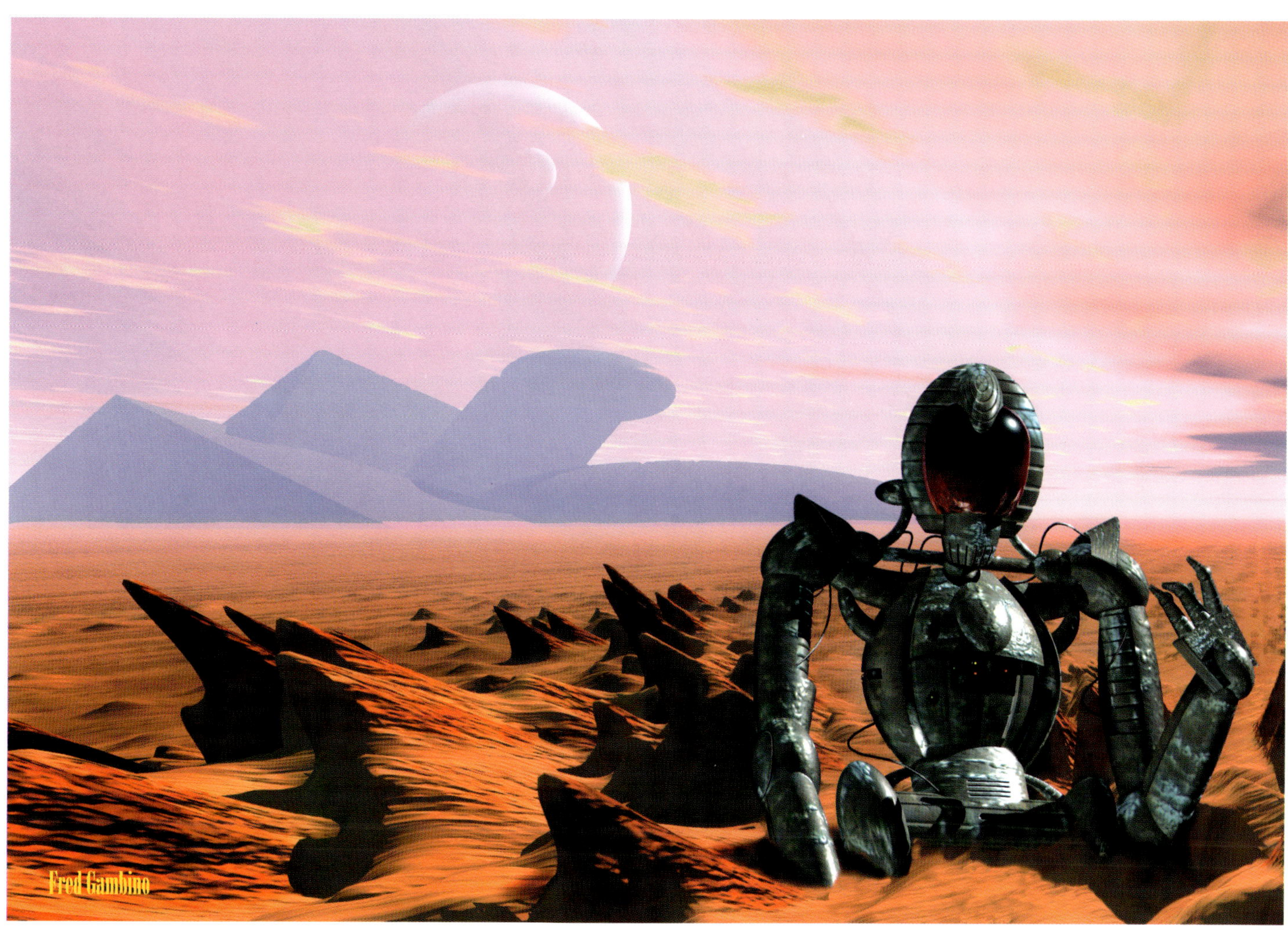

ABOVE

THE ROAD TO NIGHTFALL

Robert Silverberg
HarperCollins UK
Digital

This was my very first printed digital cover and as such has a lot that I feel could be improved upon. There was a heavy use of Bryce in the background, including the pyramid structures, and it shows what was then my most complicated model, the robot, built in Sketch. You may notice that some elements were recycled into the androids in *Ringing the Changes* (see page 81).

 Fred Gambino

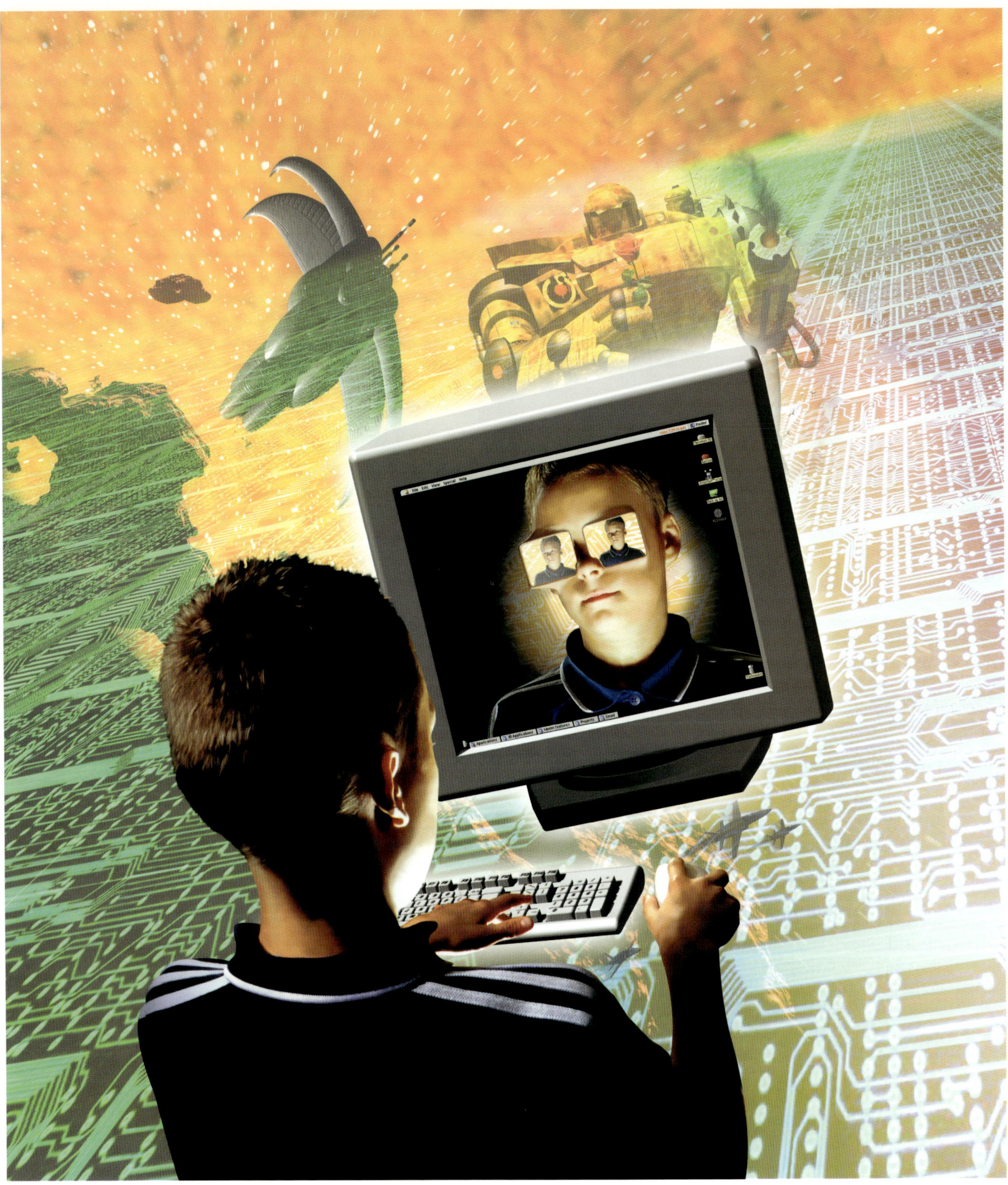

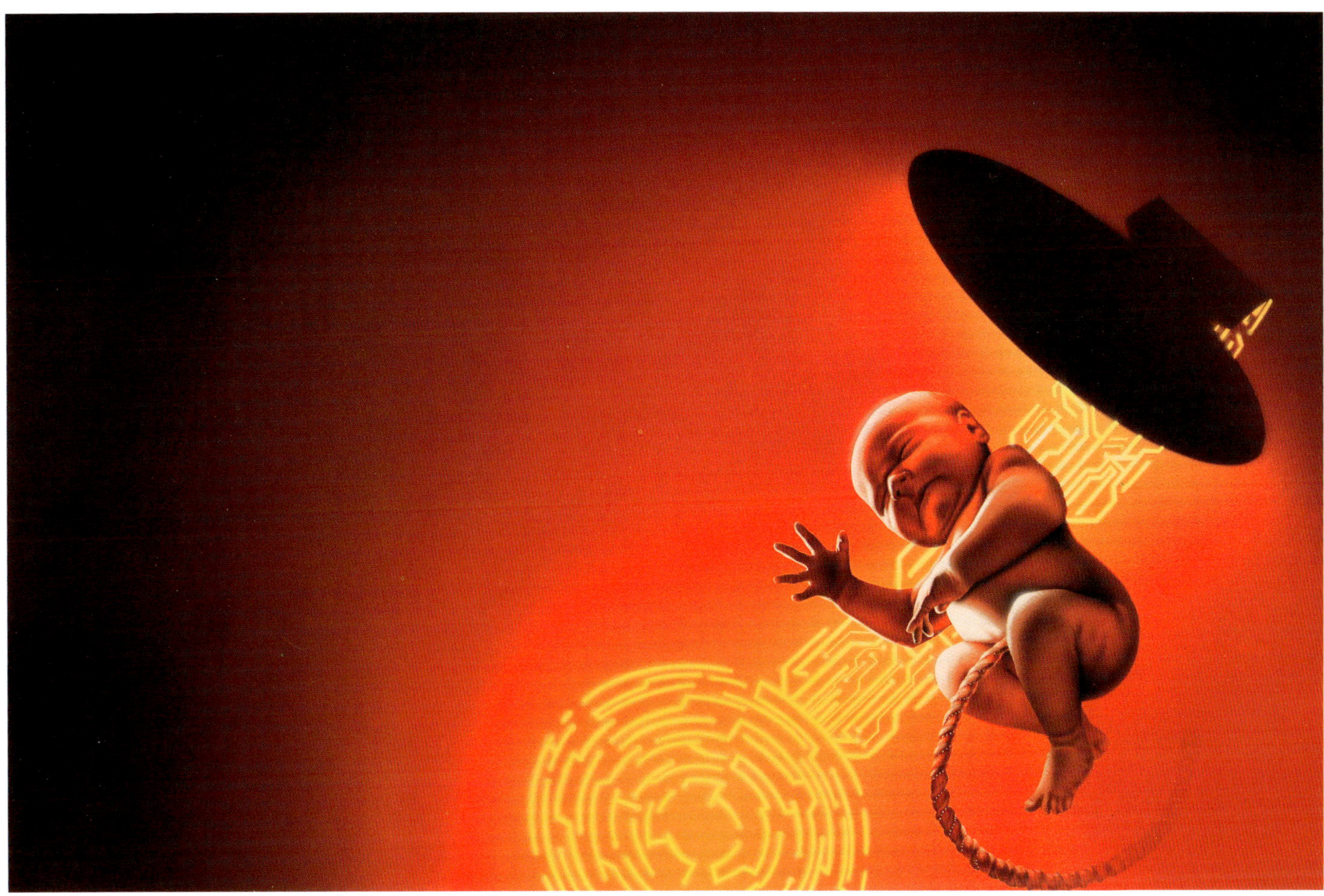

OPPOSITE

COMPUTER KIDS

Der Spiegel
Digital

This is one of a number of covers I have done for the German magazine *Der Spiegel*. The idea was theirs, my brief was to visualize it in a convincing manner.

As ever, the deadline was extremely tight, but in the best magazine tradition I was able to call upon 'stock illustration' – lifting elements from previous jobs and recycling them into the background.

I photographed my niece's son Liam for the main character. The computer is a 3D model, produced previously for a different job. Stock illustration has made huge inroads into the amount of illustration commissioned in recent years, so if you can't beat them, join them.

ABOVE

OTHERNESS

David Brin
Little, Brown UK
Acrylic

This was my very first David Brin cover. The various short stories in this compilation inspired several roughs, and one that I particularly liked is still waiting for the right job to come along. This was one of the few times that I 'borrowed' photographic reference from a book instead of producing my own, as actual babies were in short supply at the time. The final pose is a combination of several images from a variety of baby books borrowed from the local library.

The illustration is based upon a story where babies are inculcated with information in the womb. I'm aware that the device shown here would require a very large womb; however, I was more interested in using the idea as a springboard from which to produce an eye-catching cover. The teaching device was a model made from black card with the circuitry drawn on with silver marker.

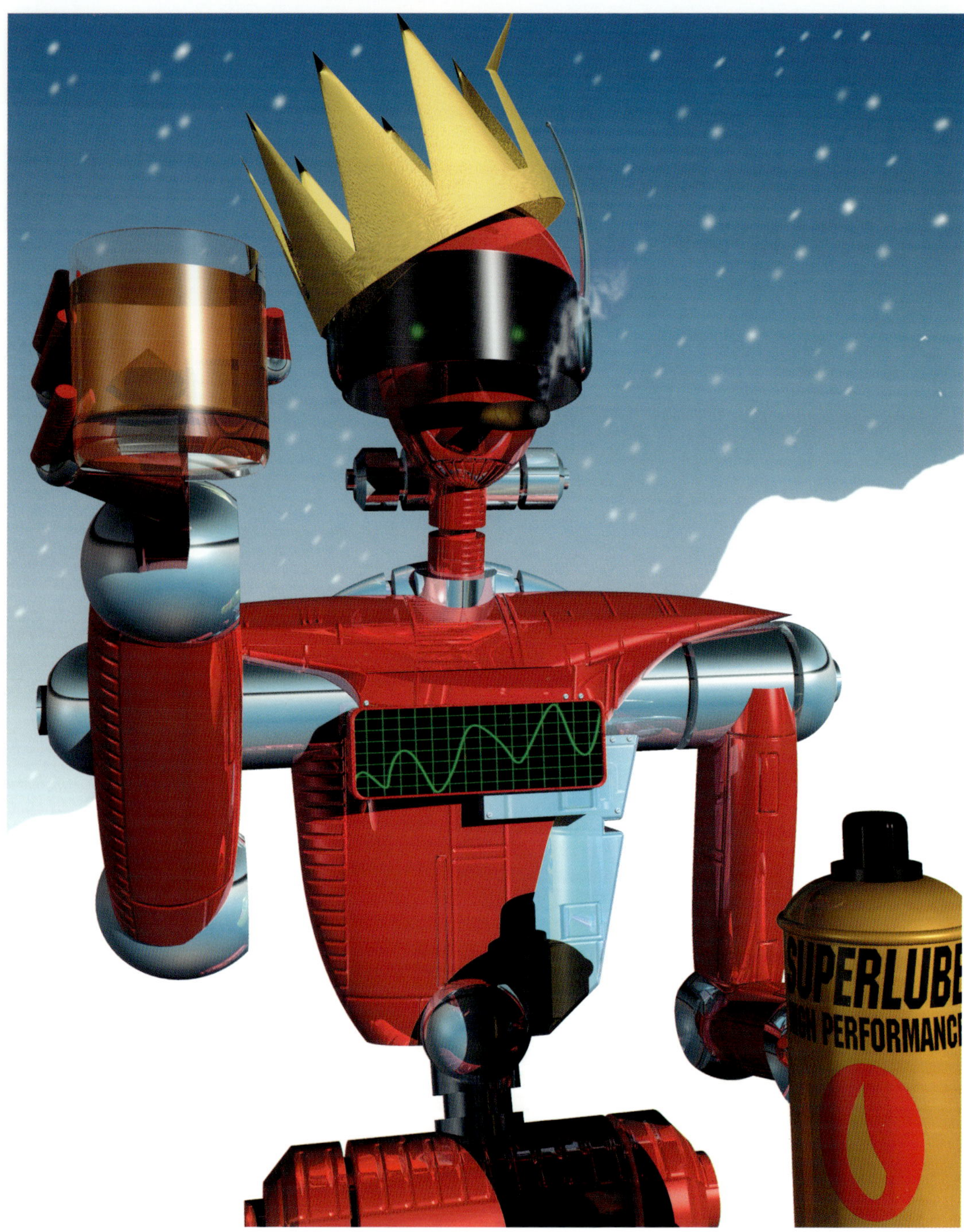

ABOVE

PARTY ROBOT

Self-promotion
Digital

For several years now, I have been producing my own Christmas cards. I send them to clients and close friends and every year the time to think up a new one seems to come round ever more quickly. This image was originally conceived for such an occasion.

Bernstein and Andriulli, my American agent, has a large collection of so-called 'stock' illustration – generic images that can be employed for a variety of uses. With a little alteration, this image made a good addition. In the Yuletide version, the graph on his chest reads 'Happy Christmas'.

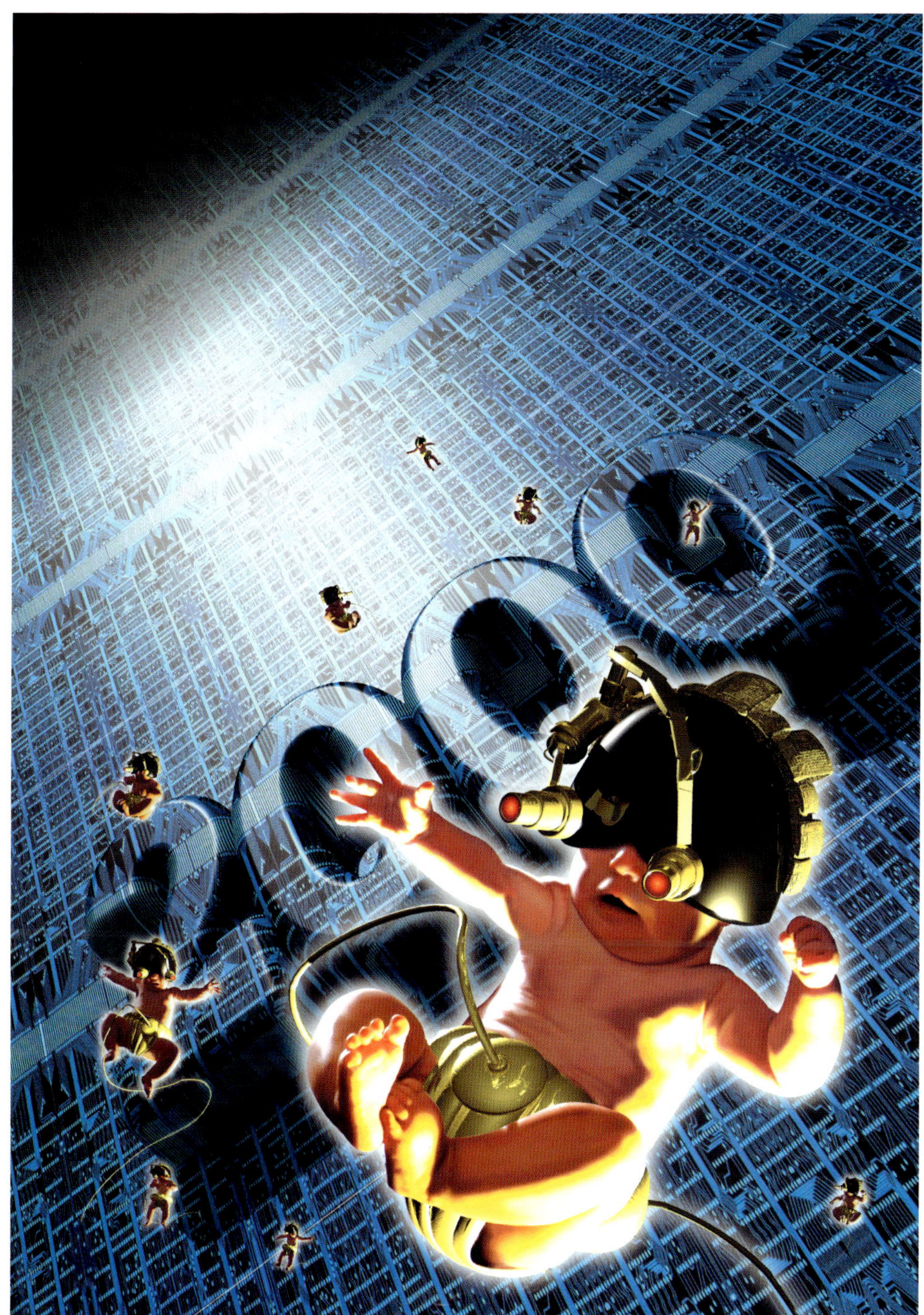

LEFT

MILLENNIUM BABIES

Asimov's Science Fiction
Digital

One of the few literary SF magazines left, both *Asimov's* and its stablemate *Analog* continue to be a showcase for that dying art, the short story. This one was for, not surprisingly, their Millennium edition. The image was based upon an idea of the art director's, in which she stipulated a baby wearing some kind of VR helmet, with '2000' incorporated into the background.

I thought, VR helmet = cyberspace, put the two together and we have a number of online infants floating over a rather stylized visualization of cyberspace. Luckily for me, some friends of mine had the foresight to produce a baby that was just the right age at just the time I needed her. Baby Isobel, definitely a natural, performed brilliantly, even managing to reach forward as I had depicted in the rough, as if reaching for some object only she could see in her VR world.

The finished image was a composite of three photos, which combined to produce almost exactly what I had envisioned.

OVERLEAF

DREAM PARK

Larry Niven and Steven Barnes
Pan
Acrylic

The scenario for this cover had already been decided by the publishers. It was to include the main character surrounded by controls and screens, with two 'holographic' figures incorporated somewhere. To try and give the idea of the figures being projections of some sort, I placed them floating in mid-air. I also employed a technique that I had used to good effect previously. The shadows don't actually exist: the background shows where they are supposed to be. If the lighting is arranged properly, this has the peculiar effect of making the figures seem less than substantial, while at the same time making them appear quite three-dimensional. A variety of spatter techniques, including the use of a toothbrush, were employed to achieve the texture on the controller's chair.

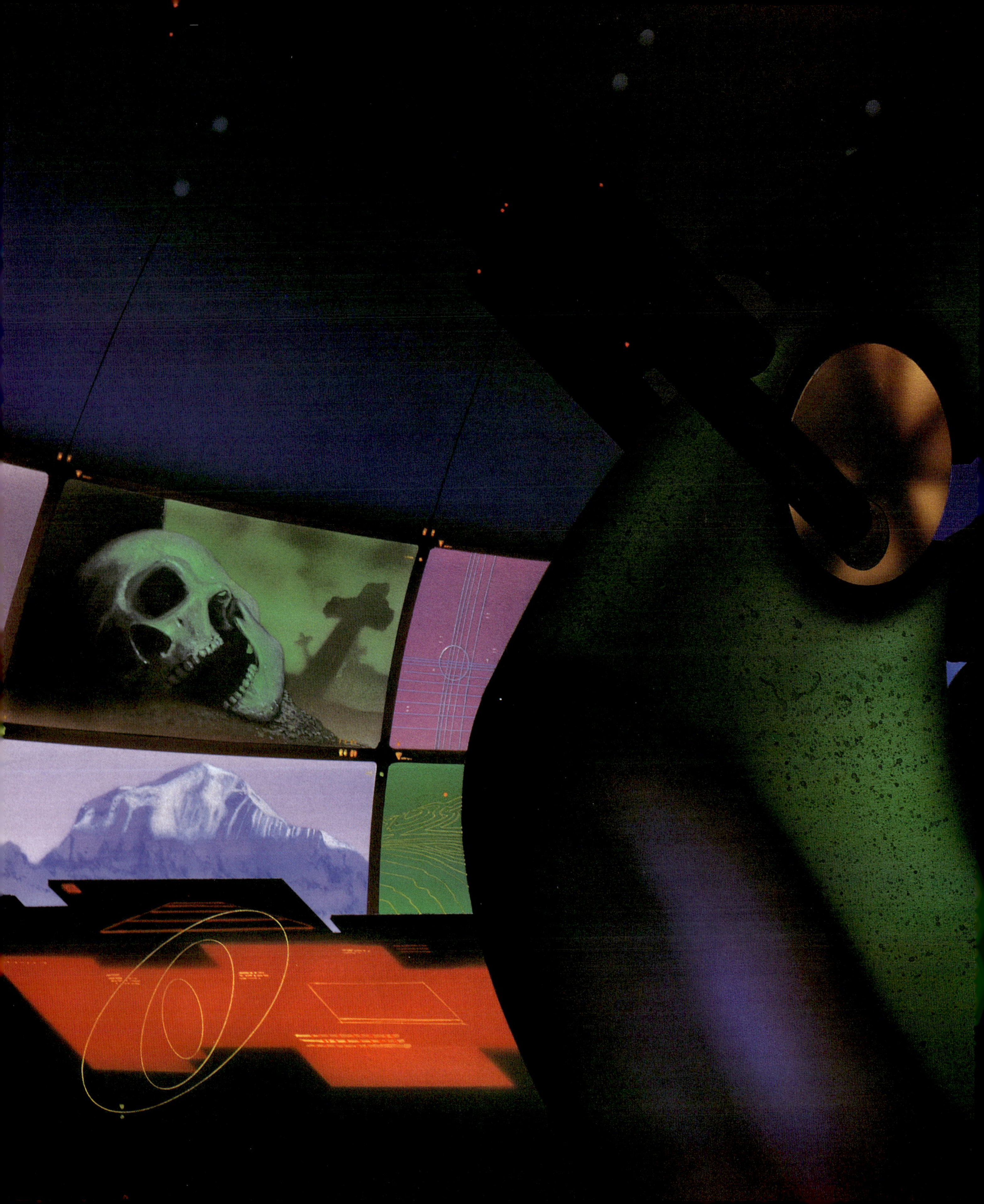

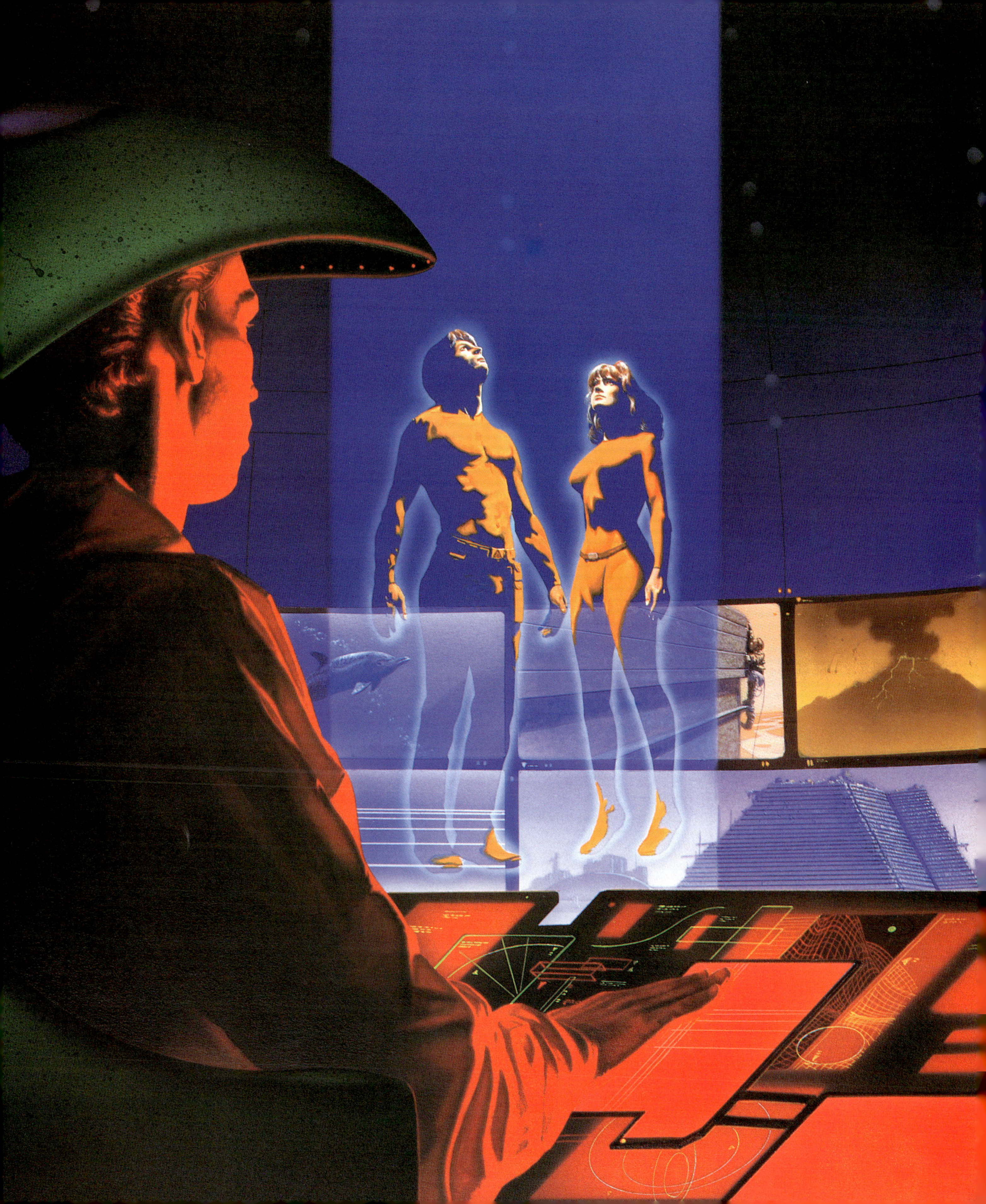

Futuropolis

By Chris Moore

Who knows what the future holds?

Here on Earth we have a few things to give a clue: the blue sky, the trees, the land, water, the air we breathe, and so on. We take these things for granted because the changes that occur in our climate do so slowly, imperceptibly. The human race has lived on earth for such a comparatively short time that one could be forgiven for thinking the Earth eternal. Recent events are at last causing us to question this assumption. However, astonishing advances in technology over the last century have accelerated progress to previously unimagined possibilities. The crystal-clear images in this chapter depict a future surviving beyond our present crises, into a time where literally anything is possible, heralding a new and exciting future for all mankind.

A few people are blessed with the ability to see into this future. An even smaller number of gifted individuals have the ability to clearly show everyone else their extraordinary vision, to gaze upon wonderful panoramas where remarkable structures pierce the sky, strange craft gliding effortlessly amongst them, where a mastery of technology defies both nature and even gravity.

The very best science-fiction art gives us a window into a possible future where we can glimpse our potential. When I look at the breathtaking vistas in this chapter I can imagine myself living in these cities, to have these spectacular buildings all around me, to live in the kind of society and order that these images suggest – a utopian existence where mankind's adaptability and relentless quest for order has resulted in a perfectly harmonious environment.

Perhaps Fred has tapped into some strange telepathic link, where someone on some distant world circling around another star in some far-off galaxy in another corner of the universe is gazing at the panorama before him and transmitting his thoughts across the stars. Maybe these places exist already; they certainly look as though they might.

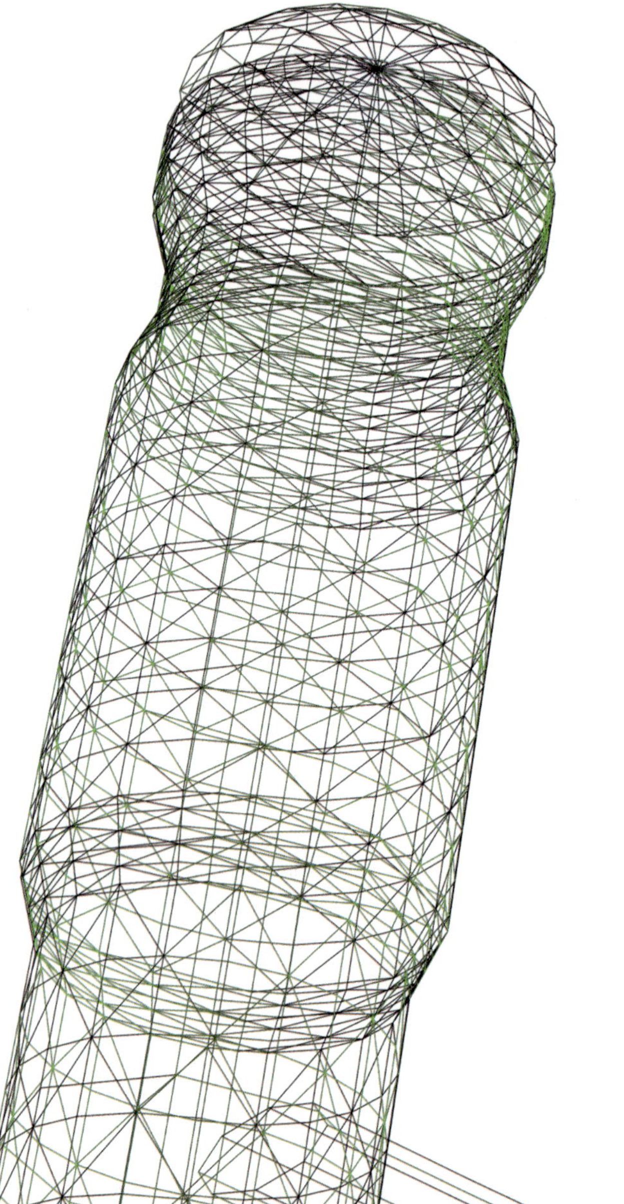

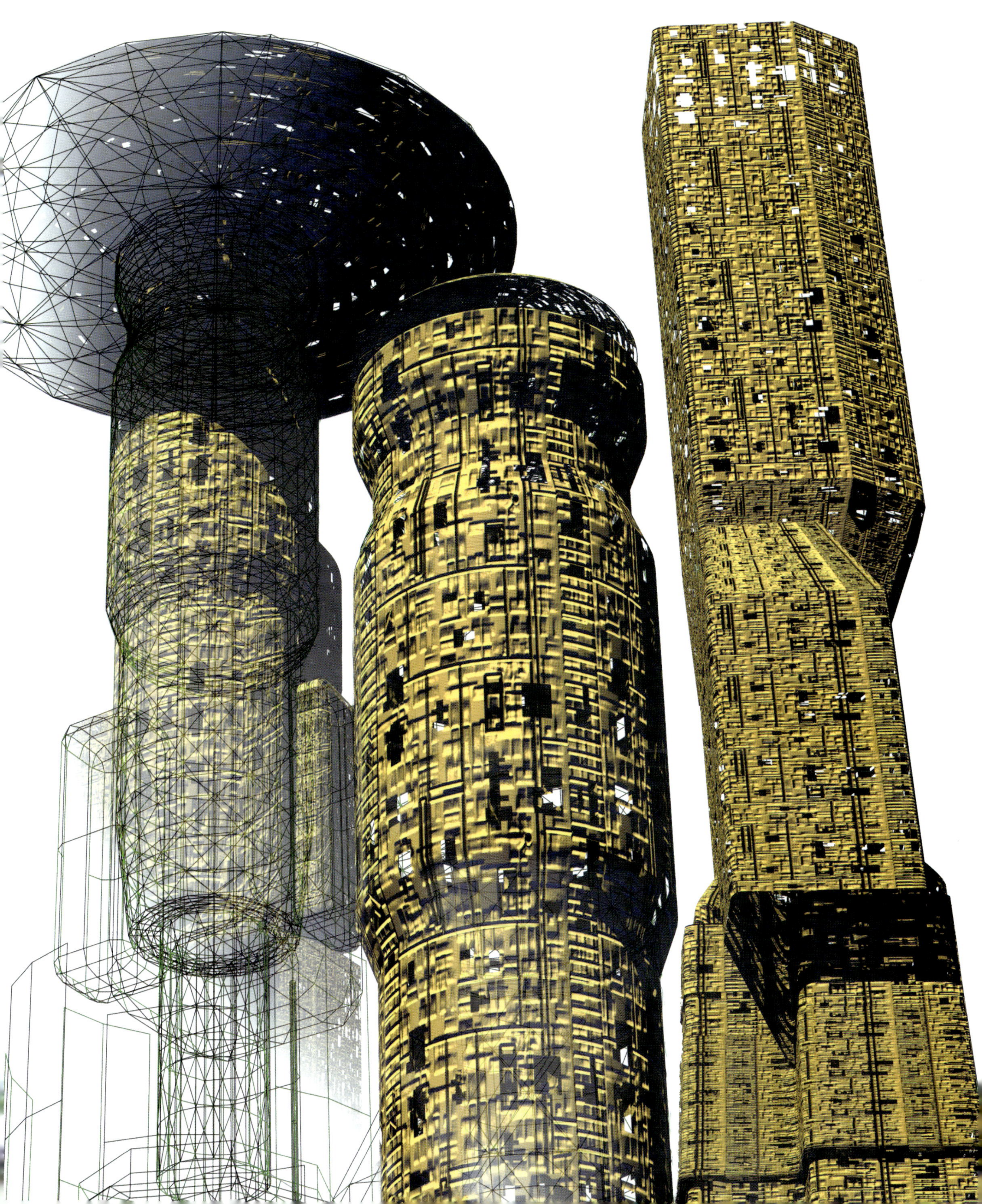

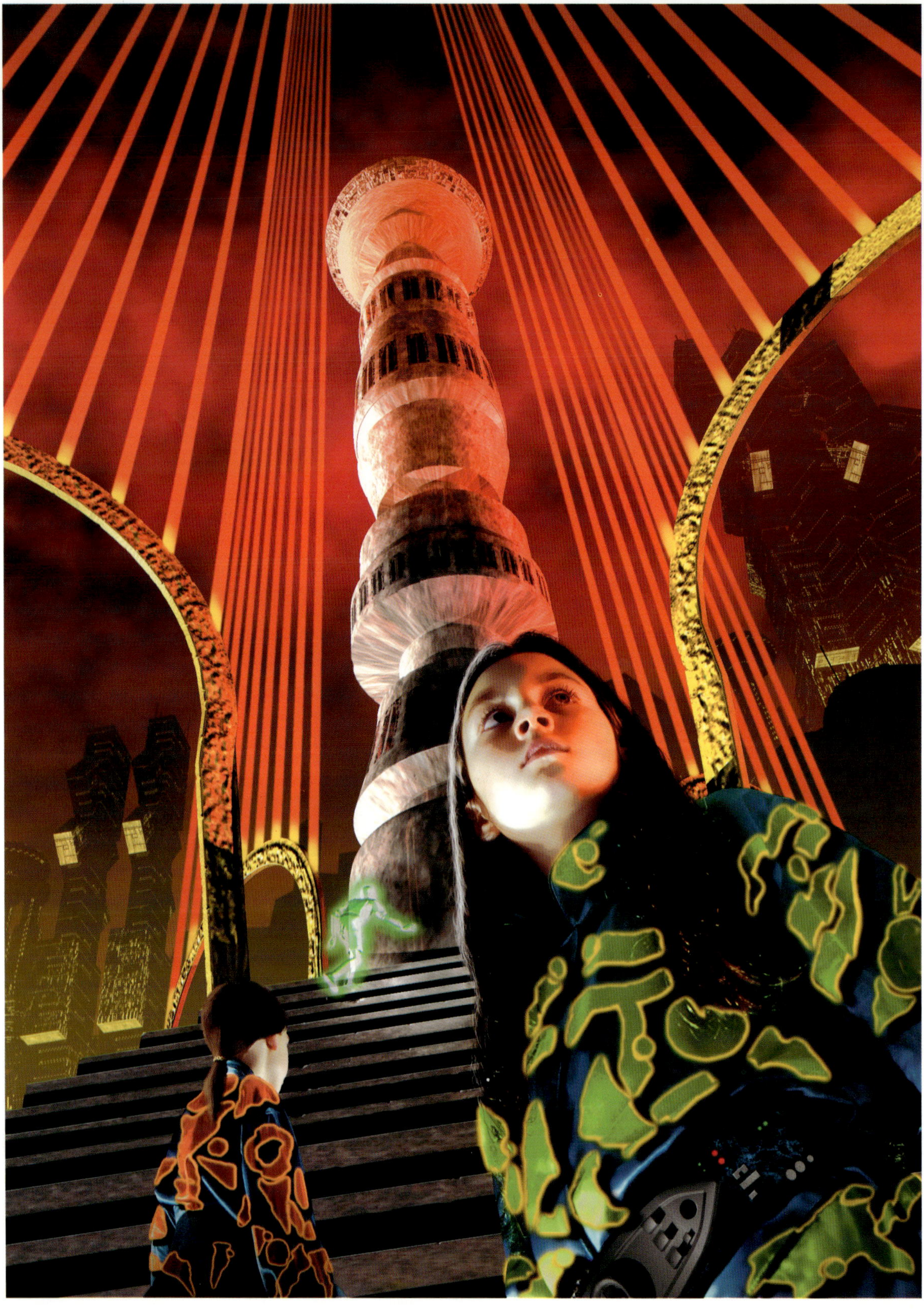

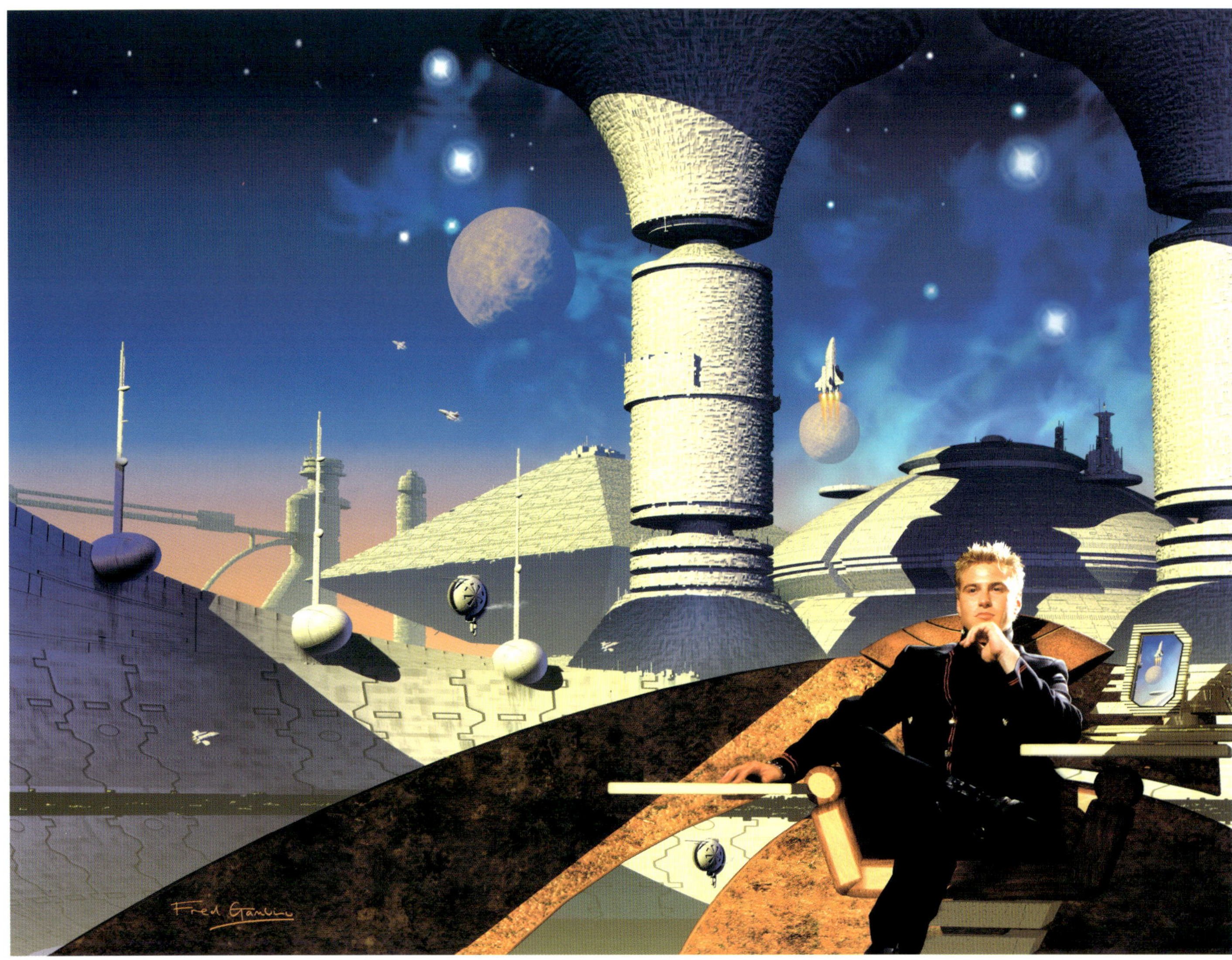

OPPOSITE

A TALE OF TIME CITY

Diana Wynne Jones
HarperCollins
Digital

I did a lot of 3D modelling for the rough on this image. Quite often, I simply colour-in pencil drawings, but when a perspective like this is involved, it pays to do the modelling from the outset. Once the geometry is built, it's easy to see how dramatic the point of view needs to be by tipping the model. Poser figures were dropped into the Sketch scene so that the perspective was consistent. Often the view that I am really happy with has the virtual camera in a position that is almost impossible to attain in the real world.

ABOVE

A CIVIL CAMPAIGN

Lois McMaster Bujold
Avon Books
Digital

This is the third cover I have done for Lois McMaster Bujold.The first was deemed a little too militaristic. In what is effectively a science-fiction love story, there would have been little in the text of that nature to seize upon anyway – hence this somewhat uncharacteristically tranquil scene.

The key thing for me was the way the light and shade in the cityscape not only serve to create atmosphere but also help to direct the viewer's eye to the focal point of the image.

I had sketched the rough out freehand and was pleasantly surprised to find that, when I came to model and light the scene, the shadows landed almost exactly where they were supposed to, needing only a small amount of retouching in Photoshop to give precisely the effect I wanted.

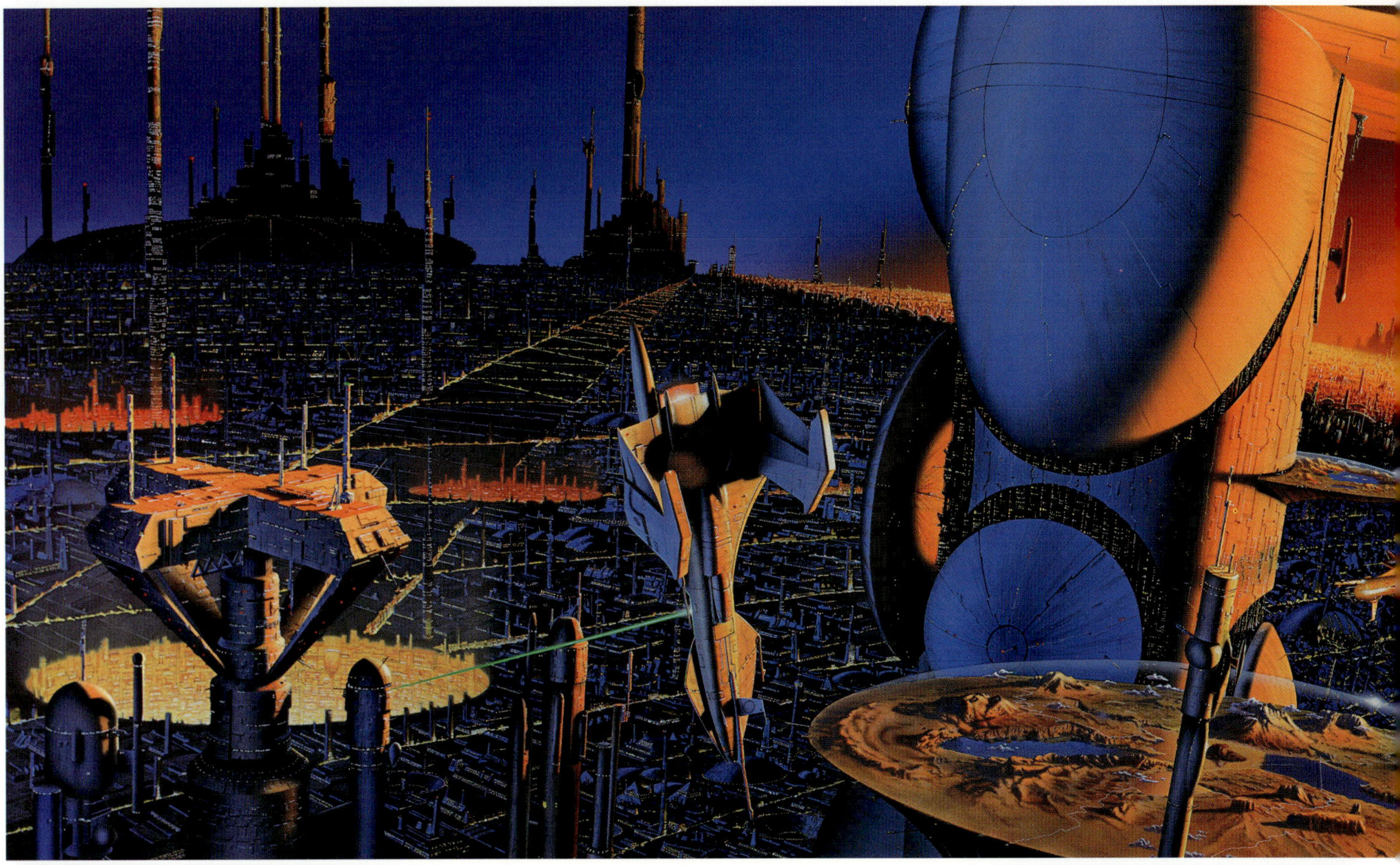

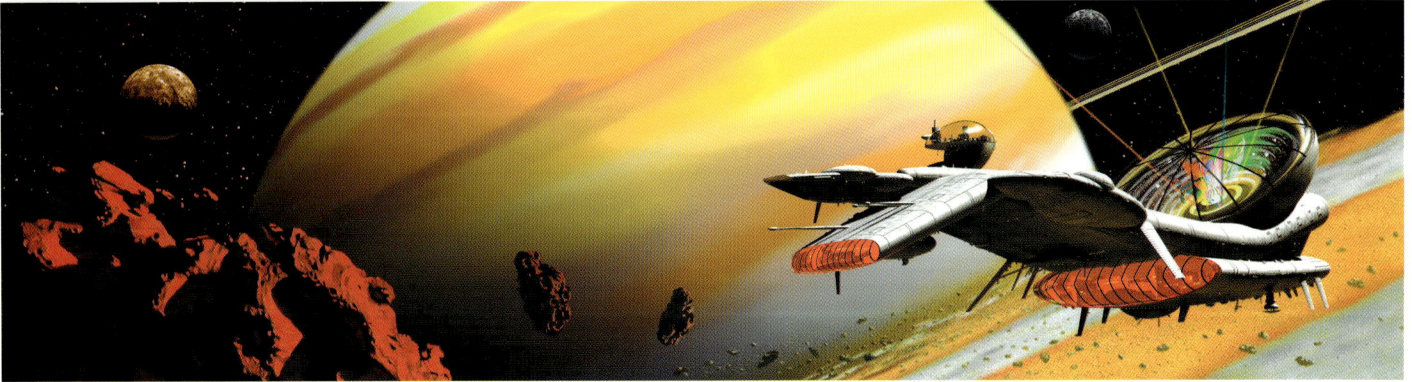

ABOVE

THE MEMORY OF WHITENESS

Kim Stanley Robinson
HarperCollins UK
Digital

I received this job while I was in the middle of a project I was helping Chris Moore with. We were doing a series of packaging illustrations for Mattel, the US toy manufacturers. This cover was conceived during a lull at Chris's studio. A letterbox format image, it developed from a small, almost abstract line drawing, where the opposing lines simply had an appealing feel. That was where the somewhat unorthodox ship design came from – a development of a few lines. It was quite interesting to then move to Sketch and actually turn it in to a solid object.

There is one sad note to this cover. This assignment came to me because of the premature death of one of the greats of science-fiction illustration, Peter Elson. He had done a superlative job on earlier Kim Stanley Robinson books. He was someone who I knew briefly at the start of our careers, and I dedicate this cover to him.

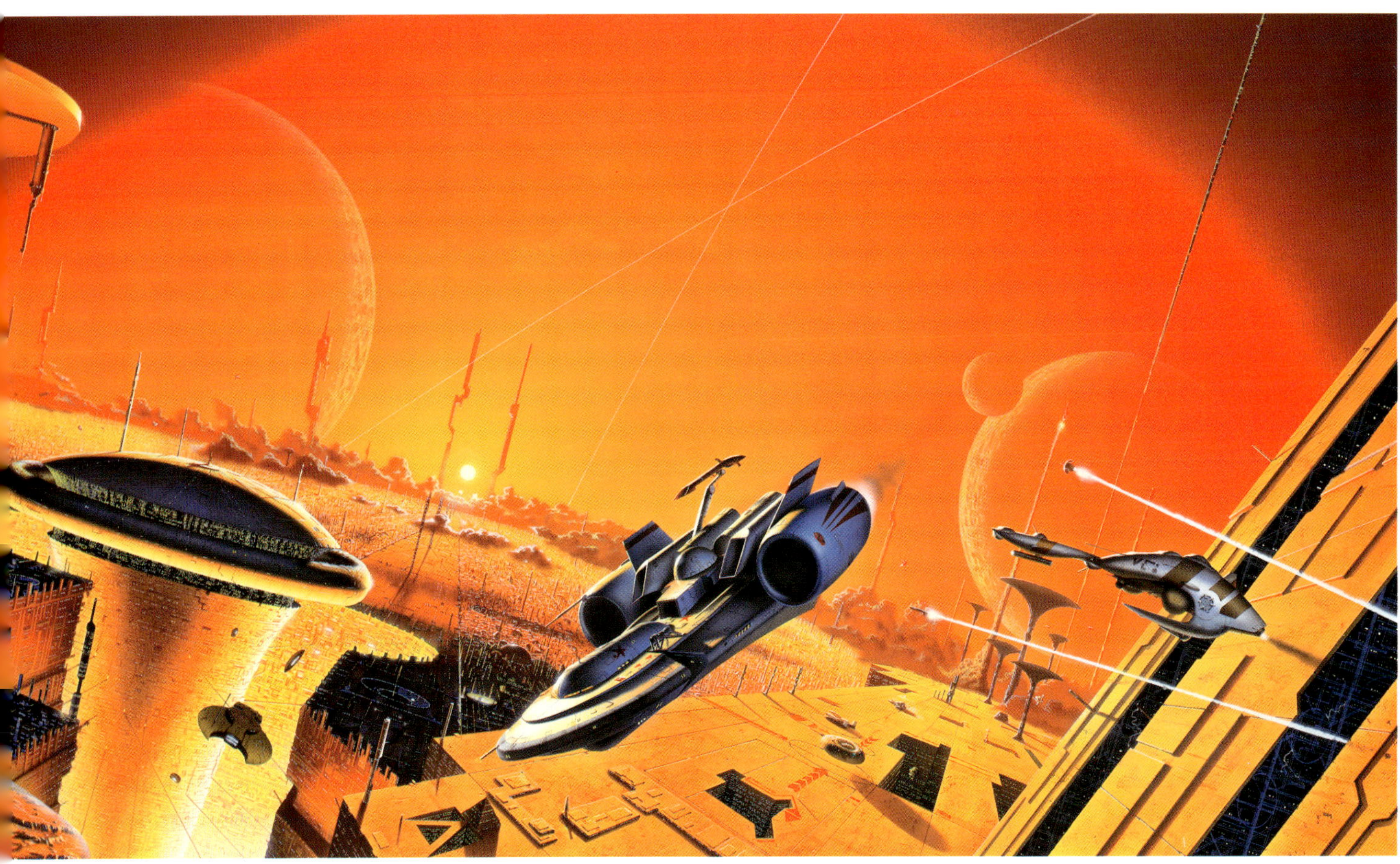

ABOVE LEFT

FOUNDATION SERIES

(Left panel)
Isaac Asimov
HarperCollins UK
Acrylic

This shows the left-hand side of a panorama of Trantor, the planet-wide city that is the centre of political power for the galactic empire in Asimov's famous epic.

Trying to convey scale on this level is extremely difficult as we have preconceived ideas about how large buildings should be. Even if we could stand and look at this scene in reality, we would be unable to grasp its true size; the human brain just isn't equipped for it. Our point of view in the image is supposedly so high that we can see the curvature of the planet, see the terminator in fact between night and day, yet structures are still rearing up around us. On this scale, some of the buildings in the background must be the size of whole countries!

One of the ways I have tried to convey something of this immense perspective is to have what, at first glance, look like small domes but which apparently have whole environments in them. The dome in the foreground contains a very Arizona-like landscape – the influence of a holiday a few weeks before.

ABOVE

FOUNDATION SERIES

(Right panel)
Isaac Asimov
HarperCollins UK
Acrylic

The right-hand panel continues the view over the terminator, so that we can see the setting sun. I painted this in two pieces because of the impracticabilities of trying to do it as one. Lack of studio space, finding a piece of illustration board big enough, getting it to London intact, all persuaded me that it would be impossible to paint it in one piece.

I also had a very tight deadline and the left-hand side had to be despatched as soon as it was finished. To get a good colour match, I attached a piece of board to the edge of the first panel and continued spraying onto it, using this strip as reference.

The painting of the two panels was an epic in itself. I had two weeks in which to complete, and it involved painting fifteen or sixteen hours a day straight through. When I finally emerged, blinking, into the sunlight, I felt as if I had been released from prison.

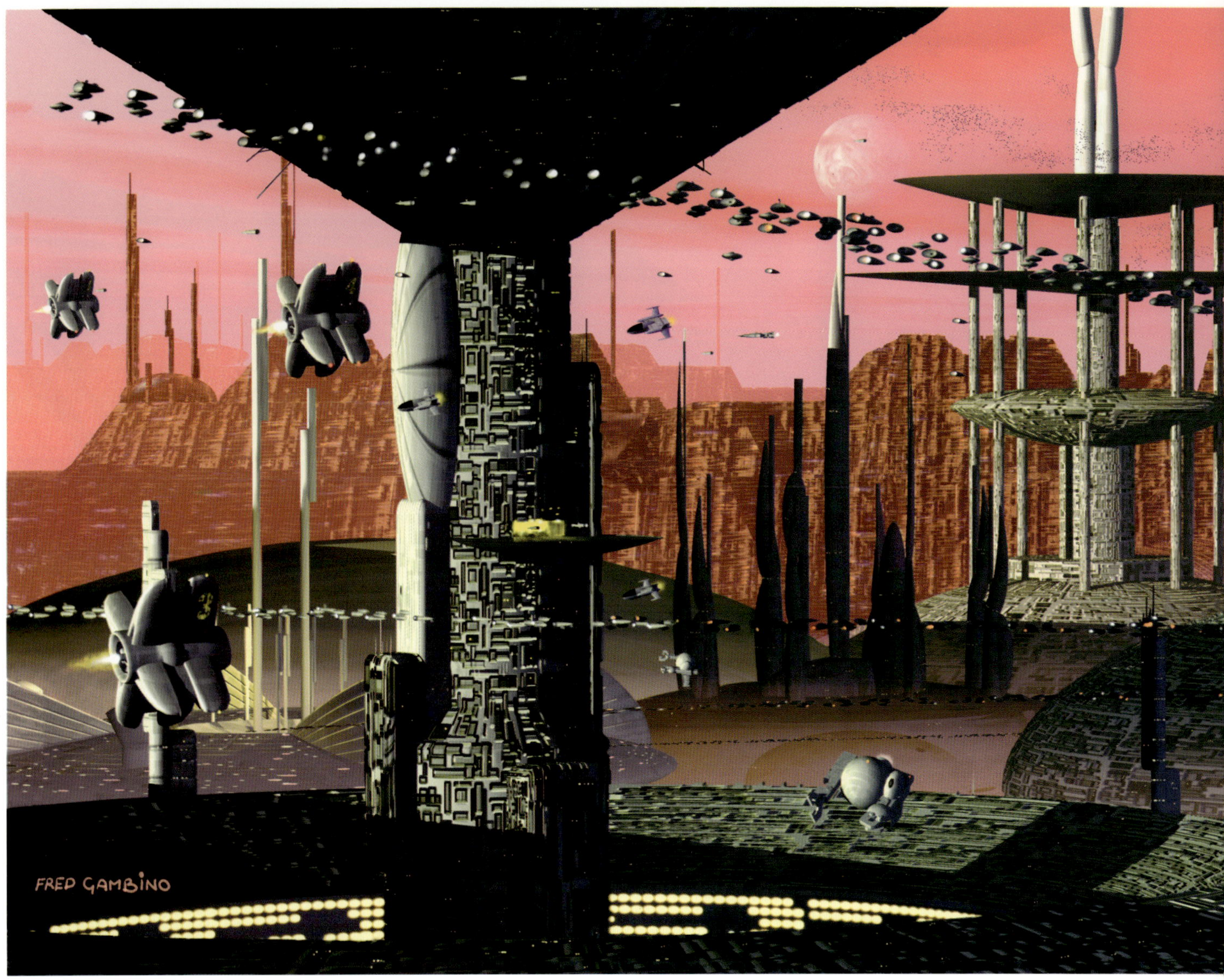

FOUNDATION'S FEAR

Gregory Benford
Little, Brown UK
Digital

Despite Asimov's death, there was to be a new Foundation Trilogy, written by three of the foremost practitioners of hard science fiction. They cover the years that precede Hari Seldon's discovery of the science of Psychohistory. The trilogy was published by Little, Brown, who again wanted views of Trantor, but needed a different look to the HarperCollins covers. I decided to tackle them digitally, to help to make a difference.

The covers were to have a letterbox format on the front, but they also wanted to use larger sections of the image on the back cover. Consequently, I generated the images at twice the dpi necessary, which meant that they could be printed at least twice the cover size, without loss of quality. The book reproductions were so small that a lot of detail was lost, so I'm glad to have the opportunity to see them printed here at a size that does them justice.

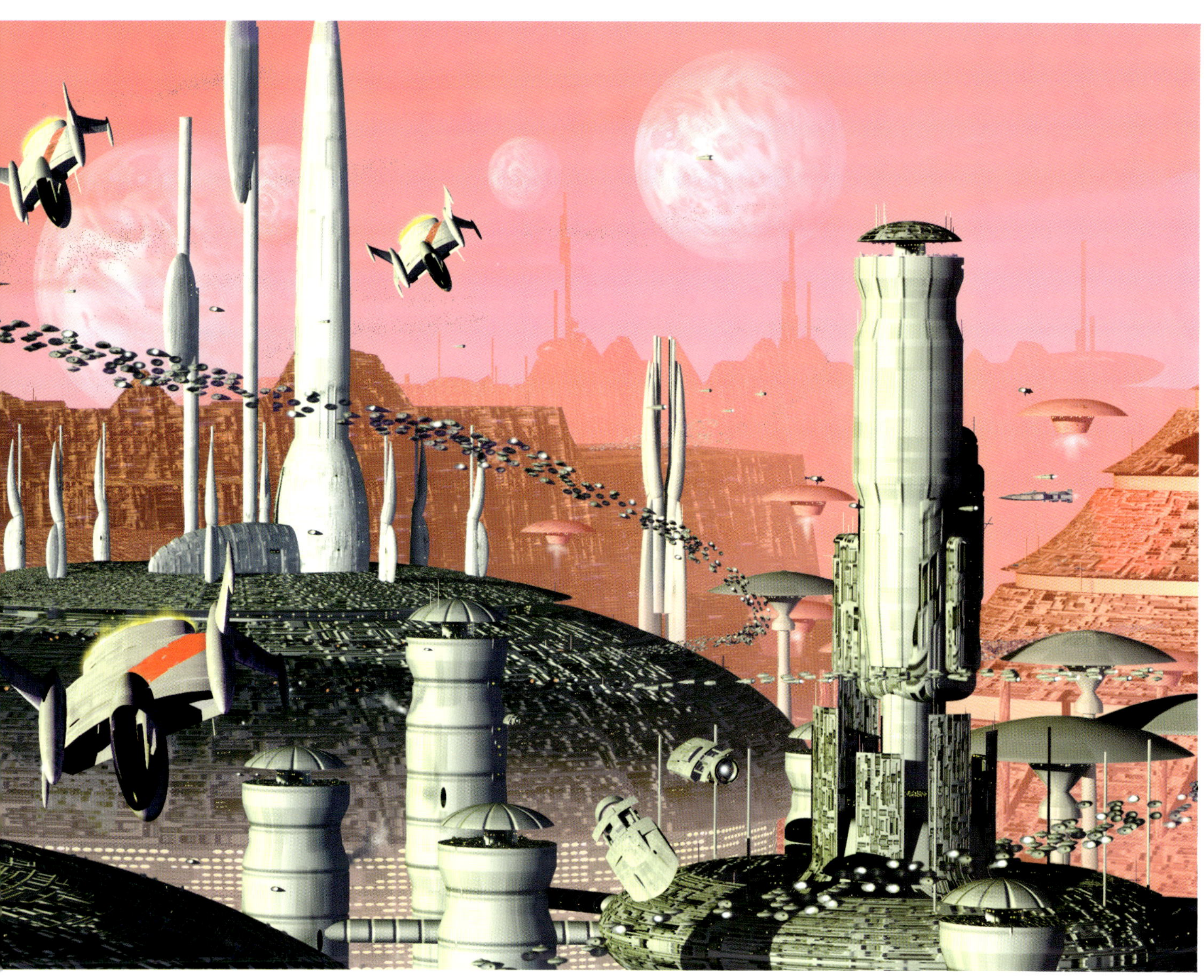

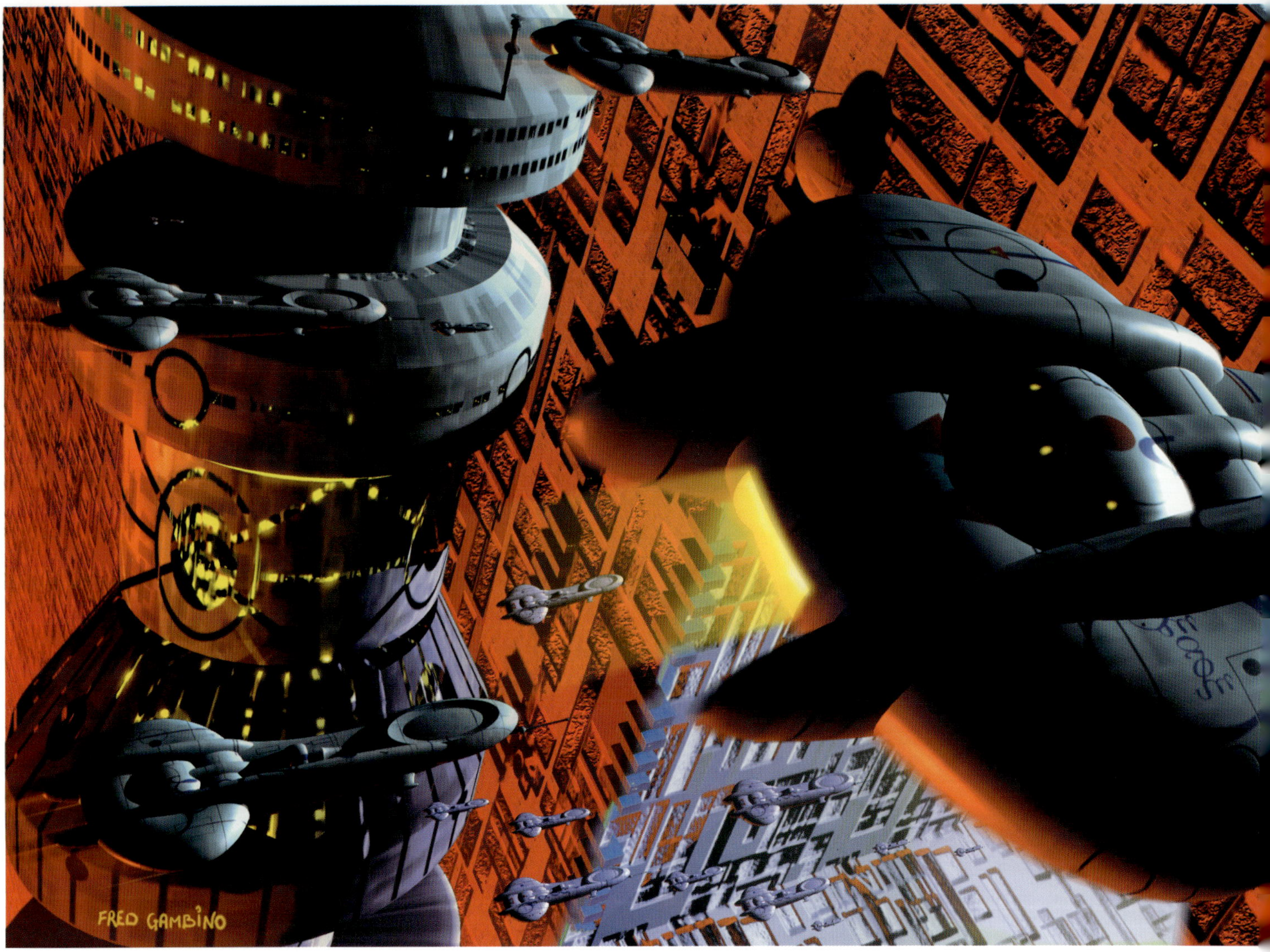

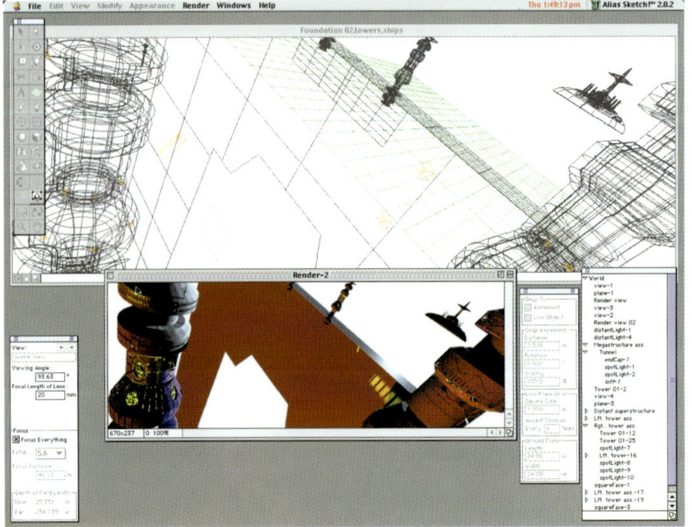
File Edit View Modify Appearance Render Windows Help
Thu 1:49:13 pm
Alias Sketch!™ 2.0.2
Foundation 02,towers,ships
Render-2
Focus Everything

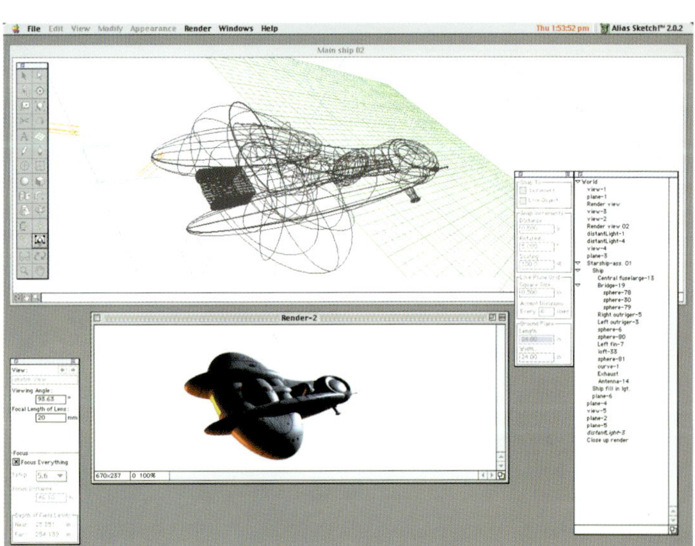
File Edit View Modify Appearance Render Windows Help
Thu 1:53:52 pm
Alias Sketch!™ 2.0.2
Main ship 02
Render-2
Focus Everything

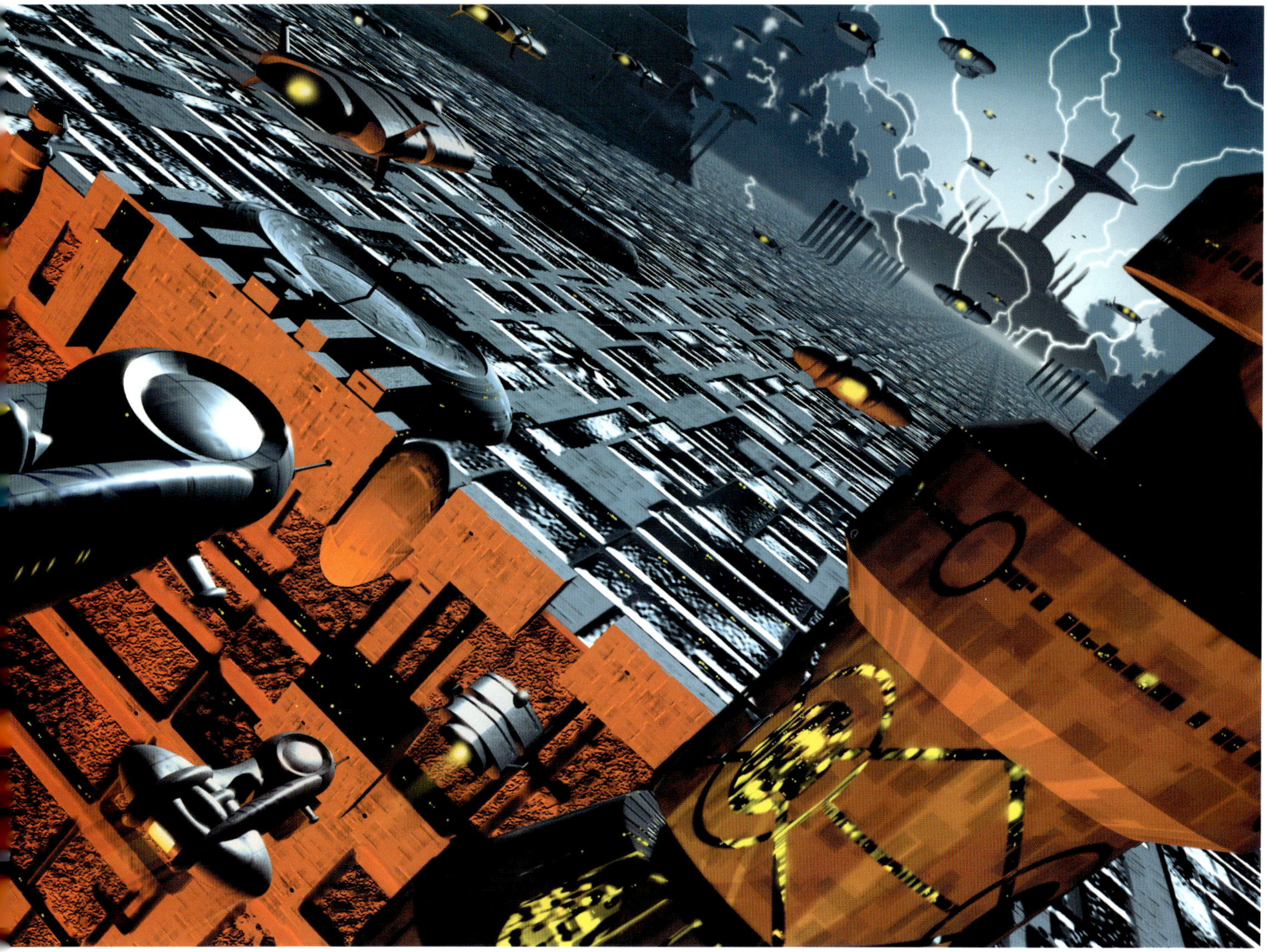

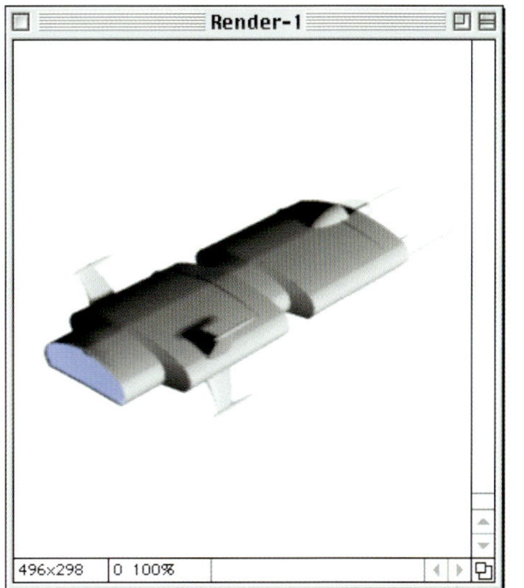

FOUNDATION AND CHAOS

Greg Bear
Little, Brown UK
Digital

The design of the second cover in the series popped into my head, almost complete, a short while after I finished the first, even though I had yet to read the manuscript. The title suggested the image, the chaos being supplied by the electrical storm in the far distance. I think, if you spend a lot of time doing this kind of work, your subconscious must carry on mulling notions over, even when you're not aware of it. Sometimes they can arrive in the form of dreams, sometimes they just pop into your head as you are driving or watching TV.

I often think that I should have a sketch book permanently on hand, to jot down ideas before they are forgotten. I've tried this, but I'm far too lazy to keep it up. However, in this instance, I did scribble the concept down before it was lost and actually had the rough ready long before the manuscript arrived.

OPPOSITE: Preliminary designs for the city and flying machines in Alias Sketch.

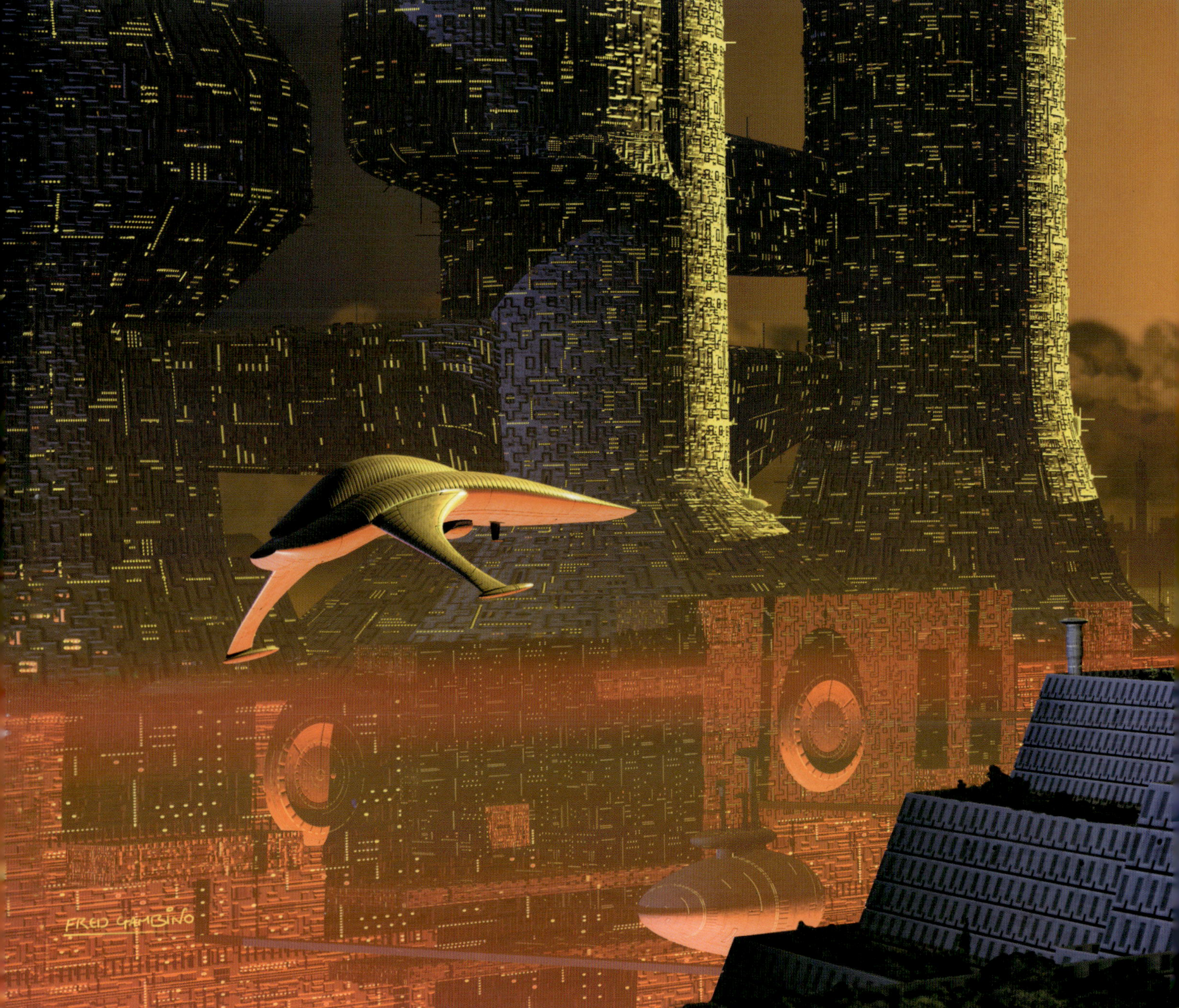

FOUNDATION'S TRIUMPH

David Brin
Little, Brown UK
Digital

By this time I was fully at home working on the computer. I had also amassed a considerable amount of 3D models, several of which were recycled into this background panorama of Trantor. As always with David Brin, there was a huge amount of descriptive text that was begging to be illustrated, but the formula had been set, and the cover had to be another view of the mega city. I chose to illustrate the emperor's palace, the only green area on the entirely metal clad surface, with the space elevator Brin describes splitting the sky in a perfectly straight line and Hari Seldon's shuttle on an approach path.

The green parkland surrounding the palace was painted freehand and, for the first time in printed form, it is possible to make out the detail on the palace and the flock of birds flying over it.

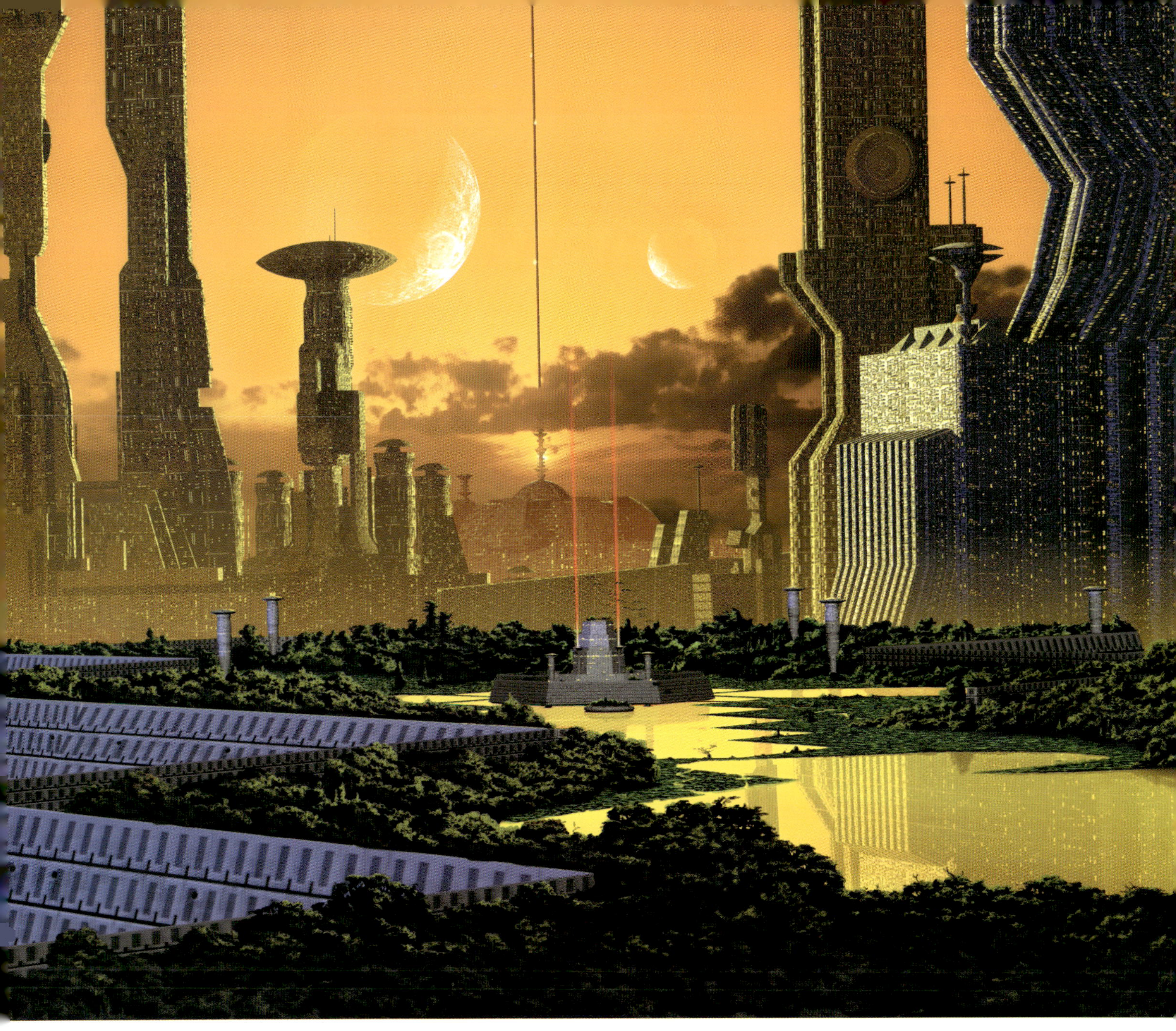

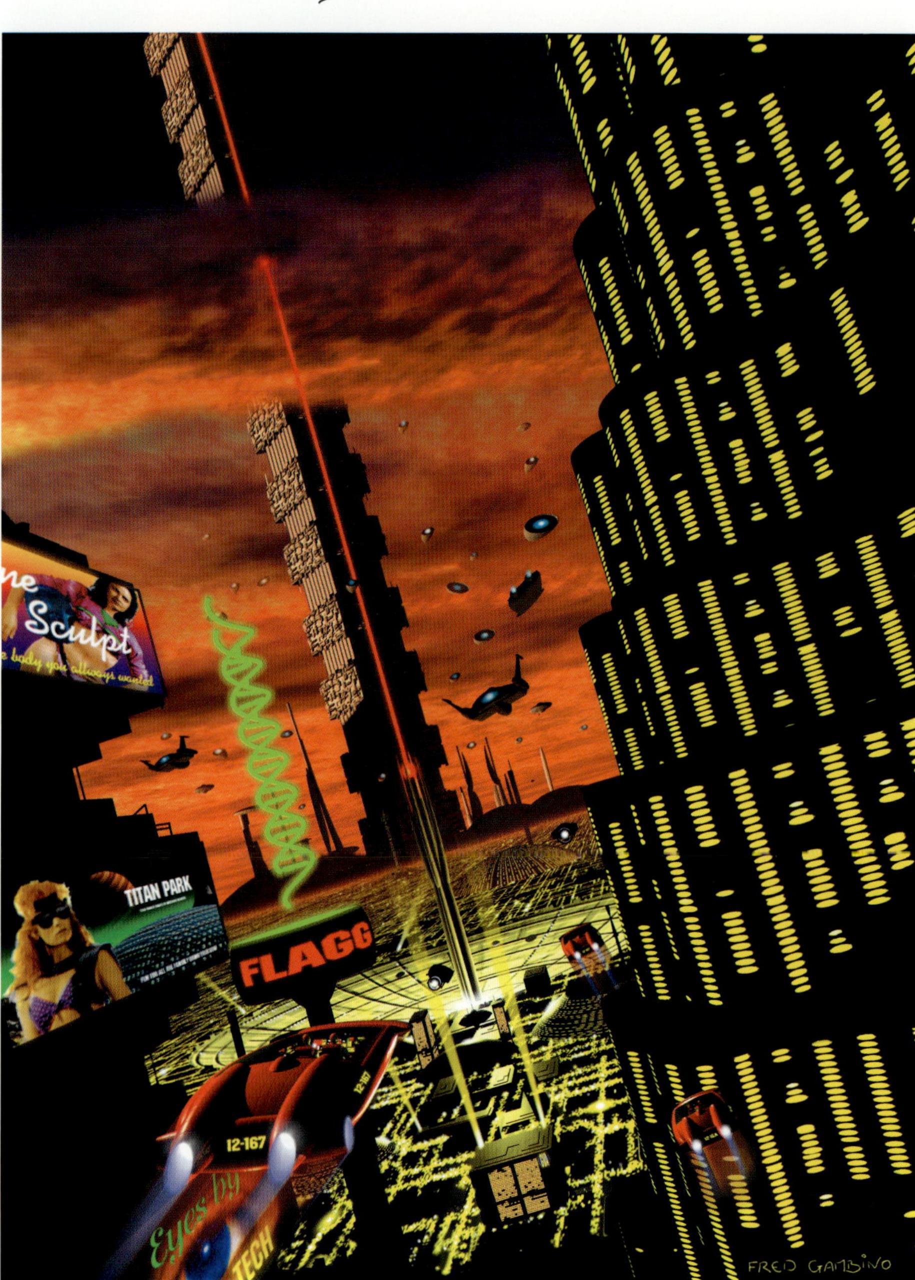

LEFT

MASQUE

F. Paul Wilson and Matthew J. Costello
Warner Books US
Digital

This was one of my first attempts to recreate digitally the kind of cityscapes that I had been doing in acrylics. The art director had been inspired to give me this job after seeing my Foundation Series covers. The brief stated that the cover should have a futuristic city with a 'Blade Runner' feel.

I was experimenting with 3D software at the time and there were no less than five programs involved in the creation of this piece, more if you include the various Photoshop plug-ins.

I have always been fanatical about detail, putting in every panel or nut and bolt in my acrylic paintings, but the amount of detail you can include in a digital image is astonishing. If I look at this image on the screen and zoom in to one hundred percent magnification, I am in detail heaven. There is a huge mass of information there that is largely lost on reproduction.

The same could be said for my paintings. I do tend to get carried away, producing detail which I find very satisfying to do but whose absence would make very little difference to the printed version.

OPPOSITE

TWILIGHT OF THE GODS

Mark Clapham and Jon De Burgh Miller
Virgin Books
Digital

This was the last in the Benny stories that I did and, as far as I know, the last in the series to be printed. The synopsis described a huge wrecked statue with the graffiti 'One God' painted on it. In the background, a city wrecked by war burns fiercely.

The statue was a Poser figure dismantled and rendered in Alias Sketch. The detail of the wrecked arm with its visible infrastructure was painted freehand. The cityscape was likewise modelled and rendered in Sketch while the sky was produced in Photoshop using a succession of cloud renders and filters.

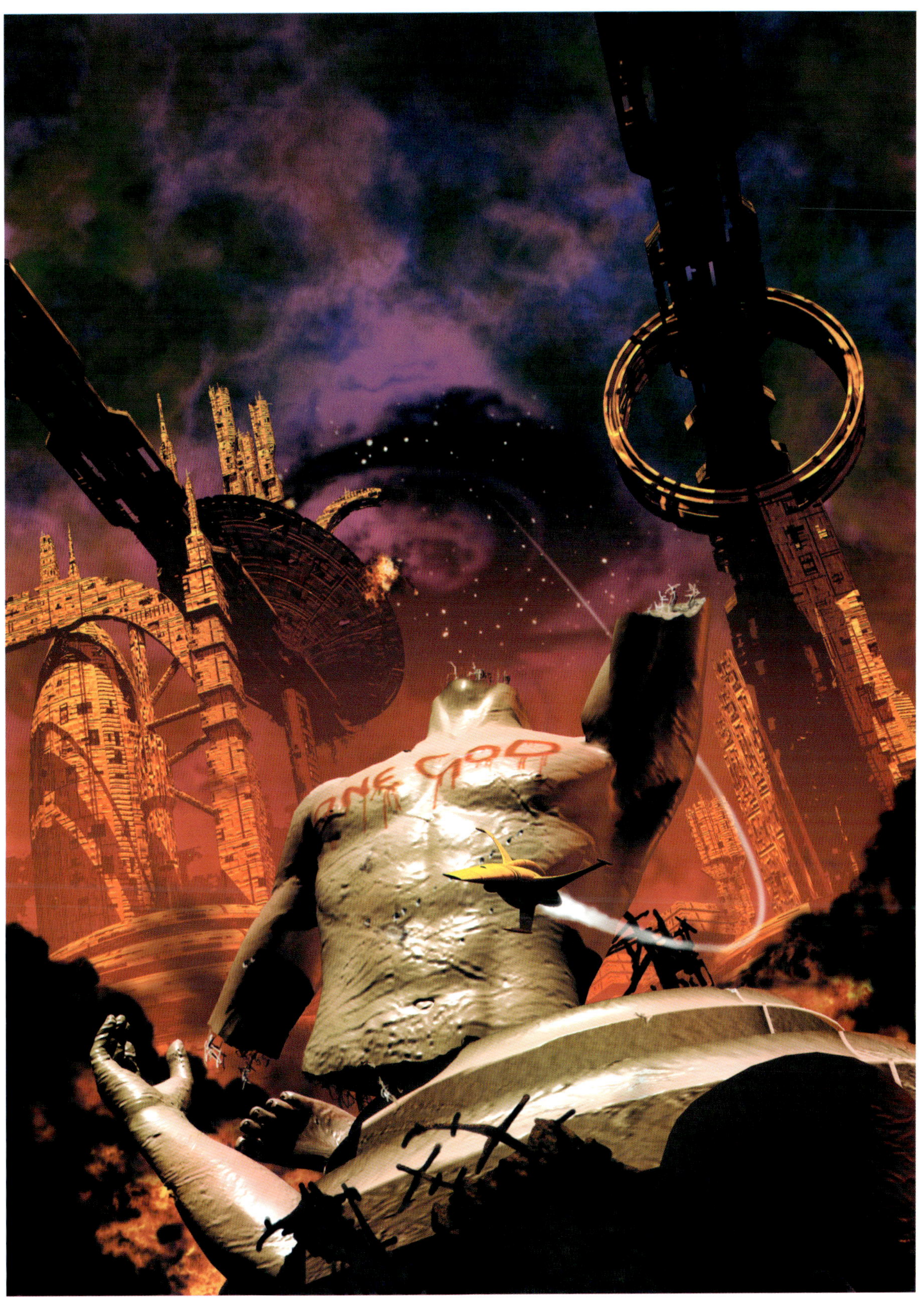
ONE GOD

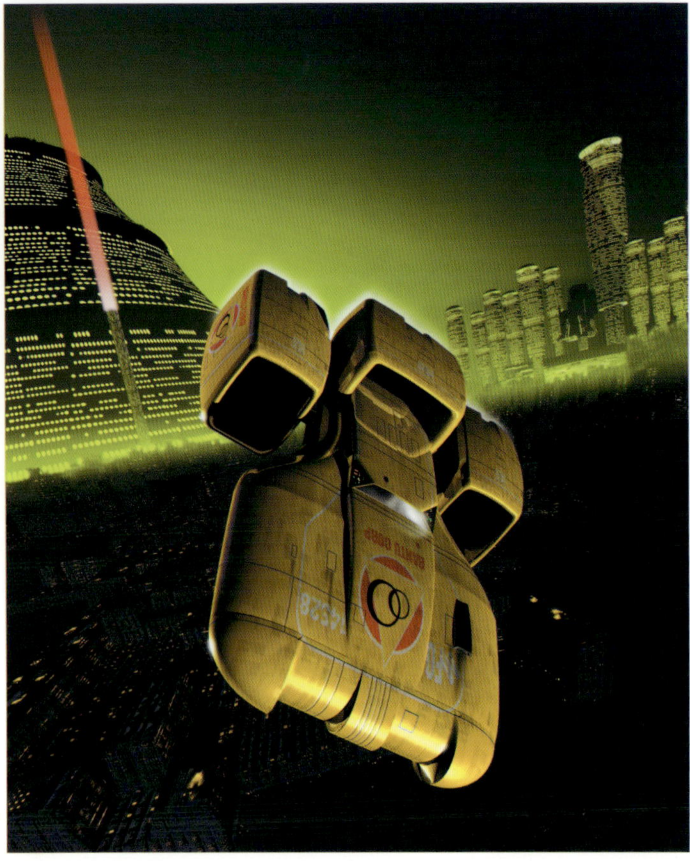

ABOVE

ANOTHER GIRL, ANOTHER PLANET

Martin Day and Len Beech
Virgin Books
Digital

This was the first in the series of books featuring Doctor Who's assistant, Bernice Summerfield. I did about half a dozen of these (see pages 31 and 106) and thoroughly enjoyed them. Although it wasn't my intention at the outset, the image ended up being almost monochromatic, which makes a change from some of my other over-the-top, almost garish, colour schemes.

RIGHT

LION TIME IN TIMBUCTOO

Robert Silverberg
HarperCollins UK
Digital

The title story of this anthology is a tale of alternative history, where the Black Death was even more virulent. Consequently, Europe doesn't become a world power but the Aztec and African civilizations do. The descriptions of Africa and the two palaces divided by the river were very evocative and I thought they would make for a very atmospheric image. The city is only mentioned vaguely in the story, but I chose to add it as an element necessary to make it clear that this was an anthology of science-fiction stories. What I was aiming to do was capture the atmosphere of the narrative rather than illustrate an actual scene.

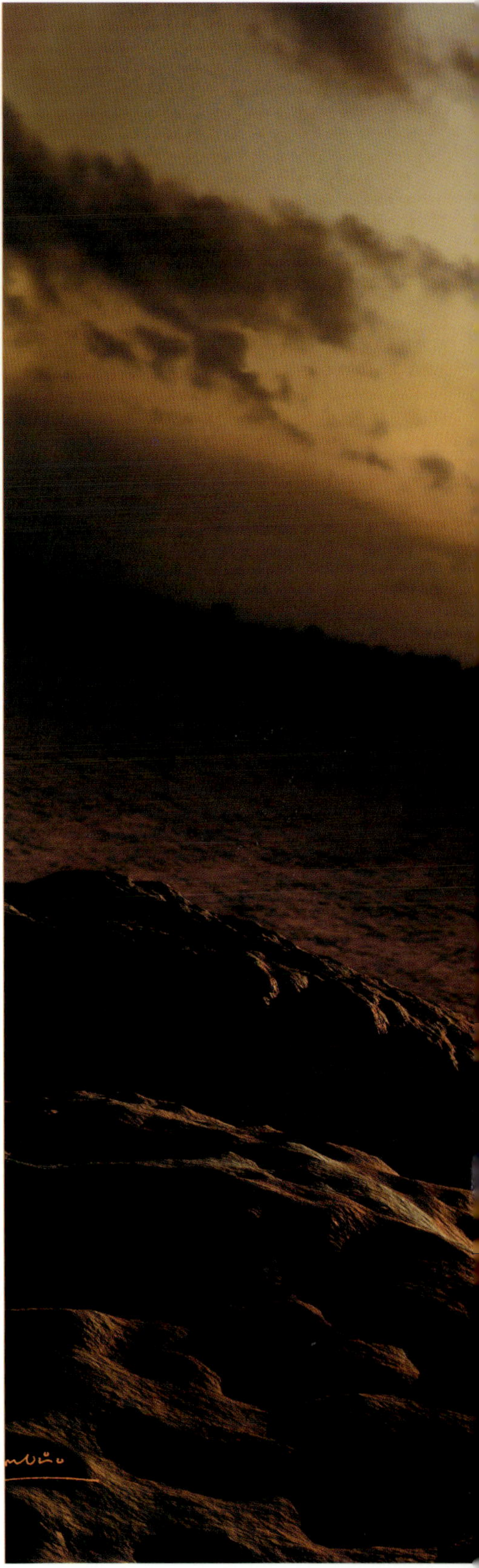

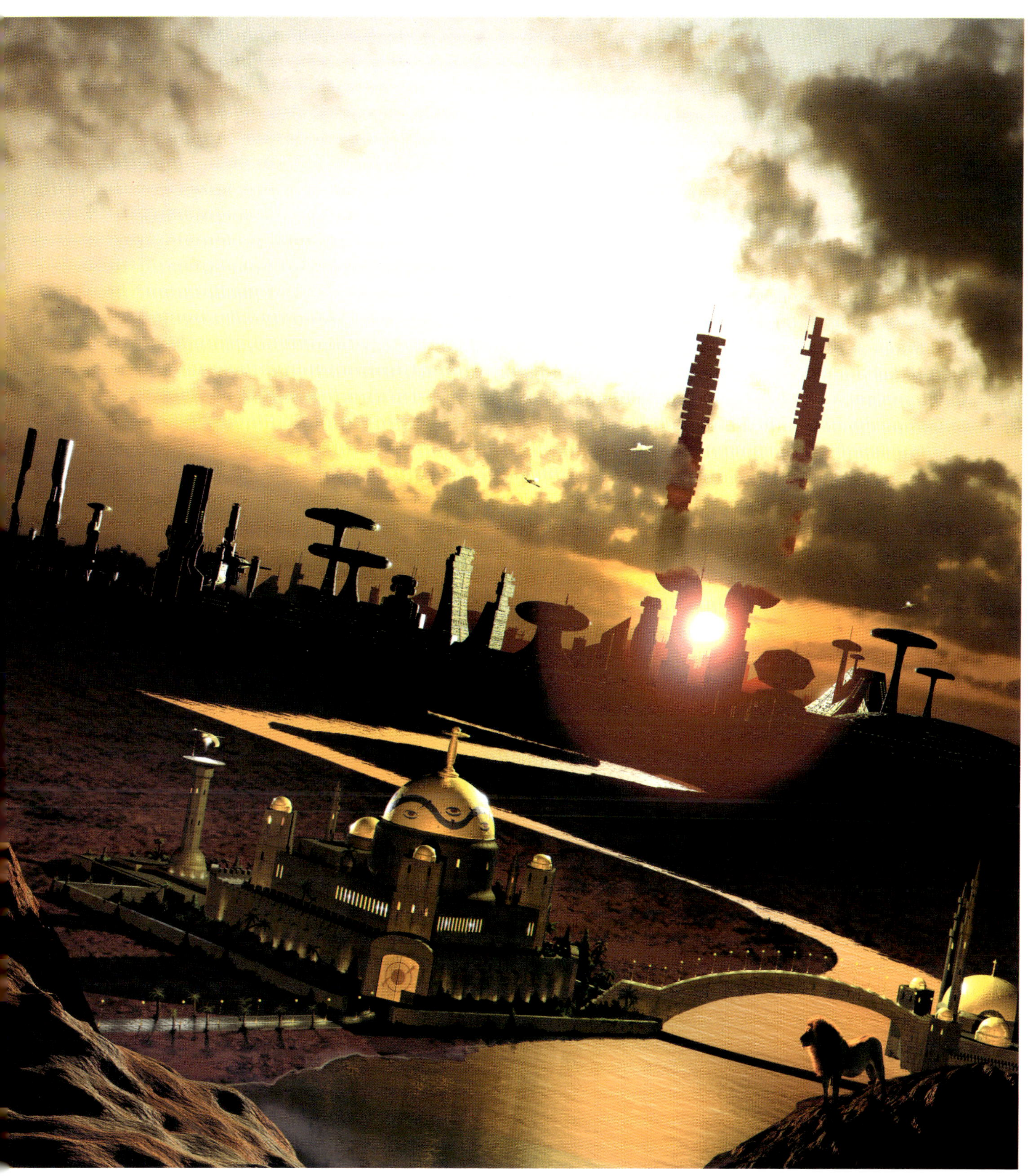

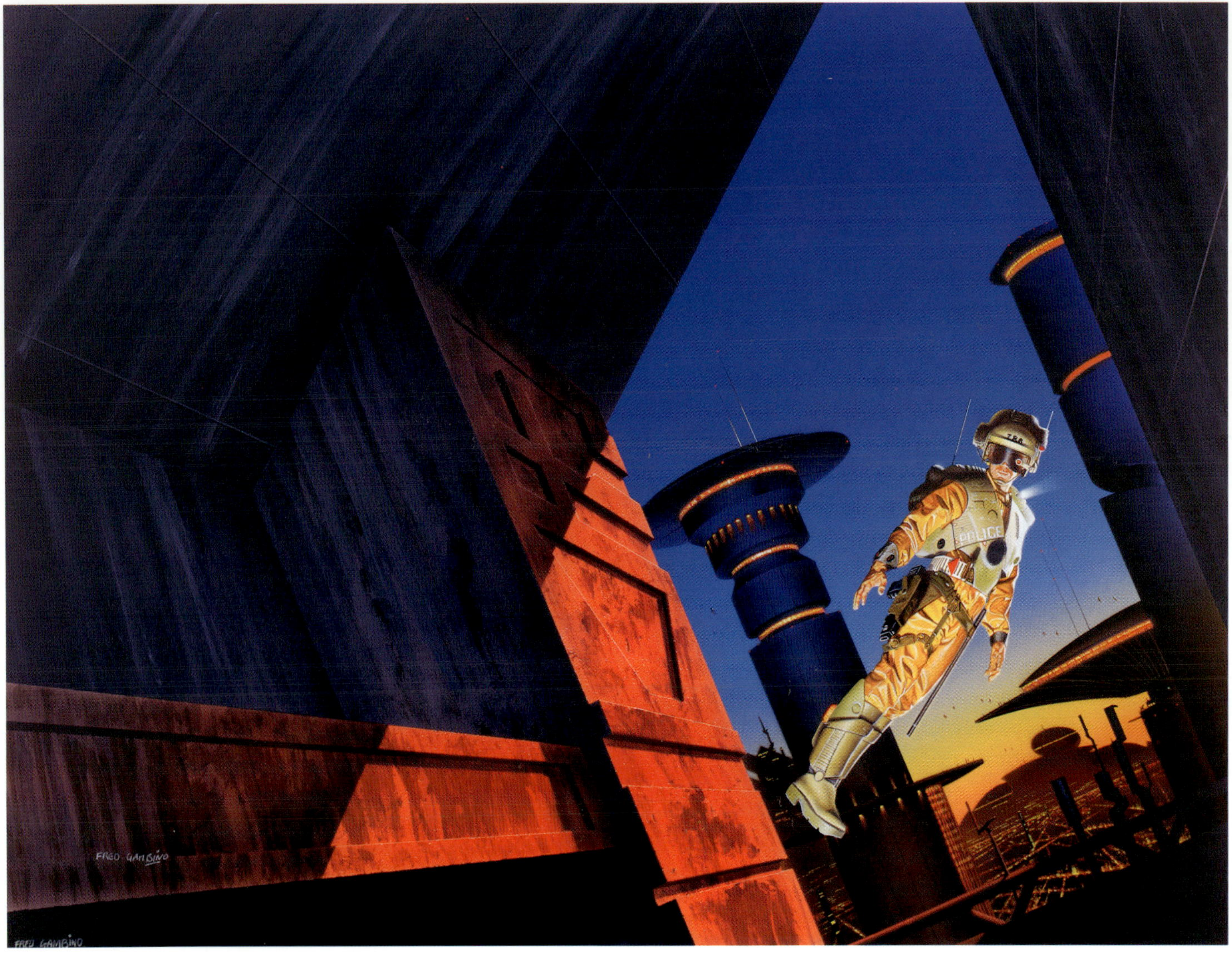

ABOVE

TERMINAL VELOCITY

Bob Shaw
Gollancz
Acrylic

I am an avid fan of Bob Shaw's writing, having read all his books as a schoolboy – *Terminal Velocity* was one of my favourites. A friend, who works for the local council, had a shiny yellow plastic suit, so, wearing that, a doctored US Air Force helmet and green wellington boots, he stood in the studio and tried to look weightless.

The anti-gravity cop in the image drifts past one of the many dangerous nooks and crannies that permeate the aerial environment of his 'beat'. I was trying to get a sense of anticipation and menace, the moment just before all hell breaks loose.

To create the city towers, I sprayed the whole of the background blue, then laid loose paper masks over it, which allowed some of the spray to creep under, giving a soft effect. My preferred material for this was scrap photographic paper. It has the wonderful property of not buckling when wet and retaining a crisp edge and it had the advantage for me of being free.

OPPOSITE

THE DOSADI EXPERIMENT

Frank Herbert
Orion
Digital

Like *The Jesus Incident* (see page 25), I had painted a cover for this novel years ago, but this image is totally different from the earlier one. After going through several permutations, a hardware cover was finally settled on. The city towers in the background show my first tentative work in Electric Image.

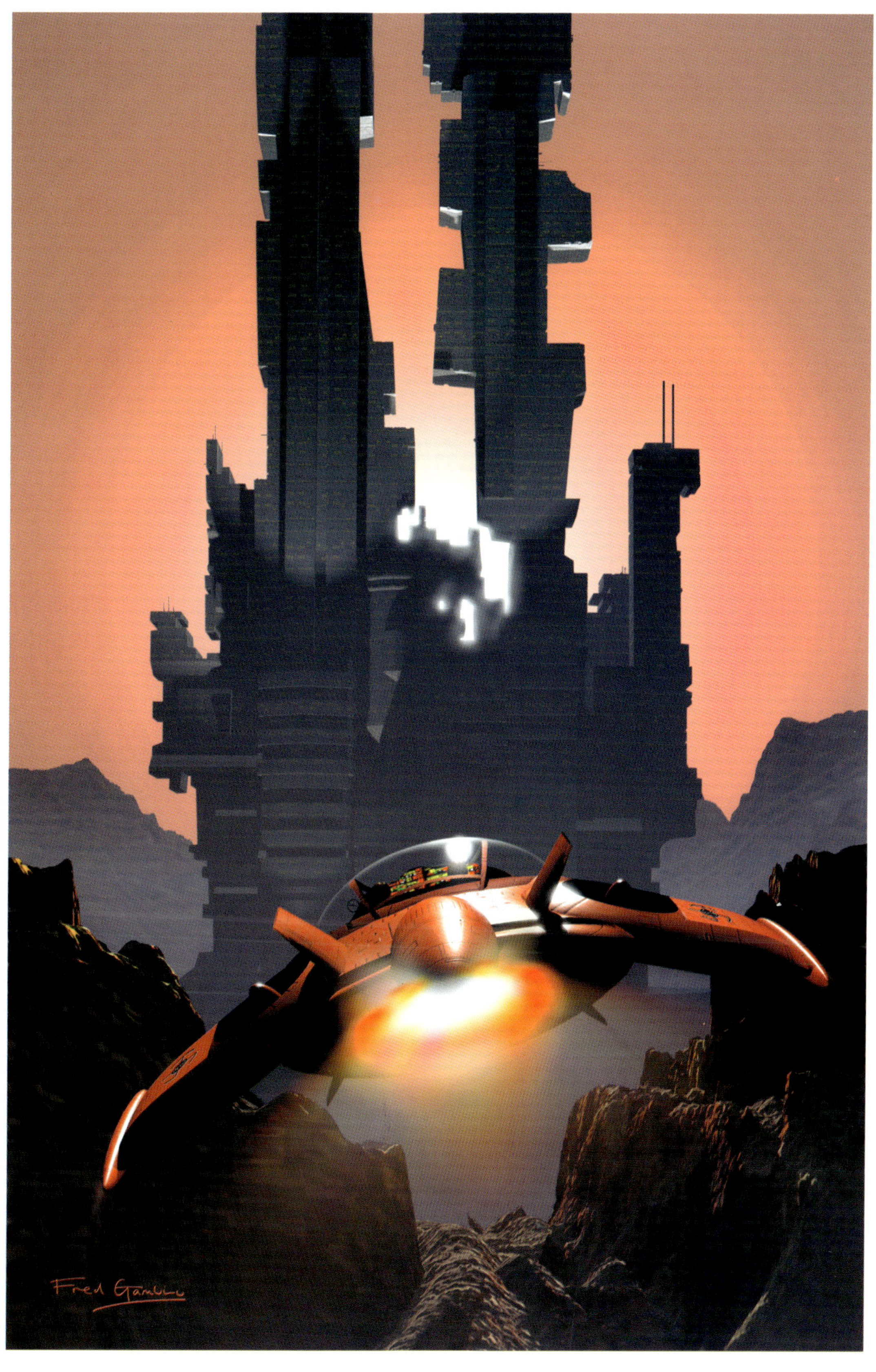

OTHER CONTINUUMS

I always wanted to be a science-fiction illustrator, but during my time, over more than two decades, I have illustrated almost every genre – from war to historical romance. I find working in these other areas as much a pleasure as working in science fiction, but over the last few years, due in part to my working digitally, my portfolio has filled with work of the science-fiction kind.

There is a sort of 'commissioning law' out there that states illustrators will only receive work directly represented by the work in their folders. Fashions in publishing have also changed and at the moment there is a trend to do more and more in-house, using stock images. The computer is also partially responsible for this, and has reduced the amount of assignments available in other areas.

Fortunately, the science-fiction community represents one of the only genres where the fans care as much about the artwork as they do about the literature. They seem hungry for all aspects of their favourite subject. This helps keep the market in commissioned science-fiction covers more buoyant. The same isn't as true for fans of crime or thriller novels. However, I still get commissions of that sort from time to time and feel that, without a glimpse of this other aspect of the illustrator's trade, this collection would not be complete.

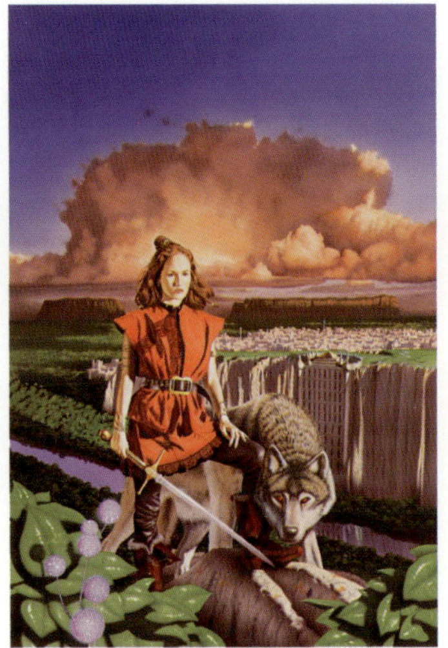

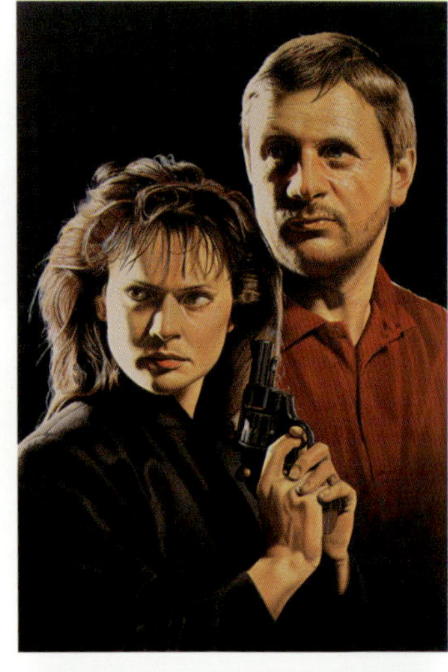

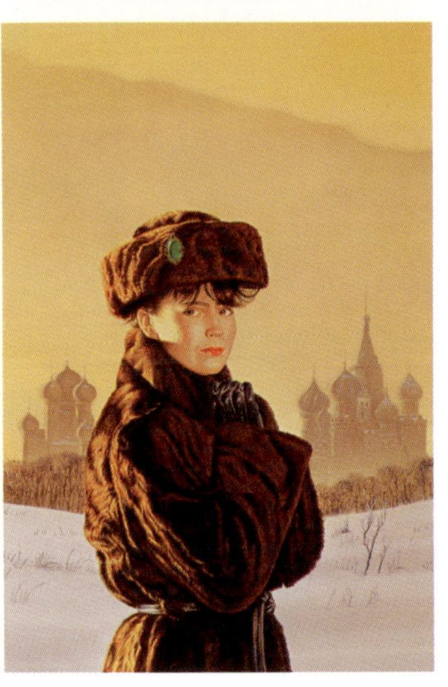

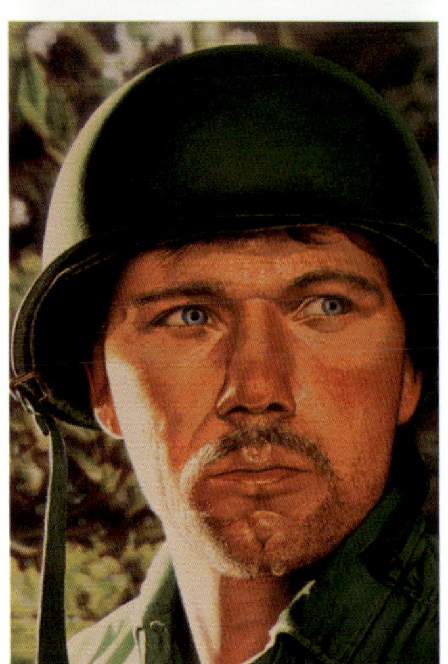

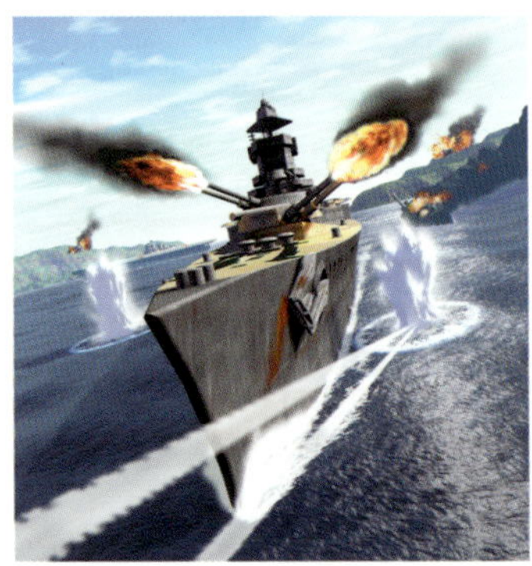

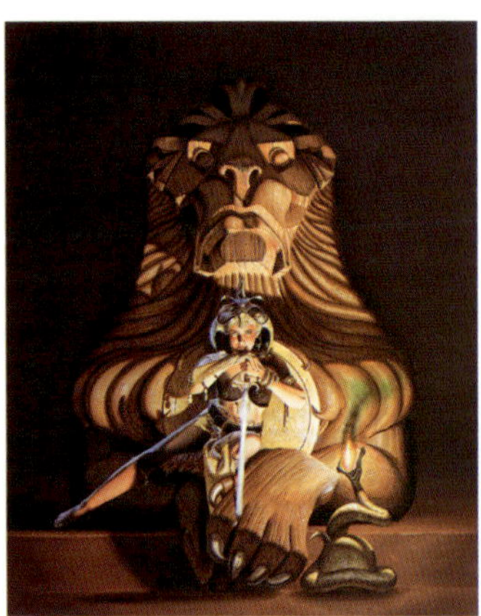

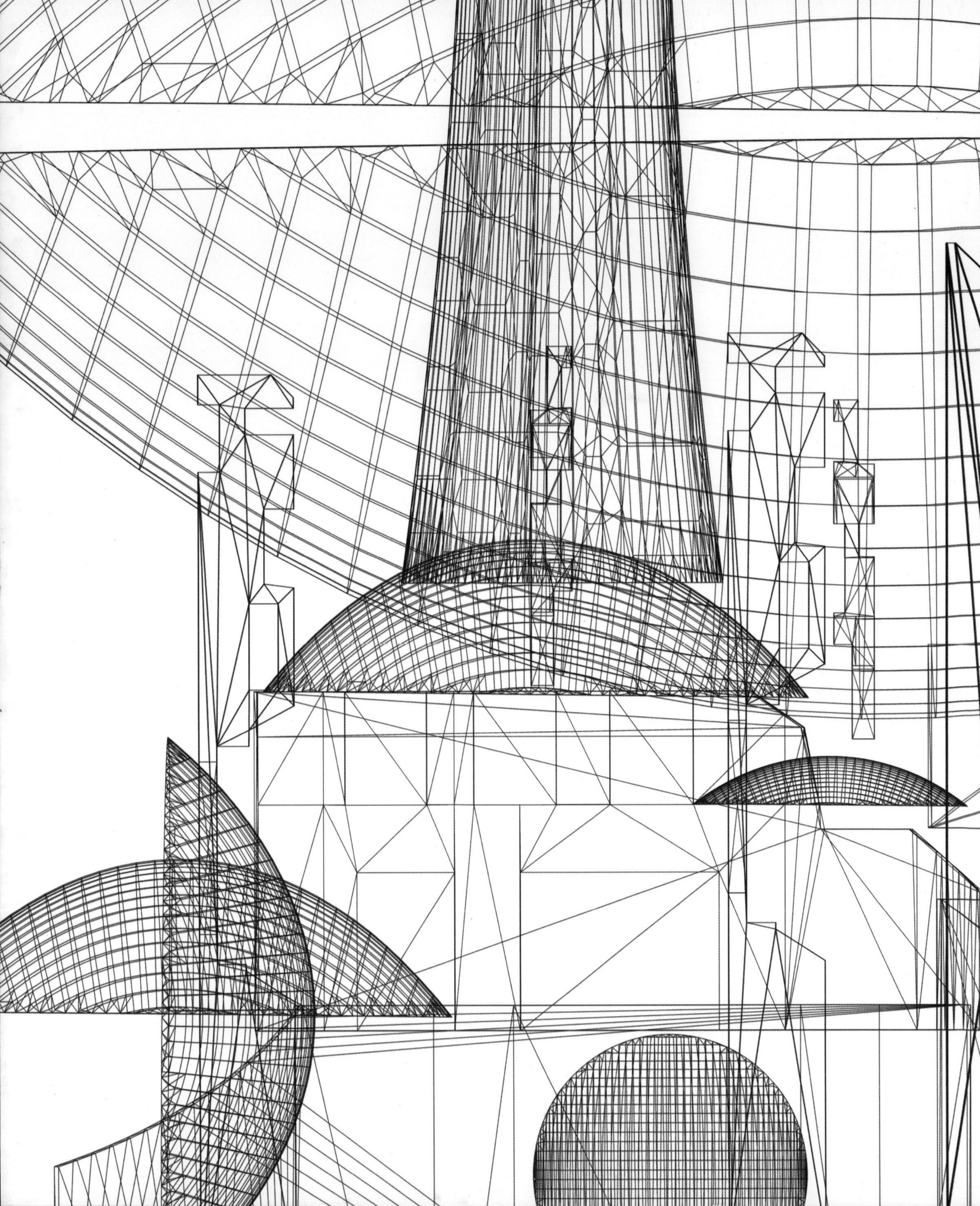